Lessons 1-60

Keyboarding & Formatting Essentials

MICROSOFT® WORD 2002 / MICROSOFT® WORD 2003

Susie H. VanHuss, Ph.D.
University of South Carolina

Connie M. Forde, Ph.D.
Mississippi State University

Donna L. Woo
Cypress College, California

THOMSON
———✶———
SOUTH-WESTERN

Australia · Canada · Mexico · Singapore · Spain · United Kingdom · United States

Keyboarding & Formatting Essentials, Microsoft® Word 2002 / Microsoft® Word 2003, Lessons 1-60
Susie H. VanHuss, Connie M. Forde, Donna Woo

VP/Editorial Director:
Jack W. Calhoun

VP/Editor-in-Chief:
Dave Shaut

Senior Publisher:
Karen Schmohe

Acquisitions Editor:
Jane Phelan

Project Manager:
Inell Bolls

Consulting Editor:
Mary Todd
Todd Publishing Services

Director Educational Marketing:
Carol Volz

Marketing Manager:
Lori Pegg

Production Editors:
Carol Spencer
Martha Conway

Production Manager:
Tricia Boies

Manufacturing Coordinator:
Charlene Taylor

Media Production Editor:
Mike Jackson

Design Project Manager:
Stacy Jenkins Shirley

Permissions Editor:
Linda Ellis

Copyeditor:
Gary Morris

Production House:
D&G Limited, LLC

Cover Designer:
Craig LaGesse Ramsdell
www.ramsdelldesign.com

Cover Images:
© PhotoDisc, Inc.

Internal Designer:
Craig LaGesse Ramsdell
www.ramsdelldesign.com

Printer:
Quebecor World, Dubuque
Dubuque, Iowa

For permission to use material from this text or product, contact us by
Tel (800) 730-2214
Fax (800) 730-2215
http://www.thomsonrights.com

For more information
contact South-Western,
5191 Natorp Boulevard,
Mason, Ohio, 45040.
Or you can visit our Internet site at:
http://www.swlearning.com

Microsoft is a registered trademark of Microsoft Corporation in the U.S. and/or other countries.

The names of all products mentioned herein are used for identification purposes only and may be trademarks or registered trademarks of their respective owners. South-Western disclaims any affiliation, association, connection with, sponsorship, or endorsement by such owners.

TABLE OF CONTENTS

THE LATEST WORD IN KEYBOARDING

Focus on the Essentials

Building a skill takes practice, and that's what you'll get with the *Keyboarding Essentials* series. More timed writings, five supplemental keyboarding lessons using the keyboarding software, and technique drills throughout.

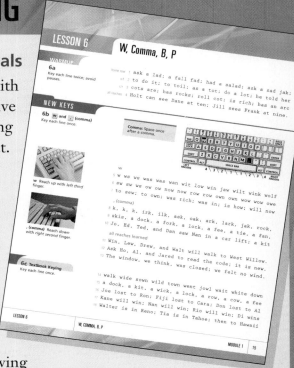

Keyboarding Pro—Now with Web Reporting, especially designed for distance education

Keyboarding Pro 4
Now with Web reporting and Spanish instruction!

Spice up your practice! *Keyboarding Pro 4* software uses graphics, games, progress graphs, videos, 3-D models for viewing proper posture and hand positions, sound effects, and a full-featured word processor to keep learning fun and meaningful. Students also have the option of e-mail or the Web for transferring their assignments to you. Instruction available in Spanish.

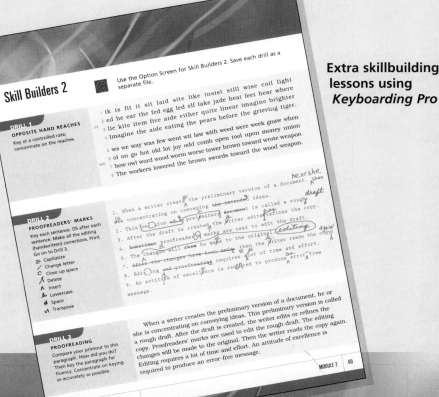

Extra skillbuilding lessons using *Keyboarding Pro*

The Latest Word
Microsoft® Word 2003 and Microsoft® Word 2002

The *Keyboarding Essentials* series teaches document formatting using the functions of Microsoft Word 2003 and 2002. Word processing commands are taught in the first lesson or two of each module and applied with simple drills. The remaining lessons provide extensive opportunities to apply the commands and reinforce new learning while extending keyboarding skills.

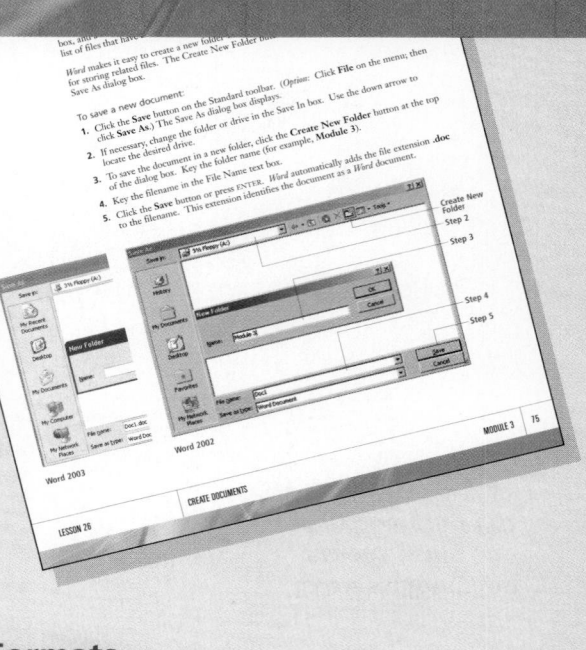

Up-to-Date Formats

New formats are explained and illustrated with callouts for proper placement.

Drills reinforce new functions.

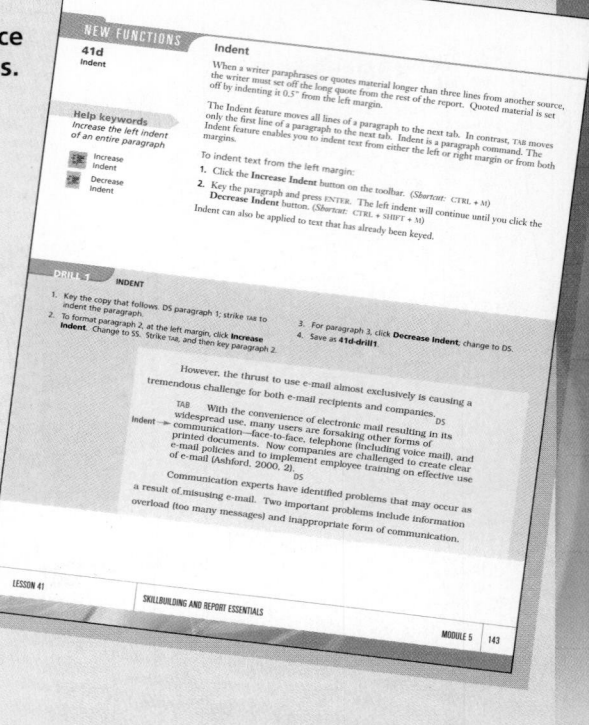

Model documents make it easy.

CLEARLY FOCUSED ON YOUR NEEDS

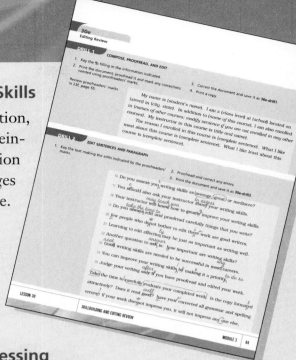

Communication Skills

Proofreading, capitalization, composition, and other language arts skills are reinforced. Supplemental Communication Skill Builder pages provide extra practice.

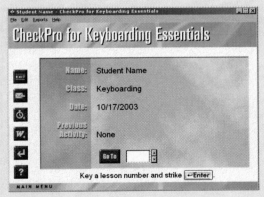

Document Processing

That's the focus of Lessons 61-120. Three new modules--18 lessons--address today's needs: Forms and Financial Documents, Promotional Document Formats, and Meeting Management.

Reference Manual

provides easy access to model documents.

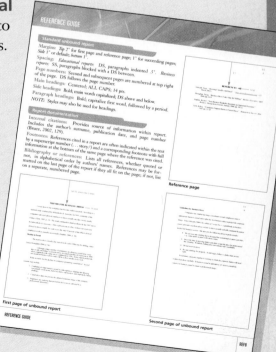

CheckPro for Keyboarding Essentials
Now with Web reporting for distance education!

Transferring student data between students and instructors just gets easier. *CheckPro for Keyboarding Essentials* is your answer to handling distance education with ease.

THE LATEST WORD IN KEYBOARDING

Product Family

Formatting & Document Processing Essentials, Lessons 61–120
0-538-72774-8
Intensive document processing text that includes many document types: budgets, financial statements, a wide variety of forms, minutes, reports, agendas, itineraries, and merged documents. A Software Training Manual reviews functions learned in L1-60.

Keyboarding & Formatting Essentials, Lessons 1–120
0-538-72796-9
Instructor's Manual & Key, Lessons 1-60 (0-538-72758-6) and *Instructor's Resource CD, Lessons 1-60* (0-538-72759-4) Solutions, data files, teaching tips, and tests—all in an easy-to-use format.

Technology Solutions

Keyboarding Pro 4
0-538-72802-7, Individual License. With Web reporting and Spanish.

CheckPro for Keyboarding Essentials
0-538-72798-5, Individual License. Now with Web reporting for your distance education needs.

MicroPace Pro, 2.0
0-538-72778-0, Individual License. Program software that correlates to *Keyboarding Essentials* and provides additional skillbuilding practice to increase technique and accuracy. Comprehensive error diagnostics.

KeyChamp, 2E
0-538-43390-6
Textbook and program software that builds speed by analyzing student's two-stroke key combinations and provides drills for building speed.

Instructor Approved

Lillie Begay
San Juan College
Farmington, New Mexico

Shirley Bennings
Augusta Technical College
Augusta, Georgia

Jane Clausen
Western Iowa Technical College
Sioux City, Iowa

Lucille Cusano
Tunix Community College
Farmington, Connecticut

Claudia Fortney
Rasmussen College
Mankato, Minnesota

Lucille Graham
San Antonio College
San Antonio, Texas

Cindy Moss
Appalachian Technical College
Jasper, Georgia

Janice Salles
Merced Community College
Merced, California

A Word from the Authors

Thank you for your support of our keyboarding texts over the past many years. We have designed this text especially for those who need a traditional keyboarding and document formatting approach. We hope our new series meets your needs.

Susie VanHuss
Connie Forde
Donna Woo

Keyboarding Pro combines the latest technology with South-Western's superior method for teaching keyboarding. The Alphabetic and Numeric and Skill modules of *Keyboarding Pro* correspond to Lessons 1-25 in *Keyboarding and Formatting Essentials*. Use Skill Builder to boost your speed and accuracy after you learn the alphabetic keys. Use the Numeric Keypad to learn the keypad by touch.

Getting Started

1. Click the **Start** button and then select **Programs**. Select the South-Western Keyboarding program group and click **Keyboarding Pro**.

2. Click anywhere on the splash screen to remove it and bring up the Log In dialog box.

The first time you use *Keyboarding Pro*, you must enter your user information and indicate where you will store your data. This process creates a student record. You will create a student record *only once* so that the results of all lessons are stored in one file.

1. From the Log In dialog box, click **New User**.

2. Enter your name (first name then last name), your Class ID, and a password. Write down the password and store it in a safe place. You will need to use this password each time you enter the program.

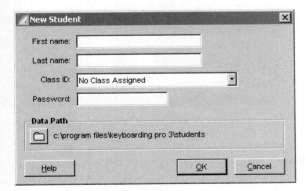

3. Specify the data location. The default storage path is **c:\Program Files\Keyboarding Pro 4\Students**. If you will be storing on Drive A or if you have a student subdirectory on the network, set the path accordingly. Click the **Folder** icon to browse to locate your folder.

4. Click **OK** to complete the registration. The program will display the Main Menu.

Each time you enter *Keyboarding Pro* after the first time, the Log In dialog box displays. Select your name and enter your password. If you do not see your name, click the **Folder** button to locate the drive where your student record is located (Drive A or your folder on the network).

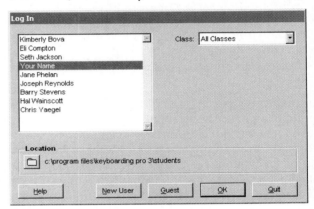

Special Features of Keyboarding Pro

 The **Open Screen** is a word processor with a timer. Available from any screen, the Open Screen allows you to practice your keyboarding or take a timed writing.

 Available from the Main menu, **Quick Review** includes numerous extra keyboarding drills for improving techniques and keyboarding skill.

 Diagnostic Writings are timed writings (1', 3', or 5') with extensive error analysis. Access Diagnostic Writings from either the Numeric and Skill or Skill Builder menu.

Send Files to Instructor: *Keyboarding Pro 4* makes it extremely easy to send your student record to your instructor. For complete information on how this feature works, go to www.collegekeyboarding.com.

WELCOME TO CHECKPRO

CheckPro verifies the accuracy of the keystrokes in drills, timed writings, and selected documents that you key beginning in Module 4. The drill practice and timed writings features are built into the *CheckPro* program. For the document exercises, *CheckPro* works in conjunction with *Microsoft Word*. You will key documents using *Word* and then *CheckPro* error-checks your work.

Getting Started with CheckPro

To launch the program, click the **Start** button and then select **Programs**. Select the South-Western Keyboarding program group and click **CheckPro for Keyboarding Essentials.** Once the splash screen is removed, the Student Registration dialog box appears.

When you first use the *CheckPro* software, you must enter your user information and indicate where you will store your data. This process creates a student record. You will create a student record only once.

1. From the Student Registration dialog box, click **New.** This launches the New Student dialog box.

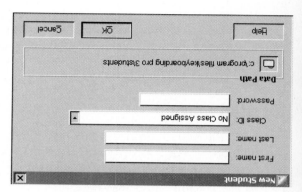

2. Enter your name and password and select your class if it is available on the drop-down list.

3. Specify the data location. The default storage path is **c:\Program Files\CheckProKE\Students.** If you will be storing on Drive A or if you have a student subdirectory on the network, set the path accordingly.

Main Screen

After you start the program and log in, the program displays the *CheckPro* main screen. The main screen is the central navigation point for the entire program. From here you can select a lesson, e-mail, a data file, or access the supplemental timings/documents. Supplemental timings refer to timed writings that are not located in a numbered lesson (for example, Skill Builders 2, 3, etc.). Supplemental documents include documents that cannot be accessed from numbered lessons (CheckPoints, projects, tests, and documents created by your instructor).

Choose a lesson by keying the lesson number or clicking on the arrows to the right of the Go To field. Then click on the **Go To** button or strike ENTER. You are now at a lesson screen, which will look *similar* to the example below.

Each time you enter *CheckPro* after the first time, the Student Registration dialog box displays. Click your name and enter your password. If you do not see your name, click the folder icon and browse either Drive A or the folder on the network where your data is being saved to locate your data record.

Lesson Screen

The lesson screen contains more activity options. Each activity corresponds directly with the activities for that lesson in your textbook. Click on the button next to an activity title to complete that activity. Drills and timed writings will be completed within the *CheckPro* software. *CheckPro* will launch *Word 2002* or *Word 2003* for you to complete documents or production tests.

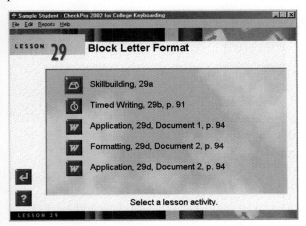

Drill Practice: For a drill practice activity, key each drill line as it appears on the screen. You can choose to repeat the activity when you finish the drill practice. A check mark appears next to the menu option on the lesson screen when you complete it.

Timed Writings: Click a **Timed Writing** button to take a timed writing. Then select the timing length and source. Key the timed writing from your textbook. The program shows the *gwam*, error rate, and actual errors when you finish the writing. You can print the timed writing report or save it to disk.

Documents and Production Tests: Select a document or assessment activity and choose **Begin new document**. You'll get a dialog box with important information, and then your word processor will be launched. *CheckPro* creates a document for you with the correct filename. The *CheckPro* toolbar will appear on top of the *Word 2002* document window. When you are finished proofreading the document, do not save the file. Instead, click on the check mark on the *CheckPro* toolbar. *CheckPro* will then save your document and

open a checked version of it back in *CheckPro* for you to review your errors. To finish an exercise or revise a checked document, select the activity and choose **Open existing document**.

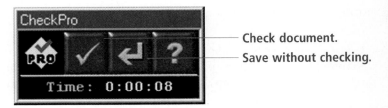

Check document.
Save without checking.

Reports

There are a number of reports available in *CheckPro*. Click on the **Reports** menu to see the selection. The Lesson Report provides a snapshot of your results for a specific lesson. Click on the **Activity Checklist** to see an overview of which activities have been completed. This report indicates the date each activity was completed, but provides no further information. Choose the **Reports** menu, **Summary Report** to view Drill, Timed Writing, Document, and Production Test summaries. All of the information for creating these reports is saved in your record file.

Special Features

CheckPro for Keyboarding Essentials makes it extremely easy to send your completed documents or student record to your instructor for evaluation. To learn more about using *CheckPro* for distance education, go to the website www.collegekeyboarding.com. A complete explanation is provided here.

The Supplemental Timed Writings button provides a way to check a timing located somewhere other than a numbered lesson (e.g. a timing located in a Skill Builder).

Select the Supplemental Documents button to complete any document exercise found in an unnumbered lesson (for example, an exercise from a project, a Communication Skill, or a document created by your instructor).

THE DESKTOP

Microsoft® Windows® is an operating system, a program that manages all other software applications on your computer and its peripherals such as the mouse and printer. Software applications that run under *Windows* have many common features. Depending on the version of your operating system, some features may look, work, or be named slightly differently on your computer.

When your computer is turned on and ready to use, a Welcome screen showing the names of every computer user on the computer will display. Click your user icon, key your password in the textbox, and then click the **Next** button to access the desktop. The illustration below shows a *Windows XP* **desktop**, which is the main working area. Your desktop will have many of the same features. Depending on what programs are on your computer and how the desktop has been arranged, it may look different.

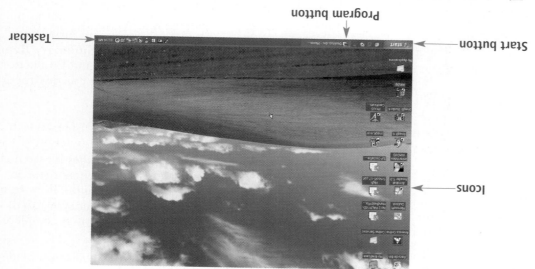

Start button ◄——

Icons ◄——

——► Taskbar

Program button

The desktop displays icons and a taskbar. Icons provide an easy way to access programs and documents that you frequently use. Desktop icons will vary. Two common icons are:

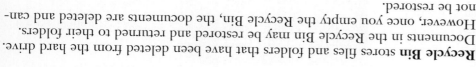

My Computer displays the disk drives, CD-ROM drives, and printers that are attached to your computer.

Recycle Bin stores files and folders that have been deleted from the hard drive. Documents in the Recycle Bin may be restored and returned to their folders. However, once you empty the Recycle Bin, the documents are deleted and cannot be restored.

The bar at the bottom of the desktop is the taskbar. **The taskbar** displays the Start button on the left, a button for each program or document that is open, and the system clock on the right (your taskbar may have additional icons). The taskbar enables you to open programs and navigate on your computer.

THE MOUSE

Windows requires the use of a mouse or other pointing device such as a touch pad built into your keyboard. The *Windows* software utilizes the left and right mouse buttons. The left button is used to select text or commands, to open files or menus, or to drag objects. The right button is used to display shortcut menus.

The pointer (arrow) ▶ indicates your location on the screen. To move the pointer, you must first move the mouse. If you have a touch pad on your keyboard, move the pointer by moving your finger on the touch pad. The mouse or touch pad is used to perform four basic actions.

Point: Move the mouse so that the pointer touches something displayed on the screen.

Click: Point to an item, quickly press the left mouse button once, and release it. You will always use the left mouse button unless directions tell you to right-click; which means click the right mouse button.

Double-click: Point to an item; quickly press the left mouse button twice, and release it.

Drag: Point to an item, then hold down the left mouse button while you move the mouse to reposition the item.

The mouse pointer changes in appearance depending on its location on the desktop and the task being performed.

| The *vertical blinking bar* indicates the current position of the cursor.

I   The *I-beam* indicates the location of the mouse pointer. To reposition the cursor at this point, you must click the mouse button.

▶   The *arrow* indicates that you can select items. It displays when the mouse is located outside the text area. You can point to a toolbar icon to display the function of that icon.

⌛   The *hourglass* indicates that *Windows* is processing a command.

↔   A *double-headed arrow* appears when the pointer is in the border of a window; it is used to change the size.

THE START BUTTON

start

The **Start** button opens the Start menu, which lists a variety of items from which to choose such as programs and documents.

The Start menu is divided into three sections and displays some of the programs and folders on your computer. The top of the menu displays the user icon and name. The middle section contains two columns of commands. The bottom section contains the Log Off and Turn Off Computer commands.

Let's take a closer look at the middle section of the Start menu. Separator lines divide sections of the Start menu. The section in the upper left is called the pinned items list, which contains an icon for your Web browser and your e-mail program. The next section below contains icons for your six most frequently used programs. The top right section contains commands to access various folders and My Computer. If your computer is connected to a network, the My Network Places command displays below My Computer. The next section contains commands to customize the computer and peripherals. The bottom section contains commands for Help, searching, and launching programs (Run).

If you do not see the program you need displayed, point to the All Programs arrow to display a full list of programs available on your computer. To open an item listed on the Start menu, point to the item and click the left mouse button. A right arrow beside a menu item indicates that a submenu with more options is available for that item. (*Note* If an icon is displayed on the desktop, you can double-click the icon to open the program, document, or folder that it represents.)

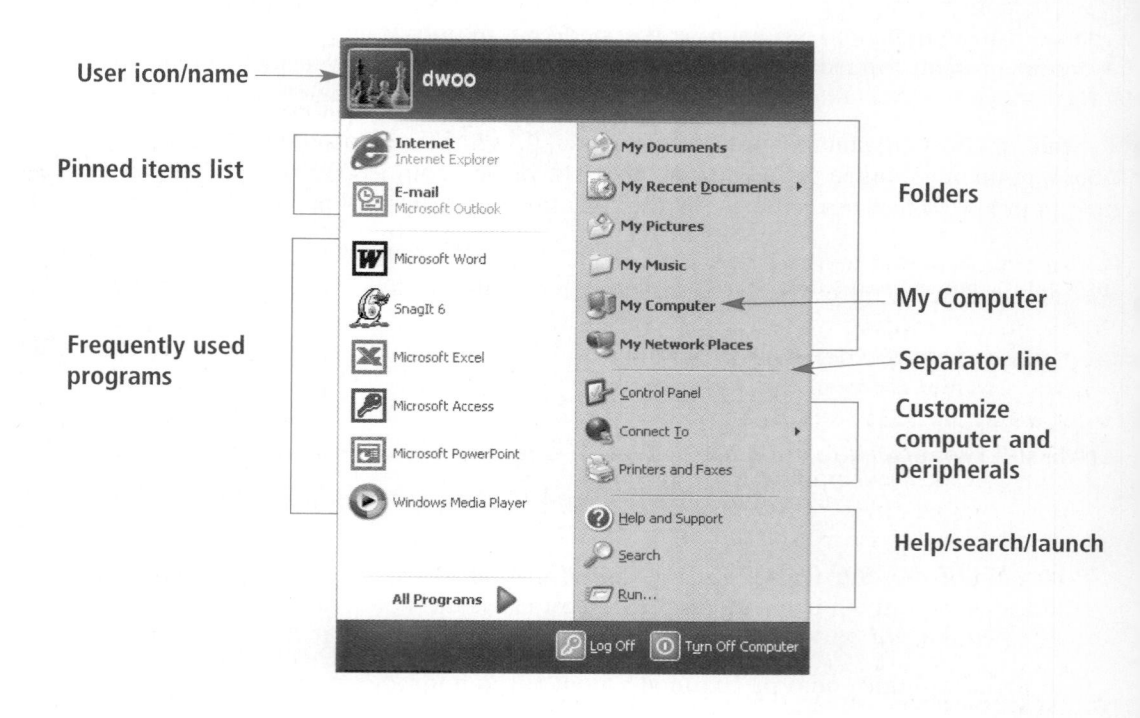

WINDOWS FEATURES

Windows displays folders, applications, and individual documents in windows. A **window** is a work area on the desktop that can be resized or moved. To resize a window, point to the border. When the pointer changes to a double-headed arrow, drag the window to the desired size. To move a window, point to the title bar, drag it to the new position, and release the mouse button.

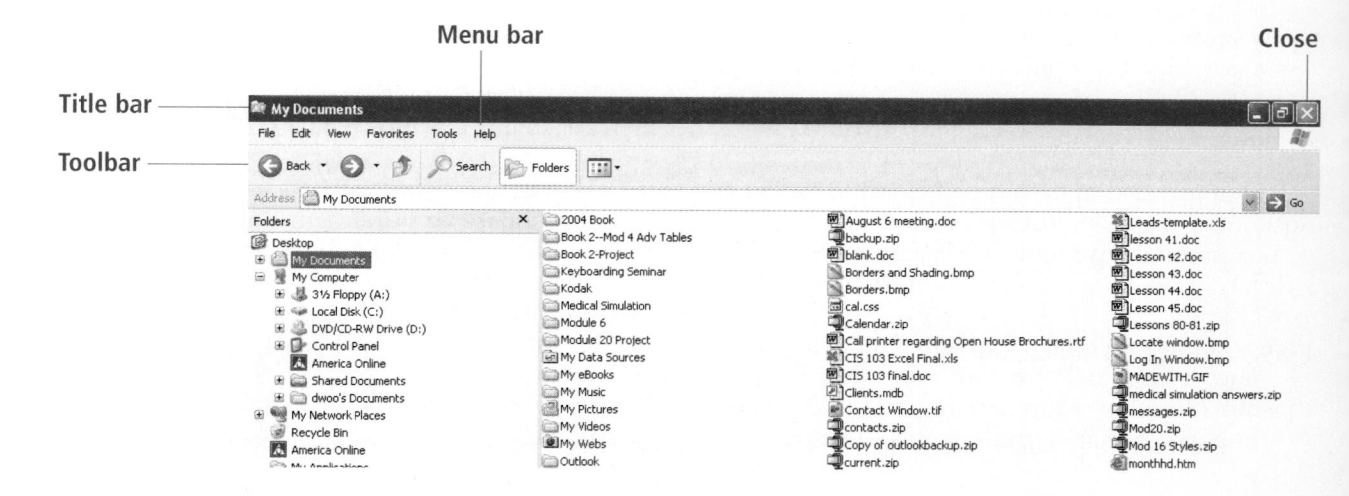

The basic features of all windows are the same. Each window contains the following:

Menu bar: Displays commands available in the software.

Toolbars: Display icons that offer a convenient way to access frequently used commands. Applications programs have different toolbars for different tasks.

Scroll bars: Enable you to see material that does not fit on one screen. You can click the arrows on the scroll bars or drag the scroll box to move through a document.

Title bar: Displays the name of the application that is currently open and the path (folder name). The Title bar also includes several buttons at the right.

> **Minimize button**: Reduces the window to a button on the taskbar. To restore the window, click the button on the taskbar.

> **Maximize button**: Enlarges a window to full-screen size.

> **Restore button**: When you maximize a window, the Maximize button is replaced with a Restore button that, when clicked, returns the window to its original size.

> **Close button**: Closes the application.

Minimize   Maximize   Close   Restore

HELP

Help is available for *Windows*. Help is also available with each software application that you use. Generally you will use the Help feature provided with the application. To access *Windows* Help, click the **Start** button, and then click **Help and Support**. You can choose from the list of Help topics displayed, or key your topic in the Search box and click the green arrow.

Index button ⎯

Search ⎯
box

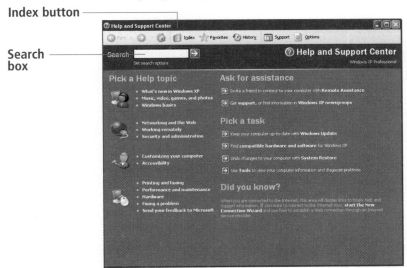

You can also click the **Index** button on the toolbar to display a list of specific items in alphabetical order. As you key the characters of the topic in the entry box, the program automatically moves to items beginning with the keyed letters. When the correct topic displays, highlight it and choose **Display**. If you prefer, you can scroll through the list of topics until you find what you are looking for.

DRILL 1

1. Click the **Start** button. Choose **Help and Support**.

2. Click **What's new in Windows XP** from the Help topics.

3. Click **Taking a tour or tutorial** in the left pane.

4. Choose **Take the Windows XP tour** in the right pane. Follow the directions on the screen to complete the *Windows XP* Tour. When finished, close the Help and Support Center.

FILE MANAGEMENT

FORMAT A DISKETTE

File Management includes the processes of creating and managing the electronic files on your computer. You will learn to format a floppy disk, understand basic file structure, manage files and folders, and log off from the computer.

Data that needs to be used again in the future must be saved on a storage device such as floppy diskettes, CD/DVD, zip disk, or the hard drive. Floppy diskettes are often used in school settings. A floppy diskette must be formatted before it can be used for storing data. Some diskettes are shipped from the manufacturer preformatted; they will not require additional formatting. If you purchase unformatted disks, they will need to be formatted before use. Formatting the disk means that the operating system will erase the disk, check for bad sectors, and place tracks and sectors on the disk so that files can be saved on the disk.

To format a disk:

The following steps will instruct you to format a high-density diskette in the A: drive. Ask your instructor what drive you are to use to format a diskette.

1. Insert the disk to be formatted in the disk drive (A:).
2. Double-click the **My Computer** icon to open the My Computer window.
3. Select the drive containing the disk to be formatted (A:).
4. Click the File menu and select **Format**; the Format dialog box displays.

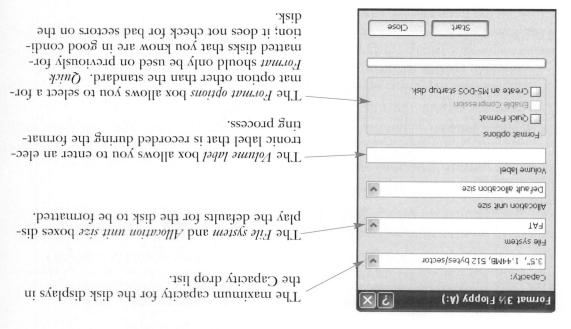

The maximum capacity for the disk displays in the Capacity drop list.

The *File system* and *Allocation unit size* boxes display the defaults for the disk to be formatted.

The *Volume label* box allows you to enter an electronic label that is recorded during the formatting process.

The *Format options* box allows you to select a format option other than the standard. *Quick Format* should only be used on previously formatted disks that you know are in good condition; it does not check for bad sectors on the disk.

5. Click the **Start** button to begin the formatting. A warning box displays so you do not format a disk that might contain data you need to keep.

6. Click **OK** when the warning box displays.

7. Click **OK** when the message box displays telling you the formatting is complete.

8. Click **Close** to close the Formatting dialog box.

9. Close the My Computer window.

DRILL 2

1. Format a 3½" floppy disk. Use your name for the volume label on the disk.

2. Double-click **My Computer** to display the My Computer dialog box.

3. Right-click **3½" Floppy (A:)** and select **Properties** from the menu.

4. Click the **General** tab in the Properties dialog box. Your name should display in the text box at the top. Notice the amount of free space on your disk. Click **OK** to remove the Properties dialog box.

5. Close the My Computer window.

UNDERSTAND THE FILE SYSTEM

As with paper files, it is important to establish a logical and easy-to-use computer file management system to organize your files efficiently so that you can find them quickly and easily. You can manage files from the desktop or from My Computer or Windows Explorer.

Computer files are stored on **disks** specified by their location. The storage drives can be identified in My Computer.

The computer in this example has a hard disk drive (C), a floppy disk drive (A), and a DVD/CD drive (D).

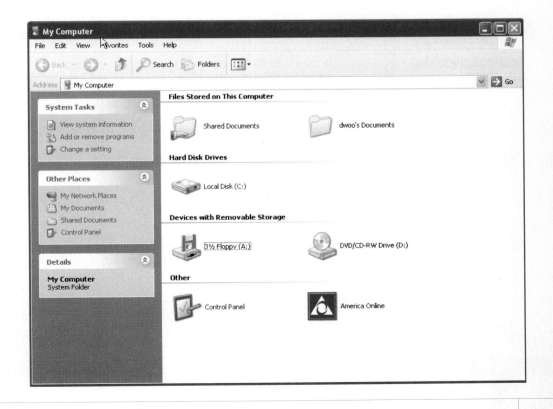

View Contents of a Drive

1. To view the contents of a drive through My Computer, double-click the **My Computer** icon on the desktop. If the **My Computer** icon is not available, choose **My Computer** from the Start menu.

2. Double-click the desired disk drive to display the contents.

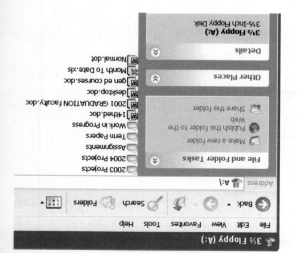

View Contents of a Folder

Folders are listed in numerical and alphabetical order. Folders with numerical names will be listed before those with alphabetic names, as shown in the figure above. To see the contents of a folder, double-click the folder. Folders may contain files, programs, and folders.

View Data and Arrange Files

Files and folders can be viewed in different ways: as Thumbnails, Tiles, Icons, List, and Details. The figure above shows the items in List View.

To change the view, click **View** on the menu, then choose a view. You may want to experiment with each of the views to decide which one you prefer.

As previously mentioned, folders are listed in alphabetical order. You can also arrange them in descending order by date, size, or type of file. To rearrange the order of files or folders, select **Details** from the View menu, and then click the heading displayed above the files or folders such as **Size**, **Type**, or **Date Modified.**

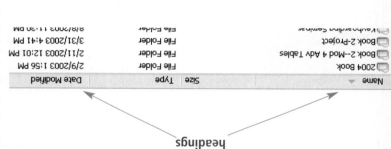

headings

Name	Size	Type	Date Modified
2004 Book		File Folder	2/9/2003 1:56 PM
Book 2--Mod 4 Adv Tables		File Folder	2/11/2003 12:01 PM
Book 2-Project		File Folder	3/31/2003 4:41 PM
Keyboarding Seminar		File Folder	8/8/2003 11:30 AM

DRILL 3

1. Insert your data CD in its drive. Use My Computer to display the contents of that CD.
2. Use the View menu to change to Thumbnails View.
3. Change the view to List View.
4. Change to Details View. Click the **Name** heading. Notice the files are displayed in ascending order.
5. Click the **Date Modified** heading to place the documents back in ascending order by date.
6. Double-click on a file folder to display the files in the folder.
7. Click the Up button on the toolbar to return to the previous level displaying the folders.
8. Click the **Back** button on the toolbar to return to the My Computer screen.

WORK WITH FOLDERS AND FILES

Folders are extremely important in organizing files. You will want to create and manage folders and the files within them so that you can easily locate them. Managing files and folders also involves renaming and deleting items.

Create Folder

Folders can be created in My Computer or in Windows Explorer.

1. To create a folder in My Computer, display the drive that is to contain the new folder.

2. Click **Make a new folder** in the left pane.

3. A new folder displays at the end of the list of files labeled **New Folder**. Delete the words *New Folder* and replace them with a new name.

4. Strike ENTER.

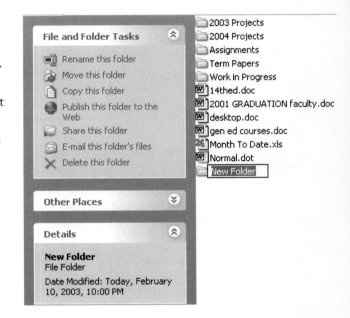

To create a folder in Windows Explorer, point to **All Programs** on the Start menu. Choose **Accessories**, and then choose **Windows Explorer**. Click the drive or folder that will contain the new folder. Select **New** from the File menu and choose **Folder**. Select and replace **New Folder** with the new name.

Name Files and Folders

Good file organization begins with giving your folders and files names that are logical and easy to understand. In the previous figure, a folder was created for Assignments, Term Papers, and Work in Progress. You may want create a folder named Module 3 to hold all work that you key in Module 3. You will save the files by the exercise name such as 26b-d1 or 26b-d2. A system like this makes finding files simple.

Rename Files and Folders

Occasionally, you may want to rename a file or folder. To do so, click the file or folder, choose **Rename this file** or **Rename this folder**, key the new name, and press ENTER. You can also rename files using the Windows Explorer menu; select the file or folder, and then choose **Rename** on the File menu.

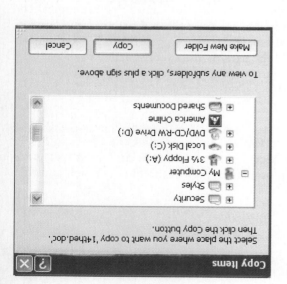

Copy Items

Select the place where you want to copy '14thed.doc'.
Then click the Copy button.

- ⊞ 🗀 Security
- ⊞ 🗀 Styles
- ⊟ 🖳 My Computer
  - ⊞ 💾 3½ Floppy (A:)
  - ⊞ 💽 Local Disk (C:)
  - ⊞ 💿 DVD/CD-RW Drive (D:)
  - ⊞ 🖪 America Online
  - 🗀 Shared Documents

To view any subfolders, click a plus sign above.

[Make New Folder]   [Copy]   [Cancel]

Move and Copy Files and Folders

1. To move or copy files using My Computer, click the file/folder to be copied or moved.

2. Click **Copy this file** or **Move this file** in the left pane. The Copy Items window displays.

3. Click the drive or the folder in which the copy is to be placed.

To copy or move files using Windows Explorer:

1. In the Windows Explorer screen, click the drive that contains the file or folder you want to move, then locate the item.

2. Be sure the place you want to move the file or folder to is visible. Press and hold down the left mouse button and drag the pointer to the new location.

To copy a file or folder, press and hold down CTRL while you drag.

Note: If you drag a file or folder to a location on the same disk, it will be moved. If you drag an item to a different disk, it will be copied. To move the item, press and hold down SHIFT while dragging.

If you wish to copy or move several items at once, click the first item; then hold down the CTRL key as you select each additional item. This allows you to copy or move all the files at one time. If the items you wish to copy or move are consecutive, click the first item, hold down SHIFT, and click the last item—now you can copy or move the entire list at once.

Delete Files and Folders

Files and folders can be deleted in My Computer or Windows Explorer. You can select and delete several files and folders at once, just as you can select several items to move or copy. If you delete a folder, you automatically delete any files and folders inside it.

To delete a file or folder and send it to the Recycle Bin, right-click the item and choose **Delete.** Answer Yes to the question about sending the item to the Recycle Bin.

Restore Deleted Files and Folders

When you delete a file or folder, the item goes to the Recycle Bin. If you have not emptied the Recycle Bin, you can restore files and folders stored there. Items deleted from the A drive will be deleted permanently and do not go to the Recycle Bin.

To restore a file in the Recycle Bin:

1. Double-click the **Recycle Bin** icon on the desktop to open the Recycle Bin window.

2. Select the file you want to restore, right-click to display the shortcut menu, and choose **Restore.** You can also choose Restore from the File menu.

3. Close the Recycle Bin window. Click the folder where the file was originally located, and it should now be restored.

LOG OFF AND SHUT DOWN

Log Off

When you are finished using the computer, you should close your user account by logging off the computer. Logging off performs three functions: (1) any applications software left often will be closed; (2) you will be prompted to save any unsaved documents; and (3) you will end your *Windows* session and allow another person to use your computer. This procedure should always be followed if your computer has more than one user account listed in the Welcome screen. It is a good idea to log off, even if you are the sole user of the computer.

To log off, click the **Start** button and click the **Log Off** button on the Start menu. Confirm the log off in the dialog box that displays. The Welcome screen displays.

Shut Down

To shut down the computer after logging off, click the **Turn off computer** button on the Welcome screen, then click the **Turn Off** button in the Turn off computer dialog box.

DRILL 4

1. Using My Computer, create a new folder on Drive A called **XP Intro**.

2. Rename the folder **Win XP**.

3. Make a copy of this folder on Drive C. (If you cannot do this, ask your instructor for the location to which you can copy.)

4. Delete the folder you created on Drive A and the copy you made on Drive C.

DRILL 5

You will need to copy files from the data CD to your floppy diskette when you perform the exercises in this book. This exercise will walk you through the steps of copying a file folder and its contents from the CD to the diskette in Drive A. You will use Windows Explorer.

1. Insert your data CD in the CD Drive and a floppy diskette in Drive A.

2. Display the Windows Explorer window.

3. Click the + symbol to the left of My Computer to display the drives on the computer.

4. Double-click the CD drive to display the contents of the CD in the right pane.

5. Click the **View** menu and select **Details**.

6. Click a file folder, hold down the left mouse button, and drag the folder to Drive A. The folder and its contents will be copied to Drive A. Next, check to see that the folder and its contents were copied to Drive A, then delete the folder.

7. Double-click **3¹/₂" Floppy (A:)** in the left pane under My Computer to display the contents of Drive A.

8. Double-click the file folder to view the files in the folder.

9. Click the **Up** button in the toolbar to display the higher level (file folders).

10. Select the file folder, click the **File** menu, and select **Delete**.

11. Click **Yes** to confirm the deletion of the folder.

12. Go back to your desktop. Ask your instructor if you should log off or shut down the computer.

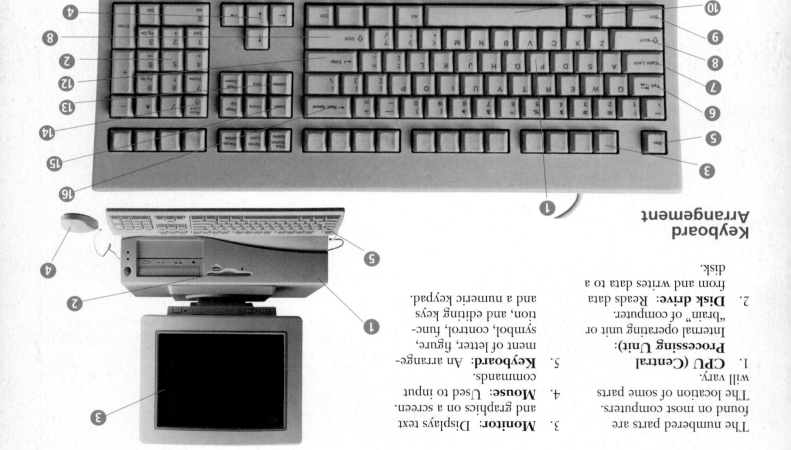

The numbered parts are found on most computers. The location of some parts will vary.

1. **CPU (Central Processing Unit):** Internal operating unit or "brain" of computer.
2. **Disk drive:** Reads data from and writes data to a disk.
3. **Monitor:** Displays text and graphics on a screen.
4. **Mouse:** Used to input commands.
5. **Keyboard:** An arrangement of letter, figure, symbol, control, function, and editing keys and a numeric keypad.

Keyboard Arrangement

1. **Alphanumeric keys:** Letters, numbers, and symbols.
2. **Numeric keypad:** Keys at the right side of the keyboard used to enter numeric copy and perform calculations.
3. **Function (F) keys:** Used to execute commands, sometimes with other keys. Commands vary with software.
4. **Arrow keys:** Move insertion point up, down, left, or right.
5. **ESC (Escape):** Closes a software menu or dialog box.
6. **TAB:** Moves the insertion point to a preset position.
7. **CAPS LOCK:** Used to make all capital letters.
8. **SHIFT:** Makes capital letters and symbols shown at tops of number keys.
9. **CTRL (Control):** With other key(s), executes commands. Commands may vary with software.
10. **ALT (Alternate):** With other key(s), executes commands. Commands may vary with software.
11. **Space Bar:** Inserts a space in text.
12. **ENTER (RETURN):** Moves insertion point to margin and down to next line. Also used to execute commands.
13. **DELETE:** Removes text to the right of insertion point.
14. **NUM LOCK:** Activates/deactivates numeric keypad.
15. **INSERT:** Activates insert or typeover.
16. **BACKSPACE:** Deletes text to the left of insertion point.

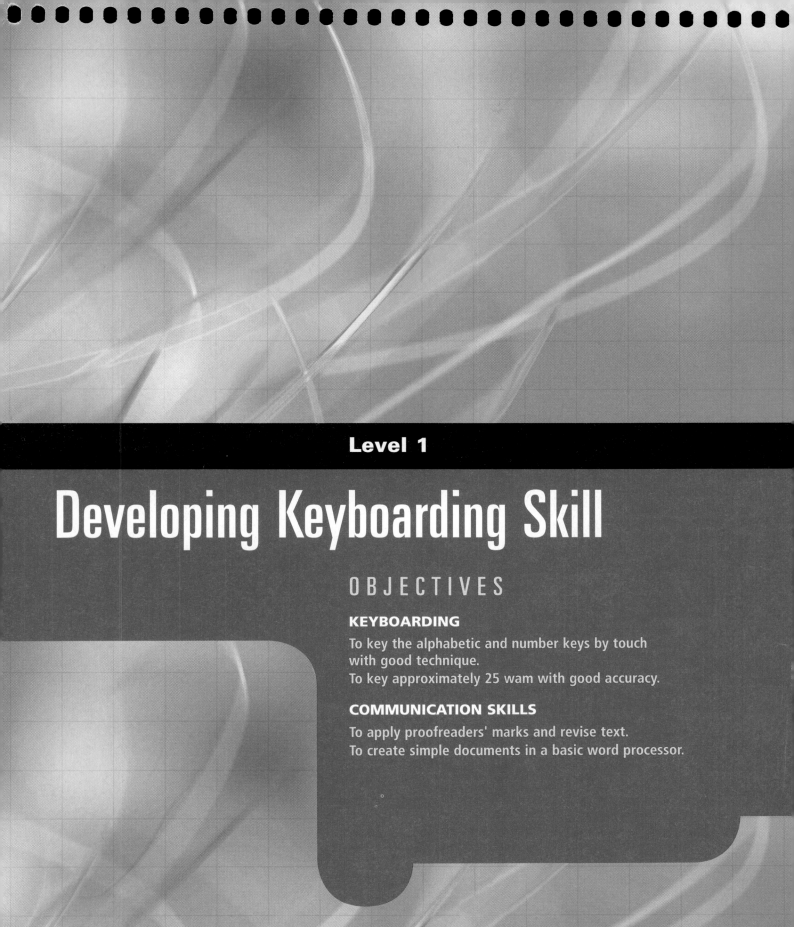

Level 1

Developing Keyboarding Skill

OBJECTIVES

KEYBOARDING

To key the alphabetic and number keys by touch
with good technique.
To key approximately 25 wam with good accuracy.

COMMUNICATION SKILLS

To apply proofreaders' marks and revise text.
To create simple documents in a basic word processor.

Internet Activities 2

Activity 3

Explore Search Engines

To find information on the World Wide Web (WWW), the best place to start is often a search engine. Search engines are used to locate specific information. Just a few examples of search engines are AltaVista, Excite, Google, AskJeeves, Lycos, and Yahoo.

 To go to a search engine, click on the **Search** button on your Web browser. (Browsers vary.)

DRILL

1. Go to the search engines on your browser. Click on the first search engine. Browse the hyperlinks available such as Maps, People Finder, News, Weather, Stock Quotes, Sports, Games, etc. Click each search engine and explore the hyperlinks.

2. Conduct the following search using Dogpile, a multithreaded search engine that searches multiple databases;
   a. Open the Web site for Dogpile (http://www.dogpile.com).
   b. In the Search entry box, key the keywords **American Psychological Association** publications; click **Go Fetch**.

3. Pick two of the following topics and search for each using three of your browser's search engines. Look over the first ten results you get from each search. Which search engine gave you the greatest number of promising results for each topic?

aerobics	antivirus software	career change
censorship	college financing	teaching tolerance

Activity 4

Search Yellow Pages

Searching the Yellow Pages for information on businesses and services is commonplace, both in business and at home. Let your computer do the searching for you the next time.

DRILL

1. Open the search engine dogpile.com. Click **Yellow Pages**.
2. Determine a city that you would like to visit. Assume you will need overnight accommodations. Use the Yellow Pages to find a listing of hotels in this city.

3. Your best friend lives in (*you provide the city*); you want to send him/her flowers. Find a listing of florists in this city.
4. You create a third scenario and find listings.

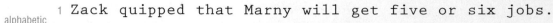

Keyboarding Assessment/Placement

WARMUP

1. Open *Keyboarding Pro*. Create a student record. (see page xviii)
2. Go to the Open Screen.
3. Key the drill twice.
4. Close the Open Screen ✕. Do not save or print the drill lines.

alphabetic
1 Zack quipped that Marny will get five or six jobs.
2 Quin Gaf's wax mock-up had just dazzled everybody.

Strike ENTER twice

figures
3 Room 2938 holds 50 people, and Room 1940 holds 67.
4 Call 803-555-0164 and then ask for extension 1928.

easy
5 Ken may go downtown now and then go to their lake.
6 Did he bid on the bicycle, or did he bid on a map?

gwam 1 3

Straight-Copy Assessment

1. Go to Skill Builder. From the Lesson menu, click the **Diagnostic Writing** button.
2. Choose 3'. Select **pretest** from the Writings list. Press TAB to begin. Key from the text.
3. Take a second 3' timing. Click the Timer to begin.
4. Print your results.

    I have a story or two or three that will carry you away   11   4
to foreign places, to meet people you have never known, to   23   8
see things you have never seen, to feast on foods available   35   12
only to a few. I will help you to learn new skills you want   47   16
and need; I will inspire you, excite you, instruct you, and   59   20
interest you. I am able, you understand, to make time fly.   71   24

    I answer difficult questions for you. I work with you   11   27
to realize a talent, to express a thought, and to determine   23   31
just who and what you are and want to be. I help you to   35   35
know words, to write, and to read. I help you to comprehend   47   40
the mysteries of the past and the secrets of the future. I   59   44
am your local library. We ought to get together often.   70   47

```
1' | 1 | 2 | 3 | 4 | 5 | 6 | 7 | 8 | 9 | 10 | 11 | 12 |
3'     |   1   |     |   2   |     |   3   |     |   4   |
```

gwam 1 3

Statistical Assessment

1. Follow the steps for the straight-copy assessment.
2. Take two 3' writings using the Diagnostic Writing feature. Choose the writing **placement2**.

    Attention Wall Street! The Zanes & Cash report for the end   4   38
of the year (Report #98) says that its last-quarter income was up   8   42
26% from the record earnings of last year. The report also says   12   46
that it was caused by a rise in gross sales of just over 4 1/3%.   16   50
The increase is the 7th in a row for last-quarter earnings; and   20   54
the chief executive of this old firm—Paul Cash—has told at   24   58
least one group that he is sure to ask the board (it will meet on   28   62
the last day of the month) for an "increase of up to $1.50 a share   32   66
as its dividend for the year."   34   68

```
1' | 1 | 2 | 3 | 4 | 5 | 6 | 7 | 8 | 9 | 10 | 11 | 12 |
3'     |   1   |     |   2   |     |   3   |     |   4   |
```

Document 7
Multi-page Report with Table

Open **steeringcommittee** from the data files. Add the text at the right to the end of the document.

Watch closely for any errors that may not be marked. Check for words that need to be changed to Canadian spelling.

Number the pages at the top right.

Prepare a title page. The report was prepared for **Nelson Chamber of Commerce by Richard R. Holmes, President**. Date the report March 15.

Save the report as **mod9-d7**, and save the title page as **mod9-d7a**.

Recommended facilitators include: *teamleaders and* (set this up as a table) *the following*

Team	Team Leaders	Facilitators
Education	Dale Coppage, Nelson BC	Ellen Obert, Spokane WA
Youth Services	Lawrence Riveria, Portland, OR	Jack Jones, Vancouver BC
Recreation	Bradley Greger, Nelson BC	Carolos Pena, Calgary AB
Economic Development	Jon Guyton, Nelson BC	Harvey Lewis
Crime	Monica Brigham, Toronto ON	Shawn McNullan, NC

After the first breakout sessions, participants will join for lunch in the H. L. Calvert Union Building. The Steering Committee recommends that Mayor Alton johnson address the topic of meeting educational challenges of the next century. A repeat of the morning breakout sessions will begin at 1:00. This repeat will allow participants to contirube to another topic. In the closing session breakout facilitators will present the goals and plans to the audience. *During*

Sponsors

The Steerting Committee has discussed the sponsorhsip of a goals conference with a number of partners in the Nelson area. The following organizations have agreed to serve as sponsors: Nelson Economic Development Foundation, Bank of Canada, Northeast Bottling Company, and Bank of Nelson, and Farthington's Clothiers.

Summary

The Steering Committee strongly recommends this goals conference. The committee will be avilable at the Camber of commerce meeting to answer any questions.

Document 8
Agenda

Format the agenda as a table. Apply the **Table Normal** format. Save it as **mod9-d8**.

Goals Conference Agenda *→ all caps*

9:30 a.m. - 9:45 a.m.	Welcome
9:45 a.m. - 10:15 a.m.	Opening Remarks
	Overview of Community Quality Initiative
	Purpose of Goals Conference
	Process
	Introduction of Community Leaders and Chamber Officers
10:15 a.m. - 10:35 a.m.	Refreshment Break
10:35 a.m. - 12 noon	Breakout Sessions
12 noon - 1:00 p.m.	Lunch
	Speaker on Educational Challenges of the 21st Century
1:00 p.m. - 2:30 p.m.	~~Goals Setting Workshops~~ Breakout Sessions
2:30 p.m. - 2:45 p.m.	Refreshment Break
2:45 p.m. - 4:00 p.m.	Presentation of Goals

get these from the report; alphabetize

Alphabetic Keys

- Key the alphabetic keys by touch.
- Key using proper techniques.
- Key at a rate of 14 gwam or more.

LESSON 1

Home Row, Space Bar, Enter, I

1a
Home Row Position and Space Bar

Practice the steps at the right until you can place your hands in home-row position without watching.

Key the drill lines several times.

Home Row Position

1. Drop your hands to your side. Allow your fingers to curve naturally. Maintain this curve as you key.

2. Lightly place your left fingers over the **a s d f** and the right fingers over the **j k l ;**. You will feel a raised element on the *f* and *j* keys, which will help you keep your fingers on the home position. You are now in **home–row position**.

Space Bar and Enter

Strike the Space Bar, located at the bottom of the keyboard, with a down-and-in motion of the right thumb to space between words.

Enter   Reach with the fourth (little) finger of the right hand to ENTER. Press it to return the insertion point to the left margin. This action creates a **hard return**. Use a hard return at the end of all drill lines. Quickly return to home position (over ;).

Key these lines

```
a  s  d  f  SPACE  j  k  l  ;  ENTER
a  s  d  f  SPACE  j  k  l  ;  ENTER
```

Document 4
Memo

Prepare this memo. Use Find and Replace to find and replace any words that should be changed to Canadian spellings. Save the memo as **mod9-d4**.

TO: Marilyn Smith, Public Relations Media Assistant | **FROM:** Anthony Baker, Public Relations Coordinator | **DATE:** Current | **SUBJECT:** Electronic Presentation

Richard Holmes has been invited to introduce our company at the March 15 meeting of the Nelson Chamber of Commerce. Please prepare a 20-minute electronic presentation for this meeting by extracting the key points from Richard's speech, which is attached.

As you prepare the presentation, remember these key points:

- Write phrases, not sentences, so that listeners focus on the key points.
- Use parallel structure and limit wraparound lines of text.
- Create *builds* to keep the audience alert.
- Add transitions between slides (suggest fade in and out).
- Add graphics and humor—we want them to remember us.

Please have the presentation ready for Richard to review by February 24. After he has made his revisions and the presentation is final, print the presentation as a handout. | xx | Attachment

Document 5
Table

Format this list of purchases as a table. Center the column headings and the data in column 1.

Calculate the total price for each item; then calculate the final total in cell D7. Save the table as **mod9-d5**.

Quantity	Description	Unit Price	Total Price
2	Posture back task chair	265.00	
2	Under-desk keyboard manager	54.00	
1	10 pack Zip 100 disks	99.95	
1	Carton laser paper (5,000 sheets, 20 lb.)	47.50	
2	Laser address labels, #5168	24.95	
	Total		

Document 6
Letter

Prepare this letter to order supplies. Copy the table you created in Document 5 into the letter. Use the current date and add an appropriate salutation.

Insert another row in the table just before the Total with this information: **2 external Zip drives at $89.99 each.** Recalculate the total.

Save the letter as **mod9-d6**.

West Coast Office Supplies
3245 Granville Street
Vancouver BC V6B 5G8

Please ship the following items, which are listed in your current office supplies catalogue.

Insert the table here (Document 5)

Please bill this to our account number 4056278. This order is urgent; therefore, ship it overnight by Loomis.

Yours truly

Allan Burgess, Purchasing Agent

NEW KEYS

1b Procedures for Learning New Keys

Apply these steps each time you learn a new key.

1c Home Row

1. Go to the Open Screen of *Keyboarding Pro*.
2. Key each line once. Press **ENTER** at the end of each line. Press **ENTER** twice to double-space (DS) between 2-line groups.
3. Close the Open Screen without saving your text.

STANDARD PLAN | for Learning New Keyreaches

1. Find the new key on the illustrated keyboard. Then find it on your keyboard.
2. Watch your finger make the reach to the new key a few times. Keep other fingers curved in home position. For an upward reach, straighten the finger slightly; for a downward reach, curve the finger a bit more.
3. Repeat the drill until you can key it fluently.

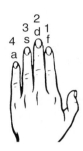

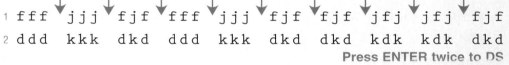

Press Space Bar once.

```
1  f f f   j j j   f j f   f f f   j j j   f j f   f j f   j f j   j f j   f j f
2  d d d   k k k   d k d   d d d   k k k   d k d   d k d   k d k   k d k   d k d
```
Press ENTER twice to DS
```
3  s s s   l l l   s l s   s s s   l l l   s l s   s l s   l s l   l s l   s l s
4  a a a   ; ; ;   a ; a   a a a   ; ; ;   a ; s   a ; a   ; a ;   ; a ;   a ; a

5  f f  j j  f f  j j  f j  f j  f j  d d  k k  d d  k k  d k  d k  d k
6  s s  l l  s s  l l  s l  s l  s l  a a  ; ;  a a  ; ;  a ;  a ;  a ;

7  f  j  d  k  s  l  a  ;
                    DS
8  ff  jj  dd  kk  ss  ll  aa  ;;

9  fff  jjj  ddd  kkk  sss  lll  aaa  jjj  ;;;
```

1d

i

1. Apply the standard plan for learning the letter *i*.
2. Keep fingers curved; key the drill once.

```
10  i  ik  ik  ik  is  is  id  id  if  if  ill  i  ail  did  kid  lid
11  i  ik  aid  ail  did  kid  lid  lids  kids  ill  aid  did  ilk
12  id  aid  aids  laid  said  ids  lid  skids  kiss  disk  dial
```

Document 2
Memo with Table

Prepare this memo to the staff.

List the words in the table in alphabetical order. Use 10% blue shading in the first row.

Save the memo as **mod9-d2**.

TO: All Staff, Spokane Branch
FROM: Marilyn Josephson, Office Manager
SUBJECT: American vs. Canadian Spelling
DATE: Current

All correspondence addressed to our Canadian office should now include Canadian spelling. Some of the differences are shown in the following table. We will need to get a list of other words that differ as well.

U.S. Spelling	Canadian Spelling
counseling	counselling
honor	honour
endeavor	endeavour
defense	defence
center	centre
check (meaning money)	cheque
color	colour
marvelous	marvellous
labor	labour
theater	theatre

Document 3
Letter

Use Find and Replace to find and replace any words that should be changed to Canadian spellings.

Save the letter as **mod9-d3**.

Current date | Chamber of Commerce | 225 Hall Street | Nelson BC V1L 5X4 | CANADA | Ladies and Gentlemen

Selkirk Communications will be relocating its headquarters from Spokane, Washington, to downtown Nelson on April 1. We are an international communications company offering the following services:

1. Written and oral communications refresher workshops
2. Customized training onsite, in our training center, or Web-based learning programs
3. Mail-order newsletters
4. Computer training on popular business software
5. Individualized or group training sessions

I would like to attend the Nelson Chamber of Commerce meeting in March to share some of the exciting ways we can help Chamber members meet their training needs. Is there time available for us on your March agenda? Please contact Anthony Baker, public relations coordinator, at our Nelson office at (604) 555-0193.

Selkirk Communications will be holding an open house during the month of April, and we will be inviting you and the Nelson community to attend. We look forward to becoming actively involved with the business community of Nelson.

Yours truly | Richard R. Holmes, President

1. Read the information at the right. Then do Lesson 1 from *Keyboarding Pro.*

STANDARD PLAN for Using Keyboarding Pro

1. Select a lesson from Alphabetic by clicking the lesson number. (Figure 1-1)
2. The first activity is displayed automatically. In Figure 1-2, *Learn Home Row* is in yellow because this activity is active. Follow the directions on screen. Key from the screen.

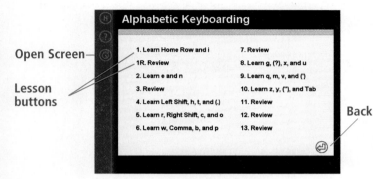

Open Screen

Lesson buttons

Figure 1-1 Alphabetic Keyboarding Lesson Menu

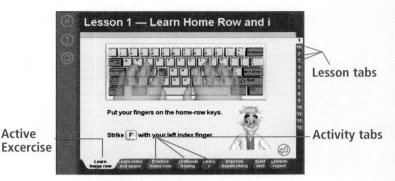

Lesson tabs

Back

Active Excercise

Activity tabs

Figure 1-2 Alphabetic Keyboarding (Lesson 1: Learn Home Row and i)

3. Key the Textbook Keying activity from your textbook (lines 13–18 below). Press ESC or the **Stop** button to continue.
4. Figure 1-3 shows the Lesson Report. A check mark opposite an exercise indicates that the exercise has been completed.
5. At the bottom, click the **Print** button to print your Lesson Report. Click the **Send File** button to send your student record to your instructor. Click the **Graph** button to view the Performance Graph.
6. Click the **Back** button twice to return to the Main menu. Then click the **Exit** button to quit the program. Remove your storage disk if necessary. Clean up the work area.

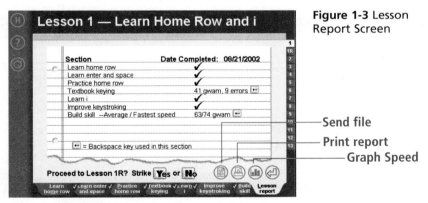

Figure 1-3 Lesson Report Screen

Send file

Print report

Graph Speed

Textbook Keying

2. Key the lines at the right in Textbook Keying. Key each line once. Strike ENTER at the end of each line.
3. When you complete the lesson, print your Lesson Report (step 5 above) and exit the software.

```
13  a  a;  al  ak  aj  s  s;  sl  sk  sj  d  d;  dl  dk  dj
14  j  ja  js  jd  jf  k  ka  ks  kd  kf  l  la  ls  ld  lf
15  a;  sl  a;sl  dkfj  a;sl  dkfj  a;sldkfj  asdf  jk
16  a;  sl  a;sl  dk  fj  dkfj  a;sl  dkfj  fkds;a;  fj
17  f  ff  j  jj  d  dd  k  kk  s  ss  l  ll  a  aa  ;  ;;  fj
18  afj;  a  s  d  f  j  k  l  ;  asdf  jkl;  fdsa  jkl;
```

MODULE 9

Selkirk Communications

- Apply keying, formatting, and word processing skills.
- Work independently and with few specific instructions.

Selkirk Communications

Selkirk Communications is a training company that is relocating its office from Spokane, Washington, to Nelson, Canada. As an administrative assistant, you will prepare a number of documents using many of the formatting and word processing skills you have learned throughout Lessons 26 to 60. Selkirk Communications uses the block letter format and unbound report style. Before you begin, add Selkirk Communications as autotext so that you do not have to key it repeatedly.

Document 1

Invitation
Format this document attractively. Use a 20-point font for the main heading and add a special text effect. Use a different font for the callouts (Place, Time, etc.), and 14-point font for the text.

Use a fancy bullet for the bulleted list. Position the document attractively on the page. Save it as **mod9-d1**.

OPEN HOUSE

Place: Selkirk Communications
         1003 Baker Street
         Nelson BC V1L 5N7

Time: 1:00-4:00 p.m.

Date: Saturday and Sunday, April 27 and 28

Selkirk Communications is excited to open its tenth international communications office in downtown Nelson. Please plan to attend our open house.

Come in and meet our friendly staff and learn how we can help meet your training needs. Selkirk Communications specializes in:

- Customized Web-based learning programs designed to meet your needs
- Instructor-led training in our classroom or your facility
- Newsletters designed to meet your needs
- Authorized training center for Microsoft Office
- Oral and written communication refresher courses

LESSON 1R

Review

1Ra Review home row

1. Open *Keyboarding Pro* software.
2. Click the ↓ next to *Class* and select your section. Click your name.
3. Key your password and click **OK**.
4. Go to *Lesson R1*.
5. Key each exercise as directed. Repeat if desired.

Note: All drill lines on this page may be keyed in the Open Screen. See 2d page 8 for instructions.

Fingers curved and upright

```
1  f j fjf jj fj fj jf dd kk dd kk dk dk dk
2  s ; s;s ;; s; s; s; aa ;; aa ;; a; a; a;

3  fj dk sl a; fjdksla; jfkdls;a ;a ;s kd j
4  f j fjf d k dkd s l sls a ; fj dk sl a;a

5  a; al ak aj s s; sl sk sj d d; dl dk djd
6  ja js jd jf k ka ks kd kf l la ls ld lfl

7  f fa fad s sa sad f fa fall fall l la lad s sa sad
8  a as ask a ad add j ja jak f fa fall; ask; add jak
```

1Rb Keyboard Review
Key each line once; repeat as time permits.

```
9  ik ki ki ik is if id il ij ia ij ik is if ji id ia
10 is il ill sill dill fill sid lid ail lid slid jail

11 if is il kid kids ill kid if kids; if a kid is ill
12 is id if ai aid jaks lid sid sis did ail; if lids;

13 a lass; ask dad; lads ask dad; a fall; fall salads
14 as a fad; ask a lad; a lass; all add; a kid; skids

15 as asks did disk ail fail sail ails jail sill silk
16 ask dad; dads said; is disk; kiss a lad; salad lid

17 aid a lad; if a kid is; a salad lid; kiss sad dads
18 as ad all ask jak lad fad kids ill kill fall disks
```

Module 8: Checkpoint

Objective Assessment

Answer the questions below to see if you have mastered the content of this module.

1. To insert clip art, choose _____ from the Insert menu.

2. To move clip art, you must first click the Text Wrapping button on the _____ toolbar.

3. A(n) _____ arrow is needed to move clip art.

4. A(n) _____ arrow is needed to size clip art.

5. To change text color, click _____ on the Formatting toolbar.

6. Text columns that flow down one column to the top of the next column are known as _____ columns.

7. To force the starting of a column, choose Break from the _____ menu.

8. To balance columns so that all columns end at the same point, insert a(n) _____ at the end of the text.

9. To add a page border to a page, choose _____ from the Format menu.

10. Page borders can be added using various _____ styles, weights, and colors.

Performance Assessment

Document 1
Newsletter

1. Open **Safety Net** from the data files.

2. Change the side margins for the entire document to .75".

3. Format the main heading, *The Safety Net*, using Arial Black font, 48 point, and dark blue text color.

4. Format the document in two equal-sized columns with lines between columns.

5. Insert a picture of a handheld cell phone positioned at the left side of the column after the cell phone is mentioned in the text.

6. Insert a picture of an individual at a computer workstation after the ergonomics seminar has been introduced.

7. Adjust the newsletter so that it will fit on one page with balanced columns.

8. Print and save the document as **checkpoint 8d-1**.

LESSON 2

E and N

WARMUP

2a

1. Open *Keyboarding Pro*.
2. Locate your student record.
3. Select Lesson 2.

1 ff dd ss aa ff dd ss aa jj kk ll ;; fj dk sl a; a;

2 fj dk sl a; fjdksla; a;sldkfj fj dk sl a; fjdksla;

3 aa ss dd ff jj kk ll ;; aa ss dd ff jj kk ll ;; a;

4 if a; as is; kids did; ask a sad lad; if a lass is

NEW KEYS

2b E and N

Key each line once; DS between groups.

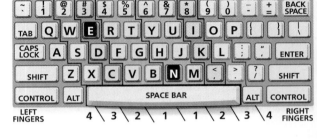

e Reach *up* with *left second* finger.

e

5 e ed ed led led lea lea ale ale elf elf eke eke ed

6 e el el eel els elk elk lea leak ale kale led jell

7 e ale kale lea leak fee feel lea lead elf self eke

n

8 n nj nj an an and and fan fan and kin din fin land

9 n an fan in fin and land sand din fans sank an sin

10 n in ink sink inn kin skin an and land in din dink

n Reach *down* with *right first* finger.

all reaches learned

11 den end fen ken dean dens ales fend fens keen knee

12 if in need; feel ill; as an end; a lad and a lass;

13 and sand; a keen idea; as a sail sank; is in jail;

14 an idea; an end; a lake; a nail; a jade; a dean is

2c Textbook Keying

Key each line once; DS between groups.

15 if a lad;

16 is a sad fall

17 if a lass did ask

18 ask a lass; ask a lad

Reach with little finger; tap Enter key quickly; return finger to home key.

19 a;sldkfj a;sldkfj a;sldkfj

20 a; sl dk fj fj dk sl a; a;sldkfj

21 i ik ik if if is is kid skid did lid aid laid said

22 ik kid ail die fie did lie ill ilk silk skill skid

1. Key a newsletter using the information that follows.

2. Set page margins for a 1" top margin and .5" side margins.

3. Key the document. Use 12-point Times New Roman for body text.

4. Format the document using two equal columns with .5" spacing between columns.

5. Create a banner heading using Comic Sans MS font, 26 point, and indigo text color.

6. Create a paragraph border around the last paragraph. Choose 5% gray shading and 2 $\frac{1}{4}$-point solid dark red shadow border.

7. Create a triple-line page border that is dark red and $\frac{1}{2}$ point.

8. Insert an appropriate clip art and center it at the bottom of the second column.

9. Preview, save as **60c-d1**, and print.

LEAGUE BASKETBALL RULES
Fourth Grade Division

1. Games consist of four 6-minute quarters. If necessary, two overtime periods are added. After two overtimes, teams will enter into a free throw shootoff.

2. Four players must be present to start a game and must arrive at least five minutes before game time.

3. An intermediate-sized ball and an eight-foot goal are used.

4. Games are half court, and each team must take it back after change of possession. When possession changes, the new offensive team will take the ball out of bounds in the back court. Each team receives three time-outs per game.

5. The clock runs continuously except for (1) the last two minutes of the fourth quarter, (2) during one-and-one free throws when the ball is handed to the shooter for the first shot, (3) during two-shot free throws when the ball is handed to the shooter for the second shot, and (4) for unusual delays according to the referee.

6. Players are limited to the same number of field goals per the grade of the league (three for third, four for fourth, etc.). However, players can make an unlimited number of free throws. Only shooting fouls result in free throws with the exception of one-and-ones after the seventh team foul.

7. All offensive players must be involved in the game. Too much one-on-one will result in an "isolation" violation.

8. All defenses must be player-to-player, but double-teaming is allowed within the three-point line. Within the lane, all defenders can go after the ball. Players may switch after picks or help if a defender loses his player.

9. Players are fouled out after committing five personal fouls.

10. Three-point shots and dunking are not allowed in this league.

For more detailed information on ball handling, passing, positions, shooting, defense, and offense, visit http://www.eteamz.com/basketball/instruction.

Ryan O'Bryant, Coach

2d Open Screen

STANDARD PLAN for the Open Screen

The **Open Screen** is a word processor that includes many features and a timer. Exercises to be keyed in the Open Screen are identified with an Open Screen icon. These exercises give you an opportunity to build your keyboarding skills, key documents, or take a timed writing. Results are not recorded in the Lesson Report. Follow the instructions in the textbook when completing these exercises.

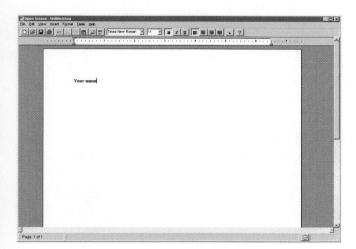

1. Click the **Open Screen** button on the Main Menu of *Keyboarding Pro*.
2. Key your name and strike ENTER twice.
3. Follow the directions in the textbook for the drill.
4. Print what you key in the Open Screen.
5. Click the **Close** button in the upper-right corner to exit the Open Screen.

Note: Any exercise keyed in the Open Screen can be saved.

SKILLBUILDING

2e Reinforcement

1. In the Open Screen, key each line twice. DS between groups of two lines.
2. Print but do not save the exercise.
3. Close the Open Screen and you will return to Lesson 2 in the software.

TECHNIQUE TIP
Keep your eyes on the textbook copy.

i

23 ik ik ik if is il ik id is if kid did lid aid ails
24 did lid aid; add a line; aid kids; ill kids; id is

n

25 nj nj nj an an and and end den ken in ink sin skin
26 jn din sand land nail sank and dank skin sans sink

e

27 el els elf elk lea lead fee feel sea seal ell jell
28 el eke ale jak lake elf els jaks kale eke els lake

all reaches

29 dine in an inn; fake jade; lend fans; as sand sank
30 in nine inns; if an end; need an idea; seek a fee;

2f End the lesson

1. Print the Lesson Report.
2. Exit the software; remove the storage disk if appropriate.

LESSON 60 Assessment

SKILLBUILDING

60a
Warmup
Key each line twice.

alphabetic	1	Jayne Cox puzzled over workbooks that were required for geometry.
figures	2	Edit pages 308 and 415 in Book A; pages 17, 29, and 60 in Book B.
one hand	3	Plum trees on a hilly acre, in my opinion, create no vast estate.
easy	4	If they sign an entitlement, the town land is to go to the girls.

| 1 | 2 | 3 | 4 | 5 | 6 | 7 | 8 | 9 | 10 | 11 | 12 | 13 |

60b
Timed Writings
Take one 3' and one 5' writing at your control level.

 all letters

gwam 3' | 5'

What is a college education worth today? If you asked that   4 | 2
question to a random sample of people, you would get a wide range of   9 | 5
responses. Many would respond that you cannot quantify the worth of 13 | 8
a bachelor's degree. They quickly stress that many factors other 18 | 11
than wages enhance the quality of life. They tend to focus on the 22 | 13
benefits of sciences and liberal arts and the appreciation they 26 | 16
develop for things that they would never have been exposed to if 31 | 18
they had not attended college. 33 | 20

Data show, though, that you can place a value on a college 37 | 22
education—at least in respect to wages earned. Less than twenty 41 | 25
years ago, a high school graduate earned only about fifty percent 45 | 27
of what a college graduate earned. Today, that number is quite 50 | 30
different. The gap between the wages of a college graduate and 54 | 32
the wages of a high school graduate has more than doubled in the 58 | 35
last twenty years. 59 | 36

The key factor in economic success is education. The new 63 | 38
jobs that pay high wages require more skills and a college degree. 68 | 41
Fortunately, many high school students do recognize the value of 72 | 43
getting a degree. Far more high school graduates are going to 76 | 46
college than ever before. They know that the best jobs are jobs 81 | 48
for knowledge workers and those jobs require a high level of skill. 85 | 51

3' | 1 | 2 | 3 | 4 |
5' | 1 | 2 | 3 |

APPLICATIONS

60c
Assessment

 Continue

 Check

With CheckPro: When you complete a document, proofread it, check the spelling, and preview for placement. When you are completely satisfied with the document, click the **Continue** button to move to the next document. You will not be able to return and edit a document once you continue to the next document. Click the **Check** button when you are ready to error-check the test. Review and/or print the document analysis results.

Without CheckPro: On the signal to begin, key the documents in sequence. When time has been called, proofread the document again and identify errors.

LESSON 3 — Review

WARMUP

3a
Key each line at a steady pace; strike and release each key quickly. Key each line again at a faster pace.

home 1 ad ads lad fad dad as ask fa la lass jak jaks alas

n 2 an fan and land fan flan sans sand sank flank dank

i 3 is id ill dill if aid ail fail did kid ski lid ilk

all 4 ade alas nine else fife ken; jell ink jak inns if;

SKILLBUILDING

3b Rhythm Builder
Key each line twice.
Lines 5–8: Think and key words. Make the space part of the word.
Lines 9–12: Think and key phrases. Do not key the vertical rules separating the phrases.

easy words

5 if is as an ad el and did die eel fin fan elf lens

6 as ask and id kid and ade aid eel feel ilk skis an

7 ail fail aid did ken ale led an flan inn inns alas

8 eel eke nee kneel did kids kale sees lake elf fled

easy phrases

9 el el|id id|is is|eke eke|lee lee|ale ale|jill jill

10 is if|is a|is a|a disk|a disk|did ski|did ski|is a

11 sell a|sell a|sell a sled|fall fad|fall fad|did die

12 sees a lake|sees a lake|as a deal|sell a sled|all a

3c Technique Practice
Key each 2-line group twice; SS.

TECHNIQUE TIP
Reach with the little finger; tap Enter key quickly; return finger to home key.

home row: fingers curved and upright

13 jak lad as lass dad sad lads fad fall la ask ad as

14 asks add jaks dads a lass ads flak adds sad as lad

upward reaches: straighten fingers slightly; return quickly to home position

15 fed die led ail kea lei did ale fife silk leak lie

16 sea lid deal sine desk lie ale like life idea jail

double letters: don't hurry when stroking double letters

17 fee jell less add inn seek fall alee lass keel all

18 dill dell see fell eel less all add kiss seen sell

1. Key the text below; SS between numbered items.
2. Create two columns of equal width; balance the columns so that both columns end at about the same point.
3. At the right of two of the numbered items, insert an appropriate graphic. Wrap text around the graphics using squaring wrapping and right alignment; size the graphic appropriately.
4. Save as **59e-d2**.

TIPS ON CULTURE AND CUSTOMS

North American business executives need knowledge of customs and practices of their international business partners. The following suggestions provide an important starting point for understanding other cultures.

1. Know the requirement of hand shaking. Taking the extra moment to shake hands at every meeting and again on departure will reap benefits.
2. Establish friendship first if important for that culture. Being a friend may be important first; conducting business is secondary. Establish a friendship; show interest in the individual and the family. Learn people's names and pronounce them correctly in conversation.
3. Understand the meaning of time. Some cultures place more importance on family, personal, and church-related activities than on business activities. Accordingly, they have longer lunches and more holidays. Therefore, they place less importance on adherence to schedules and appointment times.
4. Understand rank. Protocol with regard to who takes precedence is important; i.e., seating at meetings, speaking, and walking through doorways. Do not interrupt anyone.
5. Know the attitudes of space. Some cultures consider 18 inches a comfortable distance between people; however, others prefer much less. Adjust to their space preferences. Do not move away, back up, or put up a barrier, such as standing behind a desk.
6. Understand the attitude of hospitality. Some cultures are generous with hospitality and expect the same in return. For example, when hosting a party, prepare a generous menu; finger foods would be considered "ungenerous."
7. Share their language appropriately. Although the business meeting may be conducted in English, speak the other language in social parts of the conversation. This courteous effort will be noted.

3d Textbook Keying

Key each line once; DS between groups of two lines.

TECHNIQUE TIP
Strike keys quickly.
Strike the Space Bar Space Bar with down-and-in motion.
Strike Enter with a quick flick of the little finger.

reach review

19 ea sea lea seas deal leaf leak lead leas fleas keas
20 as ask lass ease as asks ask ask sass as alas seas
DS
21 sa sad sane sake sail sale sans safe sad said sand
22 le sled lead flee fled ale flea lei dale kale leaf
DS
23 jn jn nj nj in fan fin an; din ink sin and inn an;
24 de den end fen an an and and ken knee nee dean dee

phrases (think and key phrases)

25 and and land land el el elf elf self self ail nail
26 as as ask ask ad ad lad lad id id lid lid kid kids

27 if if|is is|jak jak|all all|did did|nan nan|elf elf
28 as a lad| ask dad| fed a jak| as all ask| sales fad

29 sell a lead|seal a deal|feel a leaf|if a jade sale
30 is a|is as if|a disk|aid all kids|did ski|is a silk

3e Reinforcement

1. In the Open Screen, key your name and strike ENTER twice.
2. Key each line once. DS between groups of two lines.
3. Print the exercise.
4. Click the **X** box in the upper-right corner to close the Open Screen.
5. Print your Lesson Report and exit.

d/e
31 den end fen ken dean dens ales fend fens keen knee
32 a deed; a desk; a jade; an eel; a jade eel; a dean

n/a
33 an an in in and and en end end sane sane sand sand
34 a land; a dean; a fan; a fin; a sane end; end land

nj
35 el eel eld elf sell self el dell fell elk els jell
36 in fin inn inks dine sink fine fins kind line lain

all reaches
37 an and fan dean elan flan land lane lean sand sane
38 sell a lead; sell a jade; seal a deal; feel a leaf

Arena Update

Get Your Shovels Ready!

The architects have put the final touches on the arena plans and the groundbreaking has been scheduled for March 18. Put the date on your calendar and plan to be a part of this exciting time. The Groundbreaking Ceremony will begin at 5:00 at the new arena site. After the ceremony, you will join the architects in the practice facility for refreshments and an exciting visual presentation of the new arena. The party ends when we all join the Western Cougars as they take on the Central Lions for the final conference game.

Cornerstone Club Named

Robbie Holiday of the Cougars Club submitted the winning name for the new premium seating and club area of the new arena. Thanks to all of you who submitted suggestions for naming the new club. For his suggestion, which was selected from over 300 names submitted, Robbie has won season tickets for next year and the opportunity to make his seat selection first. The Cornerstone Club name was selected because members of our premium clubs play a crucial role in making our new arena a reality. Without the financial support of this group, we could not lay the first cornerstone of the arena.

Cornerstone Club members have first priority in selecting their seats for both basketball and hockey in a specially designated section of the new arena. This section provides outstanding seats for both basketball games and hockey matches. Club members also have access to the Cornerstone Club before the game, during halftime, and after the game. They also receive a parking pass for the lot immediately adjacent to the arena. If you would like more information about the Cornerstone Club and how you can become a charter member of the club, call the Cougars Club office during regular business hours.

What View Would You Like?

Most of us would like to sit in our seats and try them out before we select them rather than look at a diagram of the seating in the new arena. Former Cougar players make it easy for you to select the perfect angle to watch the ball go in the basket. Mark McKay and Jeff Dunlap, using their patented Real View visualization software, make it possible for you to experience the exact view you will have from the seats you select. In fact, they encourage you to try several different views. Most of the early testers of the new seat selection

software reported that they came in with their minds completely made up about the best seats in the house. However, after experiencing several different views with the Real View software, they changed their original seat location request.

LESSON 4

Left Shift, H, T, Period

WARMUP

4a
Key each line twice SS.
Keep eyes on copy.

home row 1 al as ads lad dad fad jak fall lass asks fads all;
e/i/n 2 ed ik jn in knee end nine line sine lien dies leis
all reaches 3 see a ski; add ink; fed a jak; is an inn; as a lad
easy 4 an dial id is an la lake did el ale fake is land a

NEW KEYS

4b Left Shift and h
Key each line once.

Follow the "Standard procedures for learning new keyreaches" on p. 4 for all remaining reaches.

left shift Reach *down* with *left fourth* (little) finger; shift, strike, release.

h Reach to *left* with *right first* finger.

left shift

5 J Ja Ja Jan Jan Jane Jana Ken Kass Lee Len Nan Ned
6 and Ken and Lena and Jake and Lida and Nan and Ida
7 Inn is; Jill Ina is; Nels is; Jen is; Ken Lin is a

h

8 h hj hj he he she she hen aha ash had has hid shed
9 h hj ha hie his half hand hike dash head sash shad
10 aha hi hash heal hill hind lash hash hake dish ash

all reaches learned

11 Nels Kane and Jake Jenn; she asked Hi and Ina Linn
12 Lend Lana and Jed a dish; I fed Lane and Jess Kane
13 I see Jake Kish and Lash Hess; Isla and Helen hike

4c **Textbook Keying**
Key the drill once: Strive for good control.

14 he she held a lead; she sells jade; she has a sale
15 Ha Ja Ka La Ha Hal Ja Jake Ka Kahn La Ladd Ha Hall
16 Hal leads; Jeff led all fall; Hal has a safe lead
17 Hal Hall heads all sales; Jake Hess asks less fee;

Wrap Text Around Graphics

When graphic elements are included in documents such as newsletters, text usually wraps around the graphic.

To wrap text around graphics:

1. Insert the graphic; then place the insertion point over the graphic and right-click.
2. Select **Format picture** to display the Format Picture dialog box.
3. Click the **Layout** tab, and select the desired wrapping style (**Square**).
4. Click the desired alignment (**Right**), and then click **OK**.

DRILL 2   **WRAP TEXT AROUND GRAPHIC**

1. Open **Productivity** from the data files. Save as **59d-drill2**.

2. Go to the end of the document and select the graphic. Change handles to moving handles (click the **Text Wrapping** icon on the Picture toolbar; click **Square**).

3. Move the graphic and position it before the paragraph that begins with *Integration*. Work patiently.

4. Wrap the text around the graphic using square wrapping and center alignment.

   a. Right-click the graphic. Select **Format Picture**.

   b. Click the **Layout** tab, and select **Square** wrapping and **Center** alignment.

5. If the graphic moves to the left column, drag it back so it is positioned above the *Integration* paragraph. Be sure it is center aligned.

6. Preview and print when you are satisfied.

APPLICATIONS

59e-d1
Newsletter

1. Key the newsletter shown on the next page. Use .5" left and right margins, and apply what you have learned.

2. Key the main heading, **Arena Update**, using Albertus Extra Bold, 48 point, and dark red text color.

3. Insert clip art files, as shown in the newsletter. You may substitute any appropriate clip art you find if you cannot find the same images. Wrap the text around the graphics.

4. Use 18-point Albertus Medium type for the internal headings in the newsletter.

5. Balance columns so that all columns end at about the same place.

6. Create a double-line page border that is dark red and 1 ½ point.

7. Save the document as **59e-d1**.

4d

t and **.** (period)
Key each line once.

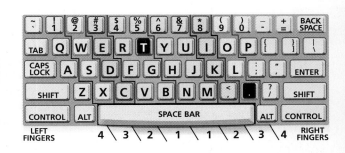

t Reach *up* with *left first* finger.

. (period) Reach *down* with *right third* finger.

Period: Space once after a period that follows an initial or an abbreviation. To increase readability, space twice after a period that ends a sentence.

t

18 t tf tf aft aft left fit fat fete tiff tie the tin
19 tf at at aft lit hit tide tilt tint sits skit this
20 hat kit let lit ate sit flat tilt thin tale tan at

. (period)

21 .1 .1 1.1 fl. fl. L. L. Neal and J. N. List hiked.
22 Hand J. H. Kass a fan. Jess did. I need an idea.
23 Jane said she has a tan dish; Jae and Lee need it.

all reaches learned

24 I did tell J. K. that Lt. Li had left. He is ill.
25 tie tan kit sit fit hit hat; the jet left at nine.
26 I see Lila and Ilene at tea. Jan Kane ate at ten.

SKILLBUILDING

4e Reinforcement

Follow the standard directions for the Open Screen (page 8).

Lines 27–34: Key each line twice; DS between groups. Try to increase your speed the second time.

Lines 35–38: Key the lines once.

reach review

27 tf .1 hj ft ki de jh tf ik ed hj de ft ki 1. tf ik
28 elf eel left is sis fit till dens ink has delt ink

h/e

29 he he heed heed she she shelf shelf shed shed she
30 he has; he had; he led; he sleds; she fell; he is

i/t

31 it is if id did lit tide tide tile tile list list
32 it is; he hit it; he is ill; she is still; she is

shift

33 Hal and Nel; Jade dishes; Kale has half; Jed hides
34 Hi Ken; Helen and Jen hike; Jan has a jade; Ken is

End the lesson

Print the lines keyed in the Open Screen and print your Lesson Report. Exit the software.

35 Nan had a sale.

36 He did see Hal.

enter

37 Lee has a desk.

38 Ina hid a dish.

TECHNIQUE TIP
Strike Enter without pausing or looking up from the copy.

59d

Columns

3 Columns

Columns

Text may be formatted in multiple columns on a page to make it easier to read. A newsletter, for example, is usually formatted in columns. Typically, newsletters are written in an informal, conversational style and are formatted with **banners** (text that spans multiple columns), newspaper columns, graphic elements, and other text enhancements. In newspaper columns, text flows down one column and then to the top of the next column. A simple, uncluttered design with a significant amount of white space is recommended to enhance the readability of newsletters.

Productivity Enhancement Program

To create columns of equal width:

1. Click the **Columns** button on the Standard toolbar.
2. Drag to select the number of columns. Using this method to create columns will format the entire document with columns of equal widths.

Column format may be applied before or after keying text. If columns are set before text is keyed, use Print Layout View to check the appearance of the text. Generally, column formats are easier to apply after text has been keyed.

Occasionally, you may want certain text (such as a banner or headline) to span more than one column.

To format a banner:

1. Select the text to be included in the banner.
2. Click the **Columns** button, and drag the number of columns to one.

To balance columns:

To balance columns so that all columns end at the same point on the page, position the insertion point at the end of the text to be balanced and insert a **Continuous section break (Insert, Break, Continuous, OK).**

To force the starting of a new column:

1. Position the insertion point where the new column is to start.
2. From the Insert menu, choose **Break**.
3. Click **Column break**.

DRILL 1　　**SIMPLE COLUMNS**

1. Open **Training** from the data files. Save it as **59d-drill1**.
2. Click **Columns** and format the document in three even columns. Preview to see how it looks.
3. Format the same document in two columns and balance the columns. Preview to check the appearance.

4. Select the heading **Productivity Enhancement Program**; click **Columns** and select one column. Double space below the heading. Apply 24 point. Center-align the heading. Save again and close.

R, Right Shift, C, O

WARMUP

5a
Key each line twice.

home keys 1 a; ad add al all lad fad jak ask lass fall jak lad

t/h/i/n 2 the hit tin nit then this kith dint tine hint thin

left shift/. 3 I need ink. Li has an idea. Hit it. I see Kate.

all reaches 4 Jeff ate at ten; he left a salad dish in the sink.

NEW KEYS

5b r and Right Shift
Key each line once.

r Reach *up* with *left first* finger.

right shift Reach *down* with *right fourth* finger; shift, strike, release.

r

5 r rf rf riff riff fir fir rid ire jar air sir lair

6 rf rid ark ran rat are hare art rant tire dirt jar

7 rare dirk ajar lark rain kirk share hart rail tart

right shift

8 D D Dan Dan Dale Ti Sal Ted Ann Ed Alf Ada Sid Fan

9 and Sid and Dina and Allen and Eli and Dean and Ed

10 Ed Dana; Dee Falk; Tina Finn; Sal Alan; Anna Deeds

all reaches learned

11 Jane and Ann hiked in the sand; Asa set the tents.

12 a rake; a jar; a tree; a red fire; a fare; a rain;

13 Fred Derr and Rai Tira dined at the Tree Art Fair.

5c Textbook Keying
Key each line once; DS between groups of two lines.

14 ir ir ire fir first air fair fire tire rid sir

15 fir jar tar fir flit rill till list stir dirt fire

DS

16 Feral is ill. Dan reads. Dee and Ed Finn see Dere.

17 All is still as Sarah and I fish here in the rain.

DS

18 I still see a red ash tree that fell in the field.

19 Lana said she did sail her skiff in the dark lake.

Skillbuilding and Newsletters

SKILLBUILDING

59a
Warmup
Key each line twice.

alphabetic	1	Jimmy Favorita realized that we must quit playing by six o'clock.
figure	2	Joell, in her 2001 truck, put 19 boxes in an annex at 3460 Marks.
double letter	3	Merriann was puzzled by a letter that followed a free book offer.
easy	4	Ana's sorority works with vigor for the goals of the civic corps.

| 1 | 2 | 3 | 4 | 5 | 6 | 7 | 8 | 9 | 10 | 11 | 12 | 13 |

59b
Technique Builder
Key each set of lines three times; work at a controlled rate.

adjacent reaches	5	Is assessing potential important in a traditional career program?
	6	I saw her at an airport at a tropical resort leaving on a cruise.
direct reach	7	Fred kicked a goal in every college soccer game in June and July.
	8	Ned used their sled on cold days and my kite on warm summer days.
double letters	9	Bobby Lott feels that the meeting at noon will be cancelled soon.
	10	Pattie and Tripp meet at the swimming pool after football drills.

59c
Timed Writings
Take two 3' writings.

Ⓐ all letters ⏱

gwam 3' | 5'

	3'	5'
Surrogate grandparents and pet therapy might not be the types	4	2
of terms that you expect to find in a medical journal, but they are	9	5
concepts that are quite popular with senior citizens. Two of the	13	8
most common problems experienced by senior citizens who do not live	18	11
with or near a family member are loneliness and the craving to feel	22	13
needed and loved.	23	14
Senior citizens who are healthy and who are stable mentally	27	16
often can have a high-quality relationship with deprived children	32	19
who do not have grandparents of their own. They often have time to	36	22
spare and the desire to give these needy children extra attention	41	24
and help with their school work and other needs. At first, it may	45	27
seem that children gain the most from relationships with seniors.	49	30
However, it soon becomes evident that the surrogate grandparents	54	32
tend to benefit as much or even more than the children.	57	34

3' | 1 | 2 | 3 | 4 |
5' | 1 | 2 | 3 |

5d

c and o
Key each line once.

c Reach *down* with *left second* finger.

o Reach *up* with right *third finger*.

c

20 c c cd cd cad cad can can tic ice sac cake cat sic
21 clad chic cite cheek clef sick lick kick dice rice
22 call acid hack jack lack lick cask crack clan cane

o

23 o ol ol old old of off odd ode or ore oar soar one
24 ol sol sold told dole do doe lo doll sol solo odor
25 onto door toil lotto soak fort hods foal roan load

all reaches learned

26 Carlo Rand can call Rocco; Cole can call Doc Cost.
27 Trina can ask Dina if Nick Corl has left; Joe did.
28 Case sent Carole a nice skirt; it fits Lorna Rich.

SKILLBUILDING

5e Keyboard Reinforcement
Key each line once SS; key at a steady pace. Repeat, striving for control.

TECHNIQUE TIP
Reach up without moving hands away from your body. Use quick keystrokes.

o/r
29 or or for for nor nor ore ore oar oar roe roe sore
30 a rose|her or|he or|he rode|or for|a door|her doll

i/t
31 is is tis tis it it fit fit tie tie this this lits
32 it is|it is|it is this|it is this|it sits|tie fits

e/n
33 en en end end ne ne need need ken ken kneel kneels
34 lend the|lend the|at the end|at the end|need their

c/o
35 ch ch check check ck ck hack lack jack co co cones
36 the cot|the cot|a dock|a dock|a jack|a jack|a cone

all reaches
37 Jack and Rona did frost nine of the cakes at last.
38 Jo can ice her drink if Tess can find her a flask.
39 Ask Jean to call Fisk at noon; he needs her notes.

●●

PAGE BORDERS

1. Open **58d-drill3**. Save as **58d-drill4**.

2. Add a page border that is dark red and ½ point.

3. Save and print.

APPLICATIONS

58e-d1
Report with Graphics

1. In a new document, format the main heading, **Trend Analysis Report**, using Arial Black font, 36 point, and indigo text color.
2. Create a subheading below the heading by keying **Market Trends** using 20-point font and adding indigo shading to the paragraph.
3. Key the bulleted list.
4. Search for clip art using the keyword **academic** and add an appropriate piece of clip art centered below the five paragraphs.
5. At the bottom of the page, key in 18-point script font **Understanding our community to prepare for our future!**
6. Save the document as **58e-d1**, and print a copy.

Trend Analysis Report

Market Analysis

- The population in the metropolitan area is growing both in the college's service area and in the demographic segments that represent the greatest market enrollment.

- The metropolitan area continues to add employment opportunities at a growth rate of 22 percent, but the area economy suffers from some of the same insecurities about the future as do other areas.

- Information technology is creating more customer potential and new demands for the delivery of coursework as well as generating new opportunities for competitors to enter this educational market.

- The pace of change is forcing people at all levels of the economy to learn new skills at the same time people are being asked to work harder—and sometimes hold more than one job.

- The new school improvement plan has not taken shape as quickly as anticipated, but a move toward mastering skills and testing for proficiencies—not rote knowledge—is gaining momentum.

LESSON 6

W, Comma, B, P

WARMUP

6a
Key each line twice; avoid pauses.

home row 1 ask a lad; a fall fad; had a salad; ask a sad jak;
o/t 2 to do it; to toil; as a tot; do a lot; he told her
c/r 3 cots are; has rocks; roll cot; is rich; has an arc
all reaches 4 Holt can see Dane at ten; Jill sees Frank at nine.

NEW KEYS

6b w and , (comma)
Key each line once.

Comma: Space once after a comma.

LEFT FINGERS 4 \ 3 \ 2 \ 1 \ 1 \ 2 \ 3 \ 4 RIGHT FINGERS

w Reach *up* with *left third* finger.

w

5 w ws ws was was wan wit low win jaw wilt wink wolf
6 sw sw ws ow ow now now row row own own wow wow owe
7 to sew; to own; was rich; was in; is how; will now

, (comma) Reach *down* with *right second* finger.

, (comma)

8 k, k, k, irk, ilk, ask, oak, ark, lark, jak, rock,
9 skis, a dock, a fork, a lock, a fee, a tie, a fan,
10 Jo, Ed, Ted, and Dan saw Nan in a car lift; a kit

all reaches learned

11 Win, Lew, Drew, and Walt will walk to West Willow.
12 Ask Ho, Al, and Jared to read the code; it is new.
13 The window, we think, was closed; we felt no wind.

6c Textbook Keying
Key each line once.

14 walk wide sown wild town went jowl wait white down
15 a dock, a kit, a wick, a lock, a row, a cow, a fee
16 Joe lost to Ron; Fiji lost to Cara; Don lost to Al
17 Kane will win; Nan will win; Rio will win; Di wins
18 Walter is in Reno; Tia is in Tahoe; then to Hawaii

Paragraph Borders and Shading

help keywords
borders and shading

Borders and shading can be added to paragraphs, pages, or selected text. Various line styles, weights, and colors can be applied to borders. Shading can be applied in a variety of colors and patterns.

> This paragraph illustrates a block border with a 1-point black line. The shading for the paragraph is 10% gray fill.

To apply a paragraph border:

TIP

Borders option available on Formatting Toolbar.

1. Click in the paragraph or select the text to be formatted with a border.
2. Click **Borders and Shading** on the Format menu, and then click the **Borders** tab.
3. Select the type of border, line style, color, and width; then click **Apply to Paragraph** and **OK**.

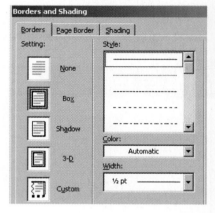

To apply shading:

1. Click in the paragraph or select the text to be shaded.
2. Click **Borders and Shading** on the Format menu, and then click the **Shading** tab.
3. Select the fill and pattern, and then apply them to the paragraph.

DRILL 3   BORDERS AND SHADING

Key the paragraph at the right. Then apply a ½-point red, double-line box border and pale blue shading to the paragraph. Save as **58d-drill3**.

> This paragraph is formatted with a ½-point red, double-line box border and pale blue shading.

Page Borders

Attractive page borders can also be added to pages using various line styles, weights, and colors.

To apply a page border:

1. Choose **Format**; then **Borders and Shading**.
2. Click the **Page Borders** tab; then choose a setting, e.g., **Box**. Choose the desired line style, line color, and line width. Click **OK**.
3. Close the document and save your changes.

6d

b and **p**
Key each line once.

b Reach *down* with *left first* finger.

p Reach *up* with *right fourth* (little) finger.

b

19 bf bf bf biff fib fib bib bib boa boa fib fibs rob
20 bf bf bf ban ban bon bon bow bow be be rib rib sob
21 a dob, a cob, a crib, a lab, a slab, a bid, a bath

p

22 p; p; pa pa; pal pal pan pan pad par pen pep paper
23 pa pa; lap lap; nap nap; hep ape spa asp leap clap
24 a park, a pan, a pal, a pad, apt to pop, a pair of

all reaches learned

25 Barb and Bob wrapped a pepper in paper and ribbon.
26 Rip, Joann, and Dick were all closer to the flash.
27 Bo will be pleased to see Japan; he works in Oslo.

SKILLBUILDING

6e Keyboard Reinforcement
Key each line once; key at a steady pace.

reach review
28 ki kid did aid lie hj has has had sw saw wits will
29 de dell led sled jn an en end ant hand k, end, kin

s/w
30 ws ws lows now we shown win cow wow wire jowl when
31 Wes saw an owl in the willow tree in the old lane.

b/p
32 bf bf fib rob bid ;p p; pal pen pot nap hop cap bp
33 Rob has both pans in a bin at the back of the pen.

6f Speed Builder
1. Follow the standard Open Screen directions on page 8.
2. Key each line twice. Work for fluency.

all reaches
34 Dick owns a dock at this lake; he paid Ken for it.
35 Jane also kept a pair of owls, a hen, and a snake.

36 Blair soaks a bit of the corn, as he did in Japan.
37 I blend the cocoa in the bowl when I work for Leo.

38 to do|can do|to bow|ask her|to nap|to work|is born
39 for this|if she|is now|did all|to see|or not|or if

To move or size clip art:

1. Select the clip art.
2. Position the insertion point over one of the handles. When the pointer turns to a double-headed arrow, drag the lower-right handle down and to the right to increase the size; drag it up and to the left to make it smaller. Drag a corner handle to maintain the same proportion.

To move clip art:

1. Select the clip art.
2. Click the **Text Wrapping** button on the Picture toolbar. Then choose **Tight** (or one of the text-wrapping options) from the drop-down list. The sizing handles change to white.
3. Position the arrow pointer on the clip art until a four-headed arrow displays. Click and drag the clip art to the desired location.

DRILL 1   CLIP ART

1. Search for roses in the clip art gallery, and insert the clip art into a new document.
2. Increase the size of the clip art to approximately double its size. Use the Horizontal and Vertical Rulers to guide you.

3. Move it to the center of the page near the top margin.
4. Create the folder **Module 8 Keys**, and save the document as **58b-drill1** in this folder. Save all exercises for Module 8 in this folder.

Text Color

A simple way to enhance the appearance of a document is to change the color of the text. For example, when creating a club meeting announcement, use club colors to attract attention, e.g., blue and gold.

To change the color of text:

1. Select the text you want to change.
2. Click the arrow next to the **Font Color** button on the Formatting toolbar. Then select the desired color.

   Note: To select the most recently used color, click the **Font Color** button.

DRILL 2   TEXT COLOR

1. Open **meeting** from the data files.
2. Change the main heading to Gill Sans Ultra Bold font and change text color to blue.

3. Add an appropriate clip art that would attract attention to the prize being awarded. Size and place the image attractively.
4. Save as **58d-drill2**.

Review

WARMUP

7a

Key each line twice; begin new lines promptly.

all 1 We often can take the older jet to Paris and back.

home 2 a; sl dk fj a;sl dkfj ad as all ask fads adds asks

1st row 3 Ann Bascan and Cabal Naban nabbed a cab in Canada.

3d row 4 Rip went to a water show with either Pippa or Pia.

SKILLBUILDING

7b Reach Mastery

Key each line once; DS between groups of three lines.

5 ws ws was was wan wan wit wit pew paw nap pop bawl

6 bf bf fb fb fob fob rib rib be be job job bat back

7 p; p; asp asp pan pan ap ap ca cap pa nap pop prow

DS

8 Barb and Bret took an old black robe and the boot.

9 Walt saw a wisp of white water renew ripe peppers.

10 Pat picked a black pepper for the picnic at Parks.

7c Rhythm Builder

Key each line once; DS between groups of three lines

words 11 a an pan so sot la lap ah own do doe el elf to tot

phrases 12 if it|to do|it is|do so|for the|he works|if he bid

sentences 13 Jess ate all of the peas in the salad in the bowl.

DS

TECHNIQUE TIP

words: key as a single unit rather than letter by letter;

phrases: say and key fluently;

sentences: work for fluency.

words 14 bow bowl pin pint for fork forks hen hens jak jaks

phrases 15 is for|did it|is the|we did a|and so|to see|or not

sentences 16 I hid the ace in a jar as a joke; I do not see it.

DS

words 17 chap chaps flak flake flakes prow prowl work works

phrases 18 as for the|as for the|and to the|to see it|and did

sentences 19 As far as I know, he did not read all of the book.

Clip art, pictures, AutoShapes, and other images are graphic elements that enhance documents such as announcements, invitations, reports, and newsletters. In this lesson, you will work with clip art and drawing tools.

Clip Art

Microsoft Word (and other applications such as *Excel*, *PowerPoint*, and *Publisher*) provides a collection of pictures, clip art, and sounds that can be added to documents. Additional clips are available online. You can also add your own clips to the collection. The clips are organized into different collections to simplify finding appropriate clip art. The Clip Organizer adds keywords to enable you to search for various types of clip art. You also have the option of selecting the collection and viewing thumbnail sketches (small pictures) of the various clip art available in each category. Once clip art has been inserted into a document, you can size it, copy and paste it, wrap text around it, or drag it to other locations.

To insert clip art:

1. Click **Insert** on the menu bar, click **Picture**, and then click **Clip Art**.

2. In the Task Pane Search text box, key the type of clip art to search for such as rabbit, baseball, or roses; then click **Search**.

3. When the results are displayed, use the scroll bar to view the thumbnail sketches. When you find the desired clip art, point to the image to display a down arrow at the right of the image, click the down arrow, and then click **Insert**. (*Option:* Click the clip art image.)

4. To display a collection of clip art from various places, choose one of the options under Other Search Options on the Task Pane.

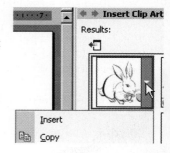

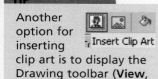

TIP

Another option for inserting clip art is to display the Drawing toolbar (**View, Toolbars, Drawing**), and click the **Insert Clip Art** button.

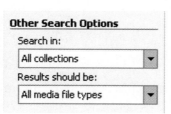

7d Technique Practice

Key each set of lines once SS; DS between 3-line groups.

▼ Space once after a period following an abbreviation.

spacing: space *immediately* after each word

20 ad la as in if it lo no of oh he or so ok pi be we
21 an ace ads ale aha a fit oil a jak nor a bit a pew
22 ice ades born is fake to jail than it and the cows

spacing/shifting ▼ ▼

23 Ask Jed. Dr. Han left at ten; Dr. Crowe, at nine.
24 I asked Jin if she had ice in a bowl; it can help.
25 Freda, not Jack, went to Spain. Joan likes Spain.

7e Timed Writings in the Open Screen

S T A N D A R D   P L A N   [for using the Open Screen Timer]

You can check your speed in the Open Screen using the Timer.

1. In the Open Screen, click the **Timer** button on the toolbar.
   In the Timer dialog box, check **Count-Down Timer** and time; click **OK**.
2. The Timer begins once you start to key and stops automatically. Do not strike ENTER at the end of a line. Wordwrap will cause the text to flow to the next line automatically.
3. To save the timing, click the **File** menu and **Save as**. Use your initals (*xx*), the exercise number, and number of the timing as the filename. Example: **xx-7f-t1** (your initials, exercise 7f, timing1).
4. Click the **Timer** button again to start a new timing.
5. Each new timing must be saved with its own name.

7f Speed Check

1. Take two 1' writings on the paragraph in the Open Screen.
2. Follow the directions in 7e. Do not strike ENTER at the ends of the lines.

Goal: 12 *wam*.

```
                   •         4         •         8         •
It  is  hard  to  fake  a  confident  spirit.  We  will  do
              12            •             16            •
better  work  if  we  approach  and  finish  a  job  and
20            •        24            •             28            •
know  that  we  will  do  the  best  work  we  can  and  then
              32
not  fret.
 |  1  |  2  |  3  |  4  |  5  |  6  |  7  |  8  |  9  |  10  |
```

7g Guided Writing

1. In the Open Screen, key each line once for fluency. Do not save your work.
2. Set the Timer in the Open Screen for 30". Take two 30" writings on each line. Do not save the timings.

Goal: to reach the end of the line before time is up.

gwam

26 Dan took her to the show.   12
27 Jan lent the bowl to the pros.   14
28 Hold the wrists low for this drill.   16
29 Jessie fit the black panel to the shelf.   18
30 Jake held a bit of cocoa and an apricot for Diane.   20
31 Dick and I fish for cod on the docks at Fish Lake.   20
32 Kent still held the dish and the cork in his hand.   20

```
 |  1  |  2  |  3  |  4  |  5  |  6  |  7  |  8  |  9  |  10  |
```

Graphic Essentials

- Enhance document format with graphics and text color.
- Create multicolumn newsletters.

LESSON 58 — Skillbuilding and Graphics

SKILLBUILDING

58a
Warmup
Key each line twice.

alphabet	1	Dave Cagney alphabetized items for next week's quarterly journal.
figures	2	Close Rooms 4, 18, and 20 from 3 until 9 on July 7; open Room 56.
upward	3	Toy & Wurt's note for $635 (see our page 78) was paid October 29.
easy	4	The auditor is due by eight, and he may lend a hand to the panel.

| 1 | 2 | 3 | 4 | 5 | 6 | 7 | 8 | 9 | 10 | 11 | 12 | 13 |

58b
Technique Builder
Key each set of lines 3 times; work at a controlled rate.

adjacent reaches	5	art try pew sort tree position copy opera maker waste three draft
	6	sat coil riot were renew forth trade power grope owner score weed
one hand	7	ad null bar poll car upon deed jump ever look feed hill noon moon
	8	get hilly are employ save phony taste union versa yummy wedge fed
balanced hand	9	aid go bid dish elan glen fury idle half jamb lend make name slam
	10	oak pay hen quay rush such urus vial works yamen amble blame pale

58c
Timed Writings
1. Key three 1' writings.
2. Key two 2' writings. Try to maintain your best 1' rate.

  all letters

	gwam	1'	2'
Good plans typically are required to execute most tasks		11	6 50
successfully. If a task is worth doing, it is worth investing		24	12 56
the time that is necessary to plan it effectively. Many people		37	18 62
are anxious to get started on a task and just begin before they		49	25 69
have thought about the best way to organize it. In the long run,		63	31 75
they frequently end up wasting time that could be spent more		75	37 81
profitably on important projects that they might prefer to tackle.		88	44 88

| 1' | 1 | 2 | 3 | 4 | 5 | 6 | 7 | 8 | 9 | 10 | 11 | 12 | 13 |
| 2' | | 1 | | 2 | | 3 | | 4 | | 5 | | 6 | |

LESSON 8

G, Question Mark, X, U

WARMUP

8a

Key each line twice. Keep eyes on copy.

all 1 Dick will see Job at nine if Rach sees Pat at one.
w/b 2 As the wind blew, Bob Webber saw the window break.
p/, 3 Pat, Pippa, or Cap has prepared the proper papers.
all 4 Bo, Jose, and Will fed Lin; Jack had not paid her.

NEW KEYS

8b g and ?

Key each line once; repeat.

Question mark: The question mark is usually followed by two spaces.

g Reach to *right* with *left first* finger.

? Left SHIFT; reach *down* with *right fourth* finger.

g

5 g g gf gaff gag grog fog frog drag cog dig fig gig
6 gf go gall flag gels slag gala gale glad glee gals
7 golf flog gorge glen high logs gore ogle page grow

?

8 ? ?; ?; ? ? Who? When? Where? Who is? Who was?
9 Who is here? Was it he? Was it she? Did she go?
10 Did Geena? Did he? What is that? Was Jose here?

all reaches learned

11 Has Ginger lost her job? Was her April bill here?
12 Phil did not want the boats to get here this soon.
13 Loris Shin has been ill; Frank, a doctor, saw her.

8c Textbook Keying

Key each line once; DS between groups.

reach review

14 ws ws hj hj tf tf ol ol rf rf ed ed cd cd bf bf p;
15 wed bid has old hold rid heed heed car bed pot pot

g

16 gf gf gin gin rig ring go gone no nog sign got dog
17 to go|to go|go on|go in|go in|to go in|in the sign

?

18 ?; ?;? who? when? where? how? what? who? It is I?
19 Is she? Is he? Did I lose Jo? Is Gal all right?

TECHNIQUE TIP

Concentrate on correct reaches.

Module 7: Checkpoint

1. The _____ feature removes text or an image from a document and places it on the Clipboard.
2. The _____ feature enables you to locate multiple uses of a word or phrase and substitute a different word or phrase for it each time it occurs.
3. The_____ is a tool that allows you to look up words and replace them with a synonym.
4. A special character that is the equivalent of two hyphens joined with no spaces is a(n) _____ dash.
5. A special character that is the equivalent of one hyphen and a space is a(n) _____ dash.
6. Use the _____ function to format a one-page document with the same amount of space in the top and bottom margin.
7. The ✂ symbol is most likely to be found on one of the _____ fonts.
8. The character effect _____ positions small text above the line of writing.
9. Drag-and-drop editing allows you to move text within the _____ .
10. To position an extra blank line (6 point) after each paragraph automatically, use the _____ function.

Performance Assessment

Document 1
Edit Report

1. Open **Sampling Plan** from the data files. Make the edits listed below.
   - Format title: center, bold, Arial 16-point font
   - Format first two side headings: bold, Arial 14-point font and the last two side headings: bold, Arial 12-point font
   - Search for *athlete* and replace with *student athlete* each time it occurs.
   - Key your name below the last line of type; right-align it; insert the date below your name.
   - Format paragraphs with 6-point spacing after paragraphs; center the page.
2. Save the document as **checkpoint7-d1**.

Document 2
Memo

1. Format the memo. Save as **checkpoint7-d2**.
2. Send the message To: **Student Athletes** From: **Jan Marks, Faculty Athletics Representative** Date: **Current** Subject: **Exit Interview**

In accordance with NCAA bylaws, the enclosed survey is sent to you as a student athlete who has completed your eligibility to compete in college athletics. This survey gives you an opportunity to share your opinions about your experience both as a student and as an athlete.

Please complete the survey and return it to me in the enclosed self-addressed envelope within two weeks. We urge you to be honest with your responses. The information is used to improve the athletics experience for future students. Your coach does not have access to this information, and your responses will be treated confidentially.

We appreciate your sharing your thoughts with us.

8d

x and **u**

Key each line once; repeat.

x Reach *down* with *left third* finger.

u Reach *up* with right first finger.

x

20 x x xs xs ox ox lox sox fox box ex hex lax hex fax
21 sx six sax sox ax fix cox wax hex box pox sex text
22 flax next flex axel pixel exit oxen taxi axis next

u

23 u uj uj jug jut just dust dud due sue use due duel
24 uj us cud but bun out sun nut gun hut hue put fuel
25 dual laud dusk suds fuss full tuna tutus duds full

all reaches learned

26 Paige Power liked the book; Josh can read it next.
27 Next we picked a bag for Jan; then she, Jan, left.
28 Is her June account due? Has Lou ruined her unit?

SKILLBUILDING

8e Reinforcement

Optional: In the Open Screen, key each line once; DS between groups. Repeat. Print.

29 nut cue hut sun rug us six cut dug axe rag fox run
30 out of the sun|cut the action|a fox den|fun at six
31 That car is not junk; it can run in the next race.

32 etc. tax nick cure lack flex walls uncle clad hurt
33 lack the cash|not just luck|next in line|just once
34 June Dunn can send that next tax case to Rex Knox.

8f Speed Check

In the Open Screen, take a 1' writing on each paragraph. Press ENTER only after you have keyed the entire paragraph. Save the timings as **xx8e-t1** and **xx8e-t2**, with *xx* being your **initials**.
Goal: 14 *wam.*

```
                 •            4           •            8           •
How a finished job will look often depends on how
          12           •           16           •           20
we feel about our work as we do it.  Attitude has
          •           24           •           28           •
a definite effect on the end result of work we do.
```
Press ENTER once
```
                 •            4           •            8           •
When we are eager to begin a job, we relax and do
          12           •           16           •           20
better work than if we start the job with an idea
          •           24           •           28           •
that there is just nothing we can do to escape it.
```

57c-d3
Memo

1. Key the memo shown below.
2. Send the memo to the **Planning Commission** from the **Community Park Site Committee**. Use the current date, and send a copy of the memo to **Mayor Charles Morgan**.
3. Use the report title from **57c-d1** as the subject of the memo.
4. Proofread, print, and save it as **57c-d3**.

The Community Park Site Committee has completed its assessment of the potential sites for the new park. Our report is attached.

The Committee unanimously recommends that the Westlake site be used for the new park. The Woodcreek site was considered acceptable, but it is not as desirable as the Westlake site. The Southside site was the least desirable of the three sites.

Please contact us if you have any questions.

57c-d4
Block Letter

1. Key the following letter in block format. Use the current date and sign your name.
2. Save it as **57c-d4**.

Ms. Margaret C. Worthington
4957 Mt. Elon Church Road
Hopkins, SC 29061-9837

Dear Ms. Worthington

The Planning Commission has authorized me to contact you to discuss the possible purchase of the 120-acre site that we discussed with you for the new Community Park. When we spoke with you yesterday, you indicated that you would be available to meet with us any afternoon next week. If it is still convenient, we would like to meet with you on Wednesday afternoon at 2:00 at the site.

Earlier you indicated that you had a recent survey and an appraisal of the property. We would appreciate it if you could have those documents available for the meeting.

If this time is not convenient, please call my office and leave a message so that I may reschedule the meeting. We look forward to working with you.

Sincerely

LESSON 9

Q, M, V, Apostrophe

WARMUP

9a
Key each line twice.

all letters 1 Lex gripes about cold weather; Fred is not joking.
space bar 2 Is it Di, Jo, or Al? Ask Lt. Coe, Bill; he knows.
easy 3 I did rush a bushel of cut corn to the sick ducks.
easy 4 He is to go to the Tudor Isle of England on a bus.

NEW KEYS

9b q and m
Key each line once; repeat.

q Reach *up* with *left fourth* finger.

m Reach *down* with *right first* finger.

q

5 q qa qa quad quad quaff quant queen quo quit quick
6 qa qu qa quo quit quod quid quip quads quote quiet
7 quite quilts quart quill quakes quail quack quaint

m

8 m mj mj jam man malt mar max maw me mew men hem me
9 m mj ma am make male mane melt meat mist amen lame
10 malt meld hemp mimic tomb foam rams mama mire mind

all reaches learned

11 Quin had some quiet qualms about taming a macaque.
12 Jake Coxe had questions about a new floor program.
13 Max was quick to join the big reception for Lidia.

9c Textbook Keying
Key each line once for control. DS between groups of two lines.

m/x 14 me men ma am jam am lax, mix jam; the hem, six men
15 Emma Max expressed an aim to make a mammoth model.

q/u 16 qa qu aqua aqua quit quit quip quite pro quo squad
17 Did Quin make a quick request to take the Qu exam?

g/n 18 fg gn gun gun dig dig nag snag snag sign grab grab
19 Georgia hung a sign in front of the union for Gib.

57c-d1
Unbound Report

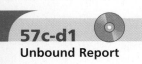

1. Open **Site Assessment** from the data files, and make the following edits:
   - Format as unbound report, SS; 6-point spacing after paragraphs.
   - Center title, apply bold, 14-point Arial type. Position heading at about 2" and add an extra blank line after the heading.
   - Format side headings in bold.
   - Use Find and Replace to find *Theme*, and replace it with *Community* each time it occurs.

2. Insert page numbers at the upper-right margin; do not show on first page.

3. Use Keep with next feature to ensure that headings are kept with the paragraphs below them.

4. Preview; make sure headings are not left alone at the bottom of a page.

5. Proofread, save as **57c-d1**, and print.

57c-d2
Leftbound Report

1. Reformat the report as a leftbound report; DS; indent paragraphs.

2. Key the table shown below making the edits indicated; position it below the last paragraph of the report. If the entire table does not fit at the bottom of the page, place it on the next page.

Site Costs *Center, bold, 14 pt. type*			
Cost Category	**Westlake**	**Southside**	**Woodcreek**
		Center column heads	
Land	$720,000	$630,000	$ 676,000
Infrastructure	175,000	210,000	180,000
Total	$805,000	$840000	$856,000

Left-align first column

3. Preview; make sure headings are not left alone at the bottom of a page.

4. Proofread, save as **57c-d2**, and print.

9d

v and ' (apostrophe)

Key each line once; repeat.

Apostrophe: The apostrophe shows (1) omission (as Rob't for Robert or it's for it is) or (2) possession when used with nouns (as Joe's hat).

v Reach *down* with *left first* finger.

' Reach to ' with *right fourth* finger.

v

20 v vf vf vie vie via via vim vat vow vile vale vote
21 vf vf ave vet ova eve vie dive five live have lave
22 cove dove over aver vivas hive volt five java jive

' (apostrophe)

23 '; '; it's it's Rod's; it's Bo's hat; we'll do it.
24 We don't know if it's Lee's pen or Norma's pencil.
25 It's ten o'clock; I won't tell him that he's late.

all reaches learned

26 It's Viv's turn to drive Iva's van to Ava's house.
27 Qua, not Vi, took the jet; so did Cal. Didn't he?
28 Wasn't Fae Baxter a judge at the post garden show?

SKILLBUILDING

9e Reinforcement

1. Follow the standard Open Screen directions on page 8.
2. Key each line twice; DS between groups. Strive to increase speed.

v/?
29 Viola said she has moved six times in five months.
30 Does Dave live on Vine Street? Must he leave now?

q/?
31 Did Viv vote? Can Paque move it? Could Val dive?
32 Didn't Raquel quit Carl Quent after their quarrel?

direct reach
33 Fred told Brice that the junior class must depart.
34 June and Hunt decided to go to that great musical.

double letter
35 Harriette will cook dinner for the swimming teams.
36 Bill's committee meets in an accounting classroom.

9f Speed Check

In the Open Screen, take two 1' writings on the paragraph. Press ENTER only after keying the entire paragraph. Save the timings as **xx-9e-t1** and **xx-9e-t2**, substituting your initials for *xx*.

```
                  .           4           .           8           .
We must be able to express our thoughts with ease
         12          .          16          .          20
if we desire to find success in the business world.
         .          24          .          28
It is there that sound ideas earn cash.
```

SKILLBUILDING

57a
Warmup
Key each line twice SS.

alphabet   1   Max Biqua watched jet planes flying in the azure sky over a cove.
figures   2   Send 105 No. 4 nails and 67 No. 8 brads for my home at 329 Annet.
3d row   3   We two were ready to type a report for our quiet trio of workers.
easy   4   Pamela owns a big bicycle; and, with it, she may visit the docks.

| 1 | 2 | 3 | 4 | 5 | 6 | 7 | 8 | 9 | 10 | 11 | 12 | 13 |

gwam   3' | 5'

57b
Timed Writings
Take one 3' and one 5' timing on the paragraphs.

  all letters

	3'	5'
Voting is a very important part of being a good citizen.	4	2
However, many young people who are eligible to vote choose not	8	5
to do so. When asked to explain or justify their decision, many	12	7
simply shrug their shoulders and reply that they have no particular	16	10
reason for not voting. The explanation others frequently give is	21	13
that they just did not get around to going to the voting polls.	25	15
A good question to consider concerns ways that we can motivate	29	18
young people to be good citizens and to go to the polls and to vote.	34	21
Some people approach this topic by trying to determine how satisfied	39	23
people are who do not vote with the performance of their elected	43	26
officials. Unfortunately, those who choose not to vote are just as	48	29
satisfied with their elected officials as are those who voted.	52	31
One interesting phenomenon concerning voting relates to the	56	34
job market. When the job market is strong, fewer young people vote	61	36
than when the job market is very bad. They also tend to be less	65	39
satisfied with their elected officials. Self-interest seems to	69	41
be a powerful motivator. Unfortunately, those who do not choose	74	44
to vote miss the point that it is in their best interest to be a	78	47
good citizen.	79	47

3' | 1 | 2 | 3 | 4 |
5' | 1 | 2 | 3 |

APPLICATIONS

57c
Assessment

 Continue

 Check

With CheckPro: When you complete a document, proofread it, check the spelling, and preview for placement. When you are completely satisfied, click the **Continue** button to move to the next document. You will not be able to return and edit a document once you continue to the next document. Click the **Check** button when you are ready to error-check the test. Review and/or print the document analysis results.

Without CheckPro: Key the documents in sequence. When time has been called, proofread all documents again and identify errors.

LESSON 10

Z, Y, Quotation Mark, Tab

WARMUP

10a
Key each line twice.

all letters	1	Quill owed those back taxes after moving to Japan.
spacing	2	Didn't Vi, Sue, and Paul go? Someone did; I know.
q/v/m	3	Marv was quite quick to remove that mauve lacquer.
easy	4	Lana is a neighbor; she owns a lake and an island.

NEW KEYS

10b z and y
Key each line once;
repeat.

z Reach *down* with *left fourth* finger.

y Reach *up* with *right first* finger.

z

5 za za zap zap zing zig zag zoo zed zip zap zig zed

6 doze zeal zero haze jazz zone zinc zing size ozone

7 ooze maze doze zoom zarf zebus daze gaze faze adze

y

8 y yj yj jay jay hay hay lay nay say days eyes ayes

9 yj ye yet yen yes cry dry you rye sty your fry wry

10 ye yen bye yea coy yew dye yaw lye yap yak yon any

all reaches learned

11 Did you say Liz saw any yaks or zebus at your zoo?

12 Relax; Jake wouldn't acquire any favorable rights.

13 Has Mazie departed? Tex, Lu, and I will go alone.

10c Textbook Keying
Key each line once. DS
between groups.

	14	Cecilia brings my jumbo umbrella to every concert.
direct reach	15	John and Kim recently brought us an old art piece.
	16	I built a gray brick border around my herb garden.

DS

	17	sa ui hj gf mn vc ew uy re io as lk rt jk df op yu
adjacent reach	18	In Ms. Lopez' opinion, the opera was really great.
	19	Polly and I were joining Walker at the open house.

The Marshall Tract   *Level 2 Heading*

The Marshall tract consists of over 1,200 acres of environmentally sensitive coastal property. Approximately one-half of the tract consists of wetlands with a conservation and preservation easement on̸ the property. A portion of the remaining property has endangered species, including the red cockaded woodpecker. An eagle nest has also been spotted on the property.

Insert *The master plan calls for the retention of the property because of its potential for research and environmental education. The short-term plans call for the establishment of a system of nature trails and boardwalks and the development of a parking area for visitors. Long-term plans specify the design and construction of a research and learning center.*

The Richardson Tract   *Level 2 Heading*

The Richardson tract consists of an entire barrier island that is used for research purposes. The property currently has a very basic research and education center. The gift agreement severely restricts development of facilities on the island; therefore, it is not likely to be highly developed at any point in the future.

Midlands Properties   *Level 1 Heading*

The Midlands portfolio of property consists of more than sixty individual parcels of land. Approximately 60 percent of the land was purchased and 40 percent was received as gifts. The land is valued at $12,650,000.

The Wheeler Tract   *Level 2 Heading*

A decision has been made to sell this property. Currently, the property is being surveyed and a new appraisal has been ordered. The property will be ~~put~~ placed on the market as soon as the survey and appraisal have been completed.

The Blossom Tract   *Level 2 Heading*

The Foundation contracted to have infrastructure work completed before turning the tract over to Midlands University for development.

10d

" (quotation mark) and **TAB**

Key each line once; repeat.

" Shift; then reach to **"** with *right fourth* finger.

TAB Reach up with *left fourth* finger.

" (quotation mark)

20 "; "; " " "lingo" "bugs" "tennies"   I   like "malts."
21 "I am not," she said, "going."   I just said, "Oh?"

tab key

22   The tab key is used for indenting paragraphs
     and aligning columns.
23   Tabs that are set by the software are called
     default tabs, which are usually a half inch.

all reaches learned

24   The expression "I give you my word," or put another
25 way, "Take my word for it," is just a way I can say, "I
26 prize my name; it clearly stands in back of my words."
27 I offer "honor" as collateral.

SKILLBUILDING

10e Reinforcement

Follow the standard directions on page 8 for keying in the Open Screen. Key each line twice; DS between groups.

10f Speed Check

Take two 1' writings of paragraph 2 in the Open Screen, using wordwrap. Save as **xx-10e-t1** and **xx-10e-t2**.
Goal: 15 *wam*

TECHNIQUE TIP

Wordwrap: Text within a paragraph moves automatically to the next line. Press ENTER only to begin a new paragraph.

tab 28   Strike the tab key and begin the line without a pause
     to maintain fluency.
29   She said that this is the lot to be sent; I
     agreed with her.
30   Strike Tab before starting to key a timed
     writing so that the first line is indented.

gwam 1'

Tab → All of us work for progress, but it is not   8
always easy to analyze "progress."   We work hard   18
for it; but, in spite of some really good efforts,   28
we may fail to receive just exactly the response we   39
want.   40
Tab → When this happens, as it does to all of us,   9
it is time to cease whatever we are doing, have   18
a quiet talk with ourselves, and face up to the   28
questions about our limited progress.   How can we   38
do better?   40

| 1 | 2 | 3 | 4 | 5 | 6 | 7 | 8 | 9 | 10 |

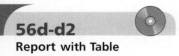
1. Open **Master Plan** from the data files. Save as **56d-d2**.

2. Center the main heading, format in bold, 16-point Arial type. Position main heading at about 2".

3. Number pages at top right margin; do not show number on the first page.

4. Format Level 1 headings with bold, 14-point Arial type. Format Level 2 headings with bold, 12-point Arial type.

5. Use 6-point spacing after paragraphs.

6. Ensure that headings are not separated from the paragraphs that follow.

7. Open **55c-d3**; select the *Property Location and Value* table and copy it; then paste it after the second paragraph in this report. Delete the blank line before and after the table title.

8. Make all edits shown below. Add text that is in script to the document.

9. Proofread and edit carefully. Check to see that you have made all edits and followed all instructions.

10. Print and resave.

Master Plan for Foundation Properties

The Midlands University Foundation properties are categorized into four classifications: Coastal Property, Midlands Property, other in-state property, and out-of-state property. The Foundation acquires property by purchasing it or by accepting gifts from donors desiring to support Midlands University.

Insert → *Generally, the Foundation retains coastal properties for research and environmental education purposes and properties in the Midlands area for future development and use by Midlands University. Usually, properties in the other two categories are held only if they are likely to appreciate significantly; otherwise, they are sold and the proceeds are used to support various University needs. Currently, no out-of-state property is being held.*

Insert table here.

Coastal Properties   *Level1 Heading*

seven

Currently the Foundation owns ~~a number of~~ different tracts of land in the Coastal Region valued at $18,325,000. Decisions on the future use of five of the tracts are pending. The master plan contains specific plans for only two of the tracts the Marshall tract and the Richardson tract.

∧ *em dash*

LESSON 11

Review

WARMUP

11a
Key each line twice SS
(slowly, then faster).

alphabet 1 Zeb had Jewel quickly give him five or six points.

" (quote) 2 Can you spell "chaos," "bias," "bye," and "their"?

y 3 Ty Clay may envy you for any zany plays you write.

easy 4 Did he bid on the bicycle, or did he bid on a map?

| 1 | 2 | 3 | 4 | 5 | 6 | 7 | 8 | 9 | 10 |

SKILLBUILDING

11b Keyboard Reinforcement
Key each line once; repeat the drill to increase fluency.

5 za za zap az az maze zoo zip razz zed zax zoa zone

6 Liz Zahl saw Zoe feed the zebra in an Arizona zoo.

7 yj yj jy jy joy lay yaw say yes any yet my try you

8 Why do you say that today, Thursday, is my payday?

9 xs xs sax ox box fix hex ax lax fox taxi lox sixes

10 Roxy, you may ask Jay to fix any tax sets for you.

11 qa qa aqua quail quit quake quid equal quiet quart

12 Did Enrique quietly but quickly quell the quarrel?

13 fv fv five lives vow ova van eve avid vex vim void

14 Has Vivi, Vada, or Eva visited Vista Valley Farms?

TECHNIQUE TIP
Work for smoothness,
not for speed.

11c Speed Builders
Key each balanced-hand line twice, as quickly as you can.

15 is to for do an may work so it but an with them am

16 am yam map aid zig yams ivy via vie quay cob amend

17 to do is for an may work so it but am an with them

18 for it|for it|to the|to the|do they|do they|do it

19 Pamela may go to the farm with Jan and a neighbor.

20 Rod and Ty may go by the lake if they go downtown.

| 1 | 2 | 3 | 4 | 5 | 6 | 7 | 8 | 9 | 10 |

APPLICATIONS

56d-d1
Edit Memo with Bullets

1. Open **Trail Design** from the data files. Save as **56d-d1**.
2. Position the first line of heading correctly.
3. Search for *sights* and replace with *sites* each time it occurs.
4. Add bullets to the list of sites.
5. Make other edits shown and add reference initials.
6. Proofread carefully and preview the document.
7. Print and resave it.

To: Trail design task force

From: Dianne Gibson

Date: Current

Subject: Trail design

Thanks *you* for participating in the Trail Design meeting last week. *I think* We did

ma*d*ke a tremendous amount of progress on this ~~fun~~ *exciting* project. Specific sights were

designated for the components of phase one of the Environmental learning center

stet ~~complex~~ and the first trail loop. Tentative sights were ~~located~~ *identified* for the phase two [2]

components including the conference center.

Ken provide*d*s us with a new lay*d* out of the property showing the following

sights that were designated during the visit.

Main *lc* Entrance
Parking ~~lot~~ *area*
Environmental Learning Center
General shelter *buildings*
Outdoor linear classroom*s*
First trail loop with key interpretative sights designated
Sustainability exhibit ~~sights~~

the positioning of Please review these sights to make sure that the layout and documentation *both*

interprets the groups ~~wishes~~ *decisions* properly. Once we recieve feed back from every one,

Ken ~~needs to~~ *will* finalize the design documents.

Our timeframe requires us to have finalized concept documents within two weeks to turn over to the architects. The architects will develop the construction documents needed to obtain the necessary permits.

11d Technique Builder

Key each line once; DS between groups.

TECHNIQUE TIP

Press CAPS LOCK to capitalize several letters. Press it again to toggle CAPS LOCK off.

enter: key smoothly without looking at fingers

21 Make the return snappily
22 and with assurance; keep
23 your eyes on your source
24 data; maintain a smooth,
25 constant pace as you key.

space bar: use down-and-in motion

26 us me it of he an by do go to us if or so am ah el
27 Have you a pen? If so, print "Free to any guest."

caps lock: press to toggle it on or off

28 Use ALL CAPS for items such as TO: FROM: SUBJECT.
29 Did Kristin mean Kansas City, MISSOURI, or KANSAS?

11e Speed Check

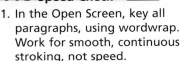

1. In the Open Screen, key all paragraphs, using wordwrap. Work for smooth, continuous stroking, not speed.
2. Save as **xx-11e**. Substitute your initals for *xx*.
3. Take a 2' writing on all paragraphs.

Goal: 16 *gwam*

To determine gross-words-a-minute (*gwam*) rate for 2':

Follow these steps if you are *not* using the Timer in the Open Screen.

1. Note the figure at the end of the last line completed.

2. For a partial line, note the figure on the scale direcly below the point at which you stopped keying.

3. Add these two figures to determine the total gross words a minute (*gwam*) you keyed.

		gwam	2'
Have we thought of communication as a kind		4	31
of war that we wage through each day?		8	35
When we think of it that way, good language		12	39
would seem to become our major line of attack.		17	44
Words become muscle; in a normal exchange or in		22	49
a quarrel, we do well to realize the power of words.		27	54

11f Enrichment

1. Go to the Skillbuilding Workshop 1, Drill 1, page 31. Choose 6 letters that cause you difficulty. Key each line twice. Put a check mark beside the lines in the book so that you know you have practiced them.

2. Save the drill as **xx-11f**. Substitute your initials for *xx*.

SKILLBUILDING

56a
Warmup
Key each line twice SS.

alphabet	1	Jacki might analyze the data by answering five complex questions.
figures	2	Memo 67 asks if the report on Bill 35-48 is due the 19th or 20th.
double letters	3	Aaron took accounting lessons at a community college last summer.
easy	4	Hand Bob a bit of cocoa, a pan of cod, an apricot, and six clams.

| 1 | 2 | 3 | 4 | 5 | 6 | 7 | 8 | 9 | 10 | 11 | 12 | 13 |

56b
Technique Builder
Key each pair of lines 3 times.
Key at a controlled rate.

First row
5 Zam name bank man came exam cave band comb six mine vent back van
6 Zack came back excited; Max made a banner for a vacant zinc mine.

Home row
7 sad lass lag had gag laggard fax hulk salad sales flask glass has
8 Dallas Klass had a jello salad; Ada asked for a large salad also.

Third row
9 were pot toy pew wept you quit power quip peer tower or rope wire
10 Terry wrote Troy for help after a power tower guide wire was cut.

56c
Timed Writings
Build/Assess Straight-Copy Skill

1. Take one 3' timed writing.
2. Take one 5' timed writing.

  all letters

	gwam	3'	5'

For many years, readers who had chosen a particular book had   4 | 2
just one question to answer. Do you want to purchase a hardcover   8 | 5
or a paperback book? It was assumed that books would be purchased   13 | 8
from a retail outlet, such as a bookstore. Currently, books are   17 | 10
being marketed and sold online. The book itself, however, is still   22 | 13
printed on paper.   23 | 14

With the technology that is on the market today, a third   27 | 16
alternative, the electronic or the so-called e-book, is emerging.   31 | 19
E-books are sold in digitized form. The book must be read from the   36 | 21
web site on a computer or on a special device designed for reading   40 | 24
e-books. Many publishers are experimenting with electronic books,   45 | 27
but only a few well-known ones have moved into the e-book market   49 | 29
in a major way. Most e-book companies are small organizations that   54 | 32
are willing to take a risk to make a profit.   56 | 34

The cost of producing and selling books in digital form is   60 | 36
far less than it is in paper form. The result is that books   65 | 39
that appeal to small markets are now feasible in digital form. The   69 | 41
cost was too great in print form. Many publishers have two key   73 | 44
concerns about the e-book market. The first is that a large number   78 | 47
of readers still are not comfortable reading from electronic media   82 | 49
for long time periods. The second factor is that they worry about   87 | 52
copyright protection. Many are very aware of the problems the music   91 | 55
industry experienced in this area.   94 | 56

3' | 1 | 2 | 3 | 4 |
5' | 1 | 2 | 3 |

LESSON 12 Review

WARMUP

12a

Key each line twice SS (slowly, then faster).

alphabet 1 Jack won five quiz games; Brad will play him next.

q 2 Quin Racq quickly and quietly quelled the quarrel.

z 3 Zaret zipped along sizzling, zigzag Arizona roads.

easy 4 Did he hang the sign by the big bush at the lake?

| 1 | 2 | 3 | 4 | 5 | 6 | 7 | 8 | 9 | 10 |

SKILLBUILDING

12b New Key Review

Key each line once; DS between groups; work for smoothness, not for speed.

b/f 5 bf bf fab fab ball bib rf rf rib rib fibs bums bee

6 Did Buffy remember that he is a brass band member?

z/y 7 za za zag zig zip yj yj jay eye day lazy hazy zest

8 Liz amazed us with the zesty pizza on a lazy trip.

q/u 9 qa qa quo qt. quit quay quad quarm que uj jug quay

10 Where is Quito? Qatar? Boqueirao? Quebec? Quilmes?

v/m 11 vf vf valve five value mj mj ham mad mull mass vim

12 Vito, enter the words vim, vivace, and avar; save.

all 13 I faced defeat; only reserves saved my best crews.

14 In my opinion, I need to rest in my reserved seat.

all 15 Holly created a red poppy and deserves art awards.

16 My pump averages a faster rate; we get better oil.

12c Textbook Keying

Key each line once; DS between groups. Work for smooth, unhurried keying.

de/ed 17 ed fed led deed dell dead deal sled desk need seed

18 Dell dealt with the deed before the dire deadline.

ol/lo 19 old tolls doll solo look sole lost love cold stole

20 Old Ole looked for the long lost olive oil lotion.

op/po 21 pop top post rope pout port stop opal opera report

22 Stop to read the top opera opinion report to Opal.

we/ew 23 we few wet were went wears weather skews stew blew

24 Working women wear sweaters when weather dictates.

TECHNIQUE TIP

Keep fingers curved and body aligned properly.

55c-d3
Edit Report

1. Save the open document (**55c-d2**) as **55c-d3**.
2. Reformat the report SS; DS between ¶s; do not indent.
3. Change to leftbound report; 1.5" left and 1.0" right margins.
4. SS the table; place a blank line before and after the title of the table.
5. Add a row at the bottom of the table; in column 2 add the total, **$34,815,000**; and in column 3, **100%**.
6. Delete the extra returns at the top of the page so that the title is on the first line; center the page.
7. Resave; print and close the document.

55c-d4
Leftbound Report

1. Open **Meade** from the data files.
2. Change format to a leftbound report.
3. Format title on first page and reference page using all caps, bold, and 14-point font. Position both for an approximate 2" top margin.
4. Make sure all ¶s are indented on the DS report.
   Format all side headings using bold type. Capitalize main words in all side headings.
5. Use the Keep with next feature to ensure that headings remain with the text that follows them and that the table is not separated from its title or divided on two pages.
6. Number pages at the top right margin; do not show number on first page.
7. Preview and check to see that all of the instructions above have been applied properly. Make any necessary corrections.
8. Save as **55c-d4** and print. Leave the document open.

55c-d5
Unbound Report

1. Save the open document (**55c-d4**) as **55c-d5**.
2. Reformat the report as an unbound report, SS. Remove all paragraph indentions.
3. Use 6-point spacing after paragraphs and side headings.
4. Change the font for all titles and headings to Arial.
5. Use the Keep with next feature to ensure that headings remain with the text that follows them and that the table is not separated from its title or divided on two pages.
6. Preview and check to see that all of the instructions above have been applied properly. Make any necessary corrections.
7. Resave and print.

SKILLBUILDING

55d
Skill Builder

Use the remaining class time to build your skills using the Skill Builder module within *Keyboarding Pro*.

12d Speed Builder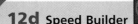

1. Key each line quickly to build stroking speed.
2. Save as **xx-L12**. (Substitute your initials for *xx*.)

TECHNIQUE TIP
Keep hands quiet; keep fingers curved and upright.

```
25 a for we you is that be this will be a to and well
26 as our with I or a to by your form which all would
27 new year no order they so new but now year who may

28 This is Lyn's only date to visit their great city.
29 I can send it to your office at any time you wish.
30 She kept the fox, owls, and fowl down by the lake.

31 Harriette will cook dinner for the swimming teams.
32 Annette will call at noon to give us her comments.
33 Johnny was good at running and passing a football.
   |  1  |  2  |  3  |  4  |  5  |  6  |  7  |  8  |  9  |  10  |
```

12e Speed Check

1. In the Open Screen, key both paragraphs using wordwrap. Work for smooth, continuous stroking, not speed.
2. Save as **xx-12e**. Substitute your initials for *xx*.
3. Take a 1' writing on paragraph 1. Save as **xx-12e-t1**.
4. Repeat step 3 using paragraph 2. Save as **xx-12e-t2**.
5. Set the Timer for 2'. Take a 2' writing on both paragraphs. Save as **xx-12e-t3**.

 all letters

Goal: 16 *wam*

Copy Difficulty

What factors determine whether copy is difficult or easy? Research shows that difficulty is influenced by syllables per word, characters per word, and percent of familiar words. Carefully controlling these three factors ensures that speed and accuracy scores are reliable—that is, increased scores reflect increased skill.

In Level 1, all timings are easy. Note "E" inside the triangle at left of the timing. Easy timings contain an average of 1.2 syllables per word, 5.1 characters per word, and 90 percent familiar words. Easy copy is suitable for the beginner who is mastering the keyboard.

```
                                        gwam  2'
              •        4        •        8
     There should be no questions, no doubt, about   5 | 35
        •       12       •         16        •
the value of being able to key; it's just a matter  10 | 40
      20      •        24      •          28      •
of common sense that today a pencil is much too slow. 15 | 45
            •        4        •        8
     Let me explain. Work is done on a keyboard      19 | 49
        •        12      •        16        •
three to six times faster than other writing and    24 | 54
        20       •        24      •        28
with a product that is a prize to read. Don't you   29 | 59
        •
agree?                                               30 | 60
    2' |     1     |     2     |     3     |     4     |     5     |
```

APPLICATIONS

55c-d2
Edit Report

1. Key the report; DS.

2. Use approximately a 2" top margin; add the title **Foundation Property in South Carolina**; center, bold.

3. Make the edits shown in the table; DS the table.

4. Save as **55c-d2** and print; leave the document open.

The Foundation owns both in-state and out-of-state property. However, the bulk of the property is located within the state. In-state property is divided into three regions—Coastal, Midlands, and Other. The following chart shows the distribution of the property by region:

Property Location and Value		
South Carolina Regions *Bold and Center headings*	Value of Property in Region	Percentage of Total Property
Coastal Region *Set right*	$18,325,000	53%
Midlands Region *align tab*	12,650,000	36%
Other Regions—In-State *at 3.5"*	3,840,000	11%

Bold (annotation above "Percentage of Total Property" heading)

Center align (annotation in Percentage column)

The total value of the property is $34,815,000. More than half of the property is located in the Coastal region. The next largest concentration is in the Midlands region.

The property values are based on the appraisal price at the time of acquisition. Properties are acquired by gift or purchase. Current market value of the property is significantly higher than the value at the time of acquisition.

LESSON 13   Review

WARMUP

13a
Key each line twice SS
(slowly, then faster).

alphabet 1 Bev quickly hid two Japanese frogs in Mitzi's box.
shift 2 Jay Nadler, a Rotary Club member, wrote Mr. Coles.
, (comma) 3 Jay, Ed, and I paid for plates, knives, and forks.
easy 4 Did the amendment name a city auditor to the firm?
| 1 | 2 | 3 | 4 | 5 | 6 | 7 | 8 | 9 | 10 |

SKILLBUILDING

13b Rhythm Builders
Key each line once SS.

word-level response: key short, familiar words as units

5 is to for do an may work so it but an with them am
6 Did they mend the torn right half of their ensign?
7 Hand me the ivory tusk on the mantle by the bugle.

letter-level response: key more difficult words letter by letter

8 only state jolly zest oil verve join rate mop card
9 After defeat, look up; gaze in joy at a few stars.
10 We gazed at a plump beaver as it waded in my pool.

combination response: use variable speed; your fingers will let you feel the difference

11 it up so at for you may was but him work were they
12 It is up to you to get the best rate; do it right.
13 This is Lyn's only date to visit their great city.
| 1 | 2 | 3 | 4 | 5 | 6 | 7 | 8 | 9 | 10 |

13c Keyboard Reinforcement
Key each line once; fingers
well curved, wrists low; avoid
punching keys with 3rd and
4th fingers.

p 14 Pat appears happy to pay for any supper I prepare.
x 15 Knox can relax; Alex gets a box of flax next week.
v 16 Vi, Ava, and Viv move ivy vines, leaves, or stems.
' 17 It's a question of whether they can't or won't go.
? 18 Did Jan go? Did she see Ray? Who paid? Did she?
. 19 Ms. E. K. Nu and Lt. B. A. Walz had the a.m. duty.
" 20 "Who are you?" he asked. "I am," I said, "Marie."
; 21 Find a car; try it; like it; work a price; buy it.

LESSON 55 — Edit Tables and Reports

SKILLBUILDING

55a
Warmup
Key each line twice SS.

1 When Jorg moves away, quickly place five dozen gloves in the box.
2 Flight 372 leaves at 10:46 a.m. and arrives in Omaha at 9:58 p.m.
3 I obtain unusual services from a number of celebrated decorators.
4 She may sign an authentic name and title to amend this endowment.
| 1 | 2 | 3 | 4 | 5 | 6 | 7 | 8 | 9 | 10 | 11 | 12 | 13 |

55b
Timed Writings
1. Key one 3' timing.
2. Key one 5' writing. Strive for control.

  all letters

	gwam	3'	5'
Reports are one of the best means by which busy executives	4	2	26
at any level of a business can keep well informed. The pertinent	8	5	29
data in reports can be used to solve a wide variety of problems	13	8	31
that arise, make any changes that may be required, analyze	16	10	34
results, and make precise, timely decisions.	19	12	36
The quality of the plans and decisions made on the basis of	23	14	39
the information found in reports depends in large measure on how	28	17	41
well the reports are produced. A good report is a thorough and	32	19	43
objective summary of all pertinent facts and figures. If reports	36	22	46
are not well produced, the firm will surely suffer.	40	24	48

3' | 1 | 2 | 3 | 4 |
5' | 1 | 2 | 3 |

APPLICATIONS

55c-d1
Edit Table

1. Open **Research Building** from the data files; save as **55c-d1**.
2. Edit the table as marked.
3. Change row height to .3" and center text vertically in the cell.
4. Resave; print.

RESEARCH BUILDING PROJECT STATUS   *Center and Bold Title*

Job	Description	Date Completed
A & E Design Work	Plans completed	September 25, 2003
Building Permits	Submit plans *for city review*	October 14, 2003
Construction *Bids*	Prepare bid documents	November 8, 2003

Add row

Award Bid   *Select final bid*   *January 10,*

13d Textbook Keying

Troublesome Pairs: Key each line once; DS between groups.

TECHNIQUE TIP

Keep hands and arms still as you reach up to the third row and down to the first row.

```
t  22  at fat hat sat to tip the that they fast last slat
r  23  or red try ran run air era fair rid ride trip trap
t/r 24  A trainer sprained an arm trying to tame the bear.

m  25  am me my mine jam man more most dome month minimum
n  26  no an now nine once net knee name ninth know never
m/n 27  Many men and women are important company managers.

o  28  on or to not now one oil toil over only solo today
i  29  it is in tie did fix his sit like with insist will
o/i 30  Joni will consider obtaining options to buy coins.

a  31  at an as art has and any case data haze tart smart
s  32  us as so say sat slap lass class just sassy simple
a/s 33  Disaster was averted as the steamer sailed to sea.

e  34  we he ear the key her hear chef desire where there
i  35  it is in tie did fix his sit like with insist will
e/i 36  An expression of gratitude for service is desired.
```

13e Speed Check

1. In the Open Screen, key the paragraphs once SS.
2. Save as **xx-13e**.
3. Take a 1' writing on paragraph 1. Save as **xx-13e-t1**.
4. Take a 1' writing on paragraph 2. Save as **xx-13e-t2**.
5. Print the better 1' writing.
6. Take a 2' writing on both paragraphs. Start over if time permits.

 all letters

Goal: 16 *gwam*

```
                                                            gwam  2"
            .           4          .           8
      The  questions  of  time  use  are  vital  ones;  we      5
    .           12          .           16
miss  so  much  just  because  we  don't  plan.                 9
            .           4          .           8
      When  we  organize  our  days,  we  save  time  for      13
        .           12          .          16
those  extra  premium  things  we  long  to  do.               17
2'|     1     |     2     |     3     |     4     |     5     |
```

54c-d4
Memo

1. Key the memo below. Make all of the corrections noted by proofreaders' marks.
2. Send the memo to **David C. Kline** from **Carolyn M. Pastides**; use the current date and the subject **Economic Development Project**.
3. Search for *Department of Commerce* and replace it with *Board of Economic Development* each time it appears.
4. Proofread carefully, preview, save as **54c-d4**, and print.

TIP
To insert a nonbreaking hyphen, click Insert, Symbol, and then Special Characters.

The meeting with representatives of the department of commerce and the representatives being recruited to move here provided a very interesting perspective on the changing approach of recruiting small, knowledge based companies rather than large manufacturing operations. The company being recruited is a recent spin off form a research project at a major university. It's stage of development could best be described as developmental.

We signed non-disclosure forms and the Department of Commerce provided us with financials provided by the company's auditor. However, the audit was not signed, and the management letter was not included. I have requested that the CFO bring to the meeting tomorrow a complete copy of the audit and proformas for two years forward. My guess is that the audit will contain a going concern clause. The company currently has a stockholders' deficit of approximately $15,000,000. Unless financing is obtained, it is unlikely that the company can continue to operate. I requested copies of contracts are agreements that would support the revenue projections in the proformas.

The technology developed by the company is exciting, and the upside potential of the joint venture appears to be very good. Documentation of prototype orders was provided. Because of the risk involved in a company at this early stage of development, it is imperative that we do a lot of due diligence before investing in this company.

Skill Builders 1

Use the Option Screen for Skill Builders. Save each drill as a separate file.

DRILL 1

Goal: reinforce key locations

Key each line at a comfortable, constant rate; check lines that need more practice; repeat those lines.

Keep
- your eyes on source copy
- your fingers curved, upright
- your wrists low, but not touching
- your elbows hanging loosely
- your feet flat on the floor

A We saw that Alan had an alabaster vase in Alabama.
B My rubber boat bobbed about in the bubbling brook.
C Ceci gave cups of cold cocoa to Rebecca and Rocco.
D Don's dad added a second deck to his old building.
E Even as Ellen edited her document, she ate dinner.
F Our firm in Buffalo has a staff of forty or fifty.
G Ginger is giving Greg the eggs she got from Helga.
H Hugh has eighty high, harsh lights he might flash.
I Irik's lack of initiative is irritating his coach.
J Judge J. J. Jore rejected Jeane and Jack's jargon.
K As a lark, Kirk kicked back a rock at Kim's kayak.
L Lucille is silly; she still likes lemon lollipops.
M Milt Mumm hammered a homer in the Miami home game.
N Ken Linn has gone hunting; Stan can begin canning.
O Jon Soto rode off to Otsego in an old Morgan auto.
P Philip helped pay the prize as my puppy hopped up.
Q Quiet Raquel quit quoting at an exquisite marquee.
R As Mrs. Kerr's motor roared, her red horse reared.
S Sissie lives in Mississippi; Lissa lives in Tulsa.
T Nat told Betty not to tattle on her little sister.
U Ula has a unique but prudish idea on unused units.
V Eva visited every vivid event for twelve evenings.
W We watched as wayworn wasps swarmed by the willow.
X Tex Cox waxed the next box for Xenia and Rex Knox.
Y Ty says you may stay with Fay for only sixty days.
Z Hazel is puzzled about the azure haze; Zack dozes.
alphabet Jacky and Max quickly fought over a sizable prawn.
alphabet Just by maximizing liquids, Chick Prew avoids flu.

| 1 | 2 | 3 | 4 | 5 | 6 | 7 | 8 | 9 | 10 |

54c-d2
Composing and Editing

1. Use the information from **54c-d1** to prepare a traditional memo to your instructor.
2. Modify the third bulleted instruction above to indicate that you have attached the printed version of your paper to this memo. Ignore the information about the electronic copy.
3. Add an attachment notation to the memo.
4. Proofread and edit the memo carefully.
5. Save the document as **54c-d2** and print it.

- Modify the third instruction above to indicate that you have attached the printed version of your paper to this memo.

- Ignore the information about the electronic copy.

54c-d3
Memo

1. Key the memo below.
2. Position the heading at about 2" and DS between paragraphs.
3. Move ¶2 so that it will be the last ¶.
4. Search for *NatureDesigns* and replace it with *NatureLink* each time it appears.
5. Use the Thesaurus to find another option for *wide-ranging* in the third sentence; select the first option.
6. Change the date in the memo from *November 10* to two weeks from today.
7. Proofread carefully, preview, save as **54c-d3**, and print.

To: Richard M. Taylor | From: Dianne Gibson | Date: Current | Subject: Trail Design

Last week, Madilyn signed the contract for the trail design for Phase 1 of our Georgetown property. NatureDesigns was selected as the contractor. This firm was chosen because of its wide-ranging experience in selecting interpretative sites, designing trails, and installing boardwalks to protect wetlands and environmentally sensitive areas.

Please let me know if you plan to participate in the initial meeting with NatureDesigns.

The first onsite meeting is scheduled for November 10. We plan to meet at the main entrance at 10:30 a.m. to tour the property and review the procedures that NatureDesigns plans to use in designing the trails near the red cockaded woodpecker (RCW) habitat. Since RCW is an endangered species, we want to balance the desires of ecotourists to observe these birds and the need to protect them.

xx | c Bruce Diamond

DRILL 2

Goal: strengthen up and down reaches

Keep hands and wrists quiet; fingers well curved in home position; stretch fingers up from home or pull them palmward as needed.

home position

1 Hall left for Dallas; he is glad Jake fed his dog.
2 Ada had a glass flask; Jake had a sad jello salad.
3 Lana Hask had a sale; Gala shall add half a glass.

down reaches

4 Did my banker, Mr. Mavann, analyze my tax account?
5 Do they, Mr. Zack, expect a number of brave women?
6 Zach, check the menu; next, beckon the lazy valet.

up reaches

7 Prue truly lost the quote we wrote for our report.
8 Teresa quietly put her whole heart into her words.
9 There were two hilarious jokes in your quiet talk.

DRILL 3

Goal: strengthen individual finger reaches

Rekey troublesome lines.

first finger

1 Bob Mugho hunted for five minutes for your number.
2 Juan hit the bright green turf with his five iron.
3 The frigates and gunboats fought mightily in Java.

second finger

4 Dick said the ice on the creek had surely cracked.
5 Even as we picnicked, I decided we needed to diet.
6 Kim, not Mickey, had rice with chicken for dinner.

third/fourth finger

7 Pam saw Roz wax an aqua auto as Lex sipped a cola.
8 Wally will quickly spell Zeus, Apollo, and Xerxes.
9 Who saw Polly? Zoe Pax saw her; she is quiet now.

DRILL 4

Goal: strengthen special reaches

Emphasize smooth stroking. Avoid pauses, but do not reach for speed.

adjacent reaches

1 Falk knew well that her opinions of art were good.
2 Theresa answered her question; order was restored.
3 We join there and walk north to the western point.

direct reaches

4 Barb Nunn must hunt for my checks; she is in debt.
5 In June and December, Irvin hunts in Bryce Canyon.
6 We decided to carve a number of funny human faces.

double letters

7 Anne stopped off at school to see Bill Wiggs cook.
8 Edd has planned a small cookout for all the troop.
9 Keep adding to my assets all fees that will apply.

| 1 | 2 | 3 | 4 | 5 | 6 | 7 | 8 | 9 | 10 |

SKILLBUILDING

54a
Warmup
Key each line twice SS.

1 Sandra quickly gave the boy a major prize for his excellent work.
2 Invoice #758 for $294 is due 2/14/03 and #315 for $67 is due now.
3 Todd and Ann meet with a committee at noon to discuss all issues.
4 He may sign both of the forms for the amendment to the endowment.

| 1 | 2 | 3 | 4 | 5 | 6 | 7 | 8 | 9 | 10 | 11 | 12 | 13 |

54b
Technique builder
Key each group of 3 lines twice.

5 Lou kicked the gray umbrella Fred gave me and broke it in pieces.
6 Cecilia jumped in the pool, kicked the side, and fractured a toe.
7 Bunny browsed in the library while June served the healthy lunch.

8 Teresa was there to operate the projection equipment on Saturday.
9 Walker sang three hymns, and Louisa taught everyone how to polka.
10 Guy and Teresa were going to buy ice cream after the polo match.

APPLICATIONS

54c-d1
Composing and Editing

1. Use the information below to compose and send an e-mail to your instructor.
2. Use the subject line **Extra Credit Assignment**.
3. Read the second bullet carefully. Select one of the 3 topics, create a new document, and save it as **54c-drill1-attach**. Key the title of your topic on the first line of this document. Close the file.
4. Proofread and edit the e-mail carefully before sending it.
5. Print a copy of your e-mail.

- Thank your instructor for providing the opportunity to complete an extra-credit assignment.

- Indicate which of the three topics available (E-Mail Etiquette, First Impressions Count, and Developing a Professional Attitude) you selected. Add a sentence indicating why you selected that topic for the three-page paper.

- Indicate that an electronic copy of your paper is attached to this e-mail and that a printed version has been placed in the appropriate assignment folder. Attach the file **54c-d1-attach** to your e-mail.

DRILL 5

Goal: improve troublesome pairs

Use a controlled rate without pauses.

d/k
1 ad add did does dish down body dear dread dabs bad
2 kid ok kiss tuck wick risk rocks kayaks corks buck
3 Dirk asked Dick to kid Drake about the baked duck.

e/i
4 deed deal den led heed made needs delay he she her
5 kit kiss kiln kiwi kick kilt kind six ribs kill it
6 Abie had neither ice cream nor fried rice in Erie.

b/v
7 fib fob fab rib beg bug rob bad bar bed born table
8 vat vet gave five ever envy never visit weave ever
9 Did Harv key jibe or jive, TV or TB, robe or rove?

t/r
10 aft after lift gift sit tot the them tax tutu tyro
11 for far ere era risk rich rock rosy work were roof
12 In Toronto, Ruth told the truth about her artwork.

u/y
13 jug just jury judge juice unit hunt bonus quiz bug
14 jay joy lay you your only envy quay oily whey body
15 Willy usually does not buy your Yukon art in July.

DRILL 6

Goal: build speed

Set the Timer for 1'.
Key each sentence for 1'.
Try to complete each sentence twice (20 *gwam* or more).
Ignore errors for now.

1 Dian may make cocoa for the girls when they visit.
2 Focus the lens for the right angle; fix the prism.
3 She may suspend work when she signs the torn form.
4 Augment their auto fuel in the keg by the autobus.
5 As usual, their robot did half turns to the right.
6 Pamela laughs as she signals to the big hairy dog.
7 Pay Vivian to fix the island for the eighty ducks.

| 1 | 2 | 3 | 4 | 5 | 6 | 7 | 8 | 9 | 10 |

DRILL 7

Goal: build speed

From the columns at the right, choose a *gwam* goal that is two to three words higher than your best rate. Set the Timer for **Variable** and then either **20"** or **30"**. Try to reach your goal.

	words	30"	20"
1 Did she make this turkey dish?		12	18
2 Blake and Laurie may go to Dubuque.		14	21
3 Signal for the oak sleigh to turn right.		16	24
4 I blame Susie; did she quench the only flame?		18	27
5 She turns the panel dials to make this robot work.		20	30

| 1 | 2 | 3 | 4 | 5 | 6 | 7 | 8 | 9 | 10 |

● ●

53e-d2
Letter

1. Open **Brady** from the data files. Save it as **53e-d2**. Make the following edits:
   - Revise the letter so that it will be formatted correctly as a modified block letter.
   - Search for the name *Debauche*; each time it appears, replace it with *DeBauche*.
   - Use the Thesaurus to find a synonym for *statistics*. Replace *statistics* with the second synonym listed.
   - Make the following correction in the first sentence of paragraph 2:
     Brad Swinton, our new vice president of Marketing, indicated. . .
   - Cut the following sentence from paragraph 2:
     I hope this will not be a problem for you.
2. Save the document again and print it.

53e-d3
Letter

1. Open document **53e-d2** that you completed in the previous activity.
2. Reformat the document as a block style letter.
3. Save it as **53e-d3** and print.

53e-d4
Letter

1. Prepare another letter for Ms. DeBauche using the same address, salutation, and closing lines that were used in **53e-d3**. Note that this letter does not contain an enclosure.
2. Key the letter below in block style format.
3. Search for *section*, and replace it each time it appears with *phase*.
4. Use the Thesaurus to find a synonym for *prolific*. Select the first option.
5. Save as **53e-d4** and print.

October 11, 200-

Our team completed its preliminary review of your proposal today. Overall, we are very pleased with the approach you have taken.

Please plan to provide the following information at our meeting on October 18:

1. Please provide a more detailed pricing plan. We would like to have each section of the project priced separately specifying hourly rate and expenses rather than the one total sum quoted.

2. How many hours do you estimate will be necessary to complete each section of the project? When would your firm be able to begin the project?

We look forward to a very prolific meeting on October 18.

DRILL 8

These writings are available as Diagnostic Writings.

1. Go to the Numeric & Skill Lesson menu and click the **Diagnostic Writing** button in the lower-right corner.
2. Choose the writing and select the length of the timing (1', 3', or 5').
3. Key the writing. If you finish before time is up, begin again.
4. Review your results.
5. (Optional) Choose the **Practice Error Words** from the Edit menu to practice errors in the writing.
6. Click the Timer icon at the bottom of the screen to begin your second attempt. Results will be entered in your Summary Report.
7. Print or save the completed Diagnostic Writing. (Sample filename: xx-Writing 1-t1).
8. To return to the program, choose Exit Diagnostic Writings from the File menu.

Goal: build staying power
1. Key each paragraph as a 1' timing.
2. Key a 2' timing on both paragraphs.

Note: The dot above text represents two words.

 all letters

Writing 1: **18** *gwam*   *gwam* 2'

Why spend weeks with some problem when just a few quiet   6

minutes can help us to resolve it.   9

If we don't take time to think through a problem, it will   15

swiftly begin to expand in size.   18

Writing 2: **20** *gwam*

We push very hard in our quest for growth, and we all   5

think that only excellent growth will pay off.   10

Believe it or not, one can actually work much too hard,   16

be much too zealous, and just miss the mark.   20

Writing 3: **22** *gwam*

A business friend once explained to me why he was often   6

quite eager to be given some new project to work with.   11

My friend said that each new project means he has to   16

organize and use the best of his knowledge and his skill.   22

Writing 4: **24** *gwam*

Don't let new words get away from you. Learn how to spell   6

and pronounce new words and when and how finally to use them.   12

A new word is a friend, but frequently more. New words   18

must be used lavishly to extend the size of your own word power. 24

2' | 1 | 2 | 3 | 4 | 5 | 6 |

continued

COMMUNICATION

53d
Composing and Editing

1. Compose a paragraph with at least two or three complete sentences to complete the three statements listed below.

2. Double-space the answers and indent each paragraph.

3. Print the paragraphs; use proofreaders' marks to edit the paragraphs carefully to improve your writing. Make the corrections.

4. Save as **53d** and print.

1. **Currently, I live in** (name and describe the city, town, or area in which you live—indicate if it is a large city, small town, or rural area and provide other descriptive information about the locale).

2. **When friends from other locations come to visit me, the places I enjoy taking them are** (describe two or three places in your area that would be interesting to show to visitors).

3. **If I could pick one place in the United States to visit, it would be** (describe one place you would like to visit and explain why you would like to go there and what you would like to see and do while you are there).

APPLICATIONS

53e-d1
Letter from Rough Draft

1. Key the letter below making all of the corrections noted.

2. Use the current date and the address and closing lines shown below. Format the letter in block style. Add an enclosure notation. Center the page.

3. Proofread, preview, save as **53e-d1**, and print.

Ms. Karen Bradley
228 High Ridge Road
Irmo, SC 29063-4187

Dear Ms. Bradley

Thank you for the opportunity to plan an exciting vacation for you and your family. We are certain that this trip will be one all of you will remember. The Greek Isles are a fun destination and you have selected outstanding pre- and post-cruise tours in Athens and Istanbul.

All of the travel arrangements have been confirmed, and a detailed itinerary and cruise brochure are enclosed. Please carefully review the itinerary to make certain that we have followed all of your instructions correctly. If any changes need to be made, please call us soon.

Your travel documents will be sent to you 2 weeks prior to departure. Please let us know if we can provide additional information for you.

Sincerely

Jane R. Todd
President

Writing 5: **26 gwam**

gwam 2'

We usually get best results when we know where we are 5
going. Just setting a few goals will help us quietly see what 12
we are doing. 13

Goals can help measure whether we are moving at a good 19
rate or dozing along. You can expect a goal to help you find 25
good results. 26

Writing 6: **28 gwam**

To win whatever prizes we want from life, we must plan to 6
move carefully from this goal to the next to get the maximum 12
result from our work. 14

If we really want to become skilled in keying, we must 19
come to see that this desire will require of us just a little 26
patience and hard work. 28

Writing 7: **30 gwam**

Am I an individual person? I'm sure I am; still, in a 5
much, much bigger sense, other people have a major voice in 12
thoughts I think and actions I take. 15

Although we are each a unique person, we all work and 21
play in organized groups of people who do not expect us to 26
dismiss their rules of law and order. 30

2' | 1 | 2 | 3 | 4 | 5 | 6 |

LESSON 53 Edit Letters

SKILLBUILDING

53a
Warmup
Key each line twice SS.

alphabet 1 Jakob will save the money required for your next big cash prizes.
fig/sym 2 I saw Vera buy 13 7/8 yards of #240 cotton denim at $6.96 a yard.
3d/4th 3 Zone 12 is impassable; quickly rope it off. Did you wax Zone 90?
easy 4 Did an auditor handle the formal audit of the firms for a profit?

| 1 | 2 | 3 | 4 | 5 | 6 | 7 | 8 | 9 | 10 | 11 | 12 | 13 |

53b
Technique Builder
Key each line twice SS.

1/2 fingers

5 Did bedlam erupt when they arrived after my speech ended quickly?
6 Joyce bought me a new bright red jacket for my birthday tomorrow.
7 Did Rebecca make the needlepoint cushion for the club room couch?
8 Much to the concern of our teacher, I did my homework on the bus.

3/4 fingers

9 Zam saw six small poodle puppies playing in the meadow last week.
10 Paxton saw a lazy lizard on the old wooden oar at Pawley's Plaza.
11 Zam Velasquez sells squid in six stores near the pool at the zoo.
12 Paul quizzed a shop owner about a patchwork quilt we saw in Waco.

all fingers

13 Jarvis Zackery played quarterback with six teams before retiring.
14 Jan Weitzel made grave errors, but he quickly fixed the problems.
15 Quinn Zack wrote just six poems and a short story before leaving.
16 Maxey Czajka will quit swimming because he performed very poorly.

53c
Timed Writings
Key two 1' timings on each ¶.
The second and third ¶s each
contain 2 more words than the
previous ¶. Try to complete
each ¶ within 1'.

  all letters

	gwam	1'	3'

Have you thought about time? Time is a perplexing commodity. Frequently we don't have adequate time to do the things we must; yet we all have just the same amount of time.

We seldom refer to the quantity of time; to a great extent, we cannot control it. We can try to set time aside, to plan, and therefore, to control portions of this valuable asset.

We should make an extra effort to fill each minute and hour with as much quality activity as possible. Time, the most precious thing a person can spend, can never be realized once it is lost.

gwam	1'	3'
12	4	40
25	8	45
35	12	48
12	16	52
24	20	56
37	24	60
12	28	64
25	32	68
37	36	72
39	36	73

1' | 1 | 2 | 3 | 4 | 5 | 6 | 7 | 8 | 9 | 10 | 11 | 12 | 13 |
3' | 1 | 2 | 3 | 4 |

Figure and Symbol Keys

- Key the numeric keys by touch.
- Use symbol keys correctly.
- Build keying speed and accuracy.
- Apply correct number expression.
- Apply proofreaders' marks.
- Apply basic Internet skills.

LESSON 14 — 1 and 8

WARMUP

14a
Key each line twice SS.
Line 2: Space once after
a series of brief questions
within a sentence.

alphabet	1 Jessie Quick believed the campaign frenzy would be exciting.
space bar	2 Was it Mary? Helen? Pam? It was a woman; I saw one of them.
3d row	3 We were quietly prepped to write two letters to Portia York.
easy	4 Kale's neighbor works with a tutor when they visit downtown.

| 1 | 2 | 3 | 4 | 5 | 6 | 7 | 8 | 9 | 10 | 11 | 12 |

SKILLBUILDING

14b
High-Frequency Words
The words at the right
are from the 100 most
used words.
Key each line once;
work for fluency.

Top 100

5 a an it been copy for his this more no office please service

6 our service than the they up was work all any many thank had

7 business from I know made more not me new of some to program

8 such these two with your about and have like department year

9 by at on but do had in letter most now one please you should

10 their order like also appreciate that there gentlemen letter

11 be can each had information letter may make now only so that

12 them time use which am other been send to enclosed have will

FUNCTION REVIEW

52d

help keywords
paragraph spacing

Space After Paragraphs

Double-spaced documents do not need additional space between paragraphs. However, to make single-spaced documents more readable, add additional space after each paragraph. You can add additional space automatically by setting the space after paragraphs to 6 points, the equivalent of one line. Each time you press ENTER, an additional line is added.

To set spacing after paragraphs:

1. Click **Paragraph** on the Format menu.
2. Select the **Indents and Spacing** tab.
3. In the Spacing section of the dialog box, increase spacing *After* from 0 to 6 pt. Click **OK**.

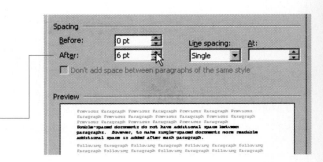

DRILL 8   PARAGRAPH SPACING

1. Open **Preview** from the data files.
2. Select all of the single-spaced paragraphs.

3. Increase the space after the paragraphs to 6 points.
4. Save the document as **52d-drill8** and print.

APPLICATIONS

52e-d1
Edit Report

1. Open **Punctuality** from the data files and save it as **52e-d1**.
2. Center the title. Change the font size to 14 point and apply bold and shadow effect.
3. In the sentence *Punctuality-Not Performance-Determines Outcome!*, change the hyphens to em dashes.
4. In the sentence that follows, replace the commas around *and by all accounts one who was unbeatable and assured to repeat the title* with em dashes.
5. Select *Punctuality—Not Performance—Determines Outcome!* in paragraph 1 and apply italic format.
6. Change spacing after paragraphs to 6 pt.
7. Move paragraph 3 between paragraphs 1 and 2.
8. Find *weak* and replace it with *lame*.
9. Select the last sentence and change the text color to red.
10. Add the following below the last paragraph: © 2003 by (*student's name*).
11. Center the page vertically.
12. Preview, print, and resave the document.

14c 1 and 8

Key each line once SS.

Note: The digit "1" and the letter "I" have separate values on a computer keyboard. Do not interchange these characters.

Abbreviations: Do not space after a period within an abbreviation, as in Ph.D., U.S., C.O.D., a.m.

1 Reach *up* with *left fourth* finger.

8 Reach *up* with *right second* finger.

1

13 1 1a a1 1 1; 1 and a 1; 1 add 1; 1 aunt; 1 ace; 1 arm; 1 aye
14 1 and 11 and 111; 11 eggs; 11 vats; Set 11A; May 11; Item 11
15 The 11 aces of the 111th Corps each rated a salute at 1 p.m.

8

16 8 8k k8 8 8; 8 kits; ask 8; 8 kites; kick 8; 8 keys; spark 8
17 OK 88; 8 bags; 8 or 88; the 88th; 88 kegs; ask 88; order 888
18 Eight of the 88 cars score 8 or better on our Form 8 rating.

all figures learned

19 She did live at 818 Park, not 181 Park; or was it 181 Clark?
20 Put 1 with 8 to form 18; put 8 with 1 to form 81. Use 1881.
21 On May 1 at 8 a.m., 18 men and 18 women left Gate 8 for Rio.

14d Reinforcement

Key each line once; DS between groups. Repeat. Key with accuracy.

figures

22 Our 188 trucks moved 1881 tons on August 18 and December 18.
23 Send Mary 181 No. 188 panes for her home at 8118 Oak Street.
24 The 188 men in 8 boats left Docks 1 and 18 at 1 p.m., May 1.

25 pop was lap pass slaw wool solo swap Apollo wasp load plaque
26 Was Polly acquainted with the equipped jazz player in Texas?
27 The computer is a useful tool; it helps you to perform well.

14e Speed Builder

Set the timer for 1'. Key each sentence as many times as possible.

Goal: to complete each sentence twice in one minute.

28 Did their form entitle them to the land?
29 Did the men in the field signal for us to go?
30 I may pay for the antique bowls when I go to town.
31 The auditor did the work right, so he risks no penalty.
32 The man by the big bush did signal us to turn down the lane.

| 1 | 2 | 3 | 4 | 5 | 6 | 7 | 8 | 9 | 10 | 11 | 12 |

To replace text:

1. Click **Edit** on the menu bar; then click **Replace**.

2. Enter the text you wish to locate in the Find what box.

3. Key the replacement text in the Replace with box.

4. Click **Find Next** to find the first occurrence of the text.

5. Click **Replace** to replace one occurrence, or click **Replace All** to replace all occurrences of the text.

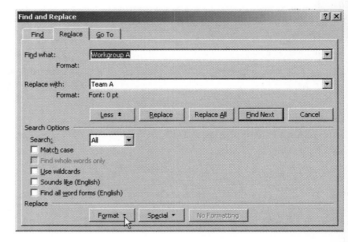

DRILL 6   FIND AND REPLACE

1. Open **Restructure** from the data files.
2. Find the word *restructuring* the first place it appears.
3. Find the second and third occurrences of *restructuring*.
4. Find *Workgroup A* and replace it with *Team A*.

5. Edit the document so that the letter is formatted correctly as a block-style letter.
6. Save the document as **52c-drill6**.

Thesaurus

TIP
An alternative way to use the Thesaurus is to position the insertion point in a word and right-click the mouse. Select **Synonyms** and then the desired word or **Thesaurus** for more information.

The Thesaurus is a tool that enables you to look up words and replace them with synonyms, antonyms, or related words.

To use the Thesaurus:

1. Position the insertion point in the word you wish to replace.

2. Click **Tools** on the menu, click **Language**, and then click **Thesaurus**.

3. If more than one meaning appears, select the appropriate meaning.

4. Select the desired synonym or antonym, and click **Replace**.

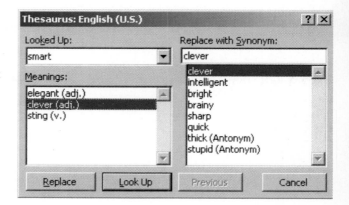

DRILL 7   THESAURUS

1. Key the following words on separate lines:
   generous   data   smart   profit
2. Replace *generous* and *data* with synonyms.
3. Replace *smart* (meaning clever) with a synonym.

4. Key **smart** again (meaning elegant), and replace it with an antonym.
5. Replace *profit* with an antonym.
6. Save the document as **52c-drill7**.

LESSON 15

5 and 0

WARMUP

15a
Key each line twice SS. For a series of capital letters, press CAPS LOCK with the left little finger. Press again to release.

alphabet	1 John Quigley packed the zinnias in twelve large, firm boxes.
1/8	2 Idle Motor 18 at 8 mph and Motor 81 at 8 mph; avoid Motor 1.
caps	3 Lily read BLITHE SPIRIT by Noel Coward. I read VANITY FAIR.
lock	4 Did they fix the problem of the torn panel and worn element?

| 1 | 2 | 3 | 4 | 5 | 6 | 7 | 8 | 9 | 10 | 11 | 12 |

adjacent reaches

5 as oil red ask wet opt mop try tree open shred operas treaty
6 were pore dirt stew ruin faster onion alumni dreary mnemonic
7 The opened red hydrants were powerful, fast, and very dirty.

outside reaches

8 pop zap cap zag wasp equip lazy zippers queue opinion quartz
9 zest waste paper exist parquet azalea acquaint apollo apathy
10 The lazy wasp passed the potted azalea on the parquet floor.

15b Technique Reinforcement
Reach up or down without moving your hands. Key each line once; repeat drill.

NEW KEYS

15c 5 and 0
Key each line once SS.

5 Reach *up* with *left first* finger.

0 Reach *up* with *right fourth* finger.

5

11 5 5f f5 5 5; 5 fans; 5 feet; 5 figs; 5 fobs; 5 furs; 5 flaws
12 5 o'clock; 5 a.m.; 5 p.m.; is 55 or less; buy 55; 5 and 5 is
13 Call Line 555 if 5 fans or 5 bins arrive at Pier 5 by 5 p.m.

0

14 0 0; :0 0 0; skip 0; plan 0; left 0; is below 0; I scored 0;
15 0 degrees; key 0 and 0; write 00 here; the total is 0 or 00;
16 She laughed at their 0 to 0 score; but ours was 0 to 0 also.

all figures learned

17 I keyed 550 pages for Invoice 05, or 50 more than we needed.
18 Pages 15 and 18 of the program listed 150, not 180, members.
19 On May 10, Rick drove 500 miles to New Mexico in car No. 08.

Drag-and-Drop Editing

Another way to edit text is to use the mouse. With **drag and drop**, you can move or copy text using the mouse. To move copy, you must first select the text, then hold down the left mouse button, and drag the text to the desired location. The mouse pointer displays a rectangle indicating that copy is being moved. Release the mouse button to "drop" the text into the desired location.

Follow a similar procedure to copy (or duplicate) text. Hold down the left mouse button and the CTRL key, and drag the text to the desired location. A plus sign indicates the text is being copied.

Copy and Paste Between Documents

Multiple documents can be opened at the same time. Each document is displayed in its own window. To move from one document to another, click **Window** on the menu; then click the document name. You may also just click the document name on the Windows taskbar. Text can then be copied and pasted between documents.

DRILL 5 **DRAG AND DROP**

1. Open **Effective Pres** from the data files.
2. Use drag-and-drop editing to make the same changes you made in **52c-drill4**.

3. Save the document as **52c-drill5**; print and close it.

Find and Replace

Find is used to locate text, formatting, footnotes, graphics, or other items within a document. **Replace** is used to find text, formatting, or other items within a document and replace them with different text, formatting, or items.

Clicking the More button on the Find or Replace tab displays a list of search options such as *Match case* or *Find whole words only*, as shown in the illustration below. The Format and Special buttons in the extended dialog box provide options for searching for formatting features or for special elements.

help keywords
find, replace

To find text:

1. Click **Edit** on the menu bar; then click **Find**.
2. Enter the text you wish to locate in the Find what box.
3. Click **Find Next** to find the next occurrence of the text.

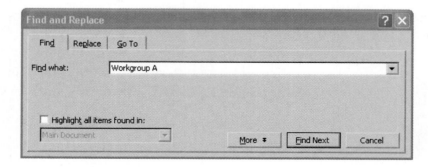

SKILLBUILDING

15d Textbook Keying
Key each line once; DS between 3-line groups.

improve figures

20 Read pages 5 and 8; duplicate page 18; omit pages 50 and 51.
21 We have Model 80 with 10 meters or Model 180 with 15 meters.
22 After May 18, French 050 meets in room 15 at 10 a.m. daily.

improve long reaches

23 Barb Abver saw a vibrant version of her brave venture on TV.
24 Call a woman or a man who will manage Minerva Manor in Nome.
25 We were quick to squirt a quantity of water at Quin and West.

15e Tab Review

1. Read the instructions to clear and set tabs.
2. Go to the Open Screen. Set a left tab at 4".
3. Practice the lines; strike TAB without watching your keyboard.

STANDARD PLAN for Setting and Clearing Tabs in the Open Screen

Preset or default tabs are displayed on the Ruler. If necessary, display the Ruler in the Open Screen. (Choose the **Show Ruler** option on the Format menu.) Sometimes you will want to remove or clear existing tabs before setting new ones.

To clear and set tabs:

1. On the menu bar, click **Format**, then **Clear All Tabs**.
2. To set tabs, select the type of tab you want to set (left, center, decimal, or right) shown at the lower-left side of the ruler.
3. Click the Ruler at the location where you want to set a tab.

Set tab 4"

         → Tab Keyboarding
has become   → Tab the primary
means of   → Tab written communication
in business and   → Tab in our personal lives.
Keyboarding is   → Tab used by persons
in every profession   → Tab and most job levels.

15f Speed Check

1. In the Open Screen, take two 1' writings on paragraph 2. Note your *gwam*. Do not save the timings.
2. Take two 1' writings on paragraph 1. Try to equal paragraph 2 rate.
3. Take one 2' writing on both paragraphs.

 all letters

	gwam	2'	3'

I thought about Harry and how he had worked for me for   6 | 4
10 years; how daily at 8 he parked his worn car in the lot;   12 | 8
then, he left at 5. Every day was almost identical for him.   18 | 12

In a quiet way, he did his job well, asking for little   23 | 15
attention. So I never recognized his thirst for travel. I   29 | 19
didn't expect to find all of those maps near his workplace.   35 | 23

help keywords
clipboard

Office Clipboard

The **Clipboard** can store up to 24 items that have been cut or copied. The Clipboard displays in the side pane. If it is not displayed, click **Edit** on the menu bar and then **Office Clipboard** to display it. Note that each item on the Clipboard is displayed for easy reference. All items on the Clipboard can be pasted at once by clicking **Paste All**. A single item can be pasted by clicking on the item and selecting **Paste** from the drop-down menu.

All items on the Clipboard can be removed by clicking the **Clear All** button. A single item can be removed by clicking the item and selecting **Delete** from the drop-down menu.

When an item is pasted into a document, the Paste button smart tag provides options for formatting the text that has been pasted.

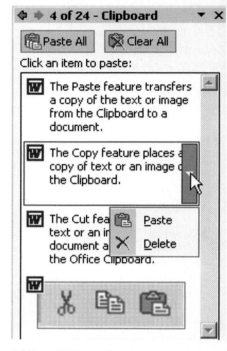

Office Clipboard

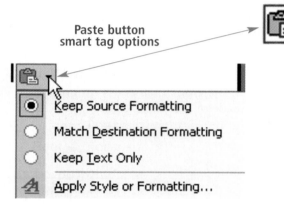

Paste button
smart tag options

To format the text using the same format as the new document, click **Match Destination Formatting**. To format the text using the same format as the document from which the text was copied, click **Keep Source Formatting**.

DRILL 4 **CLIPBOARD**

1. Open **Effective Pres** from the data files.
2. Display the Office Clipboard (**Edit**, **Office Clipboard**) and clear all items from the Clipboard.
3. Select the heading *Opening* and the paragraph that follows, and cut them.
4. Select the heading *Presentation Body* and the paragraph that follows, and cut them.
5. Select the heading *Closing* and the paragraph that follows, and cut them.
6. Place the insertion point a double space below the paragraph with the heading *Planning and Preparing Presentations* and paste all items on the Clipboard at once; adjust line spacing if necessary.
7. Save as **52c-drill4** and print the document.

---

2 and 7

16a
Key each line twice SS.

alphabet 1 Perry might know I feel jinxed because I have missed a quiz.
figures 2 Channels 5 and 8, on from 10 to 11, said Luisa's IQ was 150.
caps lock 3 Ella Hill will see Chekhov's THE CHERRY ORCHARD on Czech TV.
easy 4 The big dog by the bush kept the ducks and hen in the field.
| 1 | 2 | 3 | 4 | 5 | 6 | 7 | 8 | 9 | 10 | 11 | 12 |

NEW KEYS

16b **2** and **7**
Key each line once SS.

2 Reach *up* with *left third* finger.

7 Reach *down* with *right first* finger.

2

5 2 2s s2 2 2; has 2 sons; is 2 sizes; was 2 sites; has 2 skis
6 add 2 and 2; 2 sets of 2; catch 22; as 2 of the 22; 222 Main
7 Exactly at 2 on August 22, the 22d Company left from Pier 2.

7

8 7 7j j7 7 7; 7 jets; 7 jeans; 7 jays; 7 jobs; 7 jars; 7 jaws
9 ask for 7; buy 7; 77 years; June 7; take any 7; deny 77 boys
10 From May 7 on, all 77 men will live at 777 East 77th Street.

all figures learned

11 I read 2 of the 72 books, Ellis read 7, and Han read all 72.
12 Tract 27 cites the date as 1850; Tract 170 says it was 1852.
13 You can take Flight 850 on January 12; I'll take Flight 705.

16c Number Reinforcement
Key each line twice SS (slowly, then faster); DS between 2-line groups.

8/1 14 line 8; Book 1; No. 88; Seat 11; June 18; Cart 81; date 1881
2/7 15 take 2; July 7; buy 22; sell 77; mark 27; adds 72; Memo 2772
5/0 16 feed 5; bats 0; age 50; Ext. 55; File 50; 55 bags; band 5005
all 17 I work 18 visual signs with 20 turns of the 57 lenses to 70.
all 18 Did 17 boys fix the gears for 50 bicycles in 28 racks or 10?

1. Key the following lines as a numbered list.
2. Insert the symbols and special characters shown.
3. Save it as **52c-drill2** in the folder **Module 7 Keys**.

Special Characters
1. Parker House—Best Dining (em dash)
2. Pages 13–25 (en dash)
3. July 20 (nonbreaking space)
4. 92° F (degree and nonbreaking space)
5. Revise ¶3.

Symbols
6. ☺ Have a nice day.
7. ⇨ Room 253.
8. ✍ Sign here.
9. ✓ Yes, send today.
10. ❑ Yes   ❑ No

Cut, Copy, and Paste

 The **Cut** feature removes text or an image from a document and places it on the Office Clipboard. The **Copy** feature places a copy of text or an image from a document on the Clipboard. The **Paste** feature transfers a copy of the text or image from the Clipboard to a document.

help keywords
move or copy text; cut; copy; paste

To move text to a new location:
1. Select the text to be copied. Click **Cut** on the Standard toolbar.
2. Move the insertion point to the new location. Click **Paste** on the Standard toolbar.

To copy text to a new location:
1. Select the text to be copied. Click **Copy** on the Standard toolbar.
2. Move the insertion point to the new location. Click **Paste** on the Standard toolbar.

1. Open **Cut and Paste** from the data files.
2. Select **Cut and** in the first heading and cut it so the heading is **Paste**.
3. Select the heading **Paste** and the paragraph that follows it.
4. Move the selected copy below the last paragraph.
5. Key a line across the page.
6. Copy both paragraphs, and paste them below the line.
7. Save the document as **52c-drill3**.

SKILLBUILDING

16d Reach Review

Key each line once; fingers curved and relaxed; wrists low.

3d/4th
19 pop was lap pass slaw wool solo swap apollo wasp load plaque
20 Al's quote was, "I was dazzled by the jazz, pizza, and pool."

1st/2d
21 bad fun nut kick dried night brick civic thick hutch believe
22 Kim may visit her friends in Germany if I give her a ticket.

3d/1st
23 cry tube wine quit very curb exit crime ebony mention excite
24 To be invited, petition the six executive committee members.

16e Textbook Keying

Key each line once; DS between 3-line groups. Do not pause at the end of lines.

> **TECHNIQUE TIP**
> Think and key the words and phrases as units rather than letter by letter.

words: *think, say,* and *key* words
25 is do am lay cut pen dub may fob ale rap cot hay pay hem box
26 box wit man sir fish also hair giant rigor civic virus ivory
27 laugh sight flame audit formal social turkey bicycle problem

phrases: *think, say,* and *key* phrases
28 is it|is it|if it is|if it is|or by|or by|or me|or me|for us
29 and all|for pay|pay dues and|the pen|the pen box|the pen box
30 such forms|held both|work form|then wish|sign name|with them

easy sentences
31 The man is to do the work right; he then pays the neighbors.
32 Sign the forms to pay the eight men for the turkey and hams.
33 The antique ivory bicycle is a social problem for the chair.
| 1 | 2 | 3 | 4 | 5 | 6 | 7 | 8 | 9 | 10 | 11 | 12 |

16f Speed Check

1. Take two 1' writings on paragraph 1. Do not save.
2. Take two 1' writings on paragraph 2.
3. Take one 2' writing on both paragraphs.

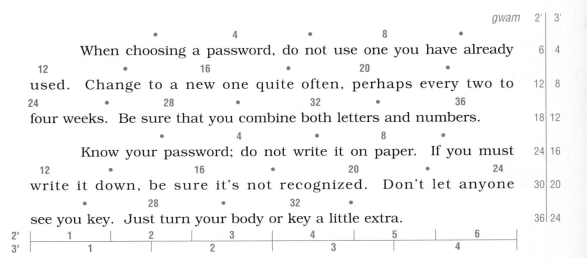

	gwam	2'	3'
When choosing a password, do not use one you have already		6	4
used. Change to a new one quite often, perhaps every two to		12	8
four weeks. Be sure that you combine both letters and numbers.		18	12
Know your password; do not write it on paper. If you must		24	16
write it down, be sure it's not recognized. Don't let anyone		30	20
see you key. Just turn your body or key a little extra.		36	24

2' | 1 | 2 | 3 | 4 | 5 | 6 |
3' | 1 | 2 | 3 | 4 |

NEW FUNCTIONS

52c

Character Effects

Character effects include a number of special attributes that enhance the appearance of text. Commonly used character effects include superscript, subscript, small caps, strikethrough, shadow, and outline. Character effects are accessed from the Font dialog box (Format menu, Font). Color and underline style are also available on the Font tab. Select existing text and click the appropriate effect to apply it, or turn the effect on before keying and off after keying.

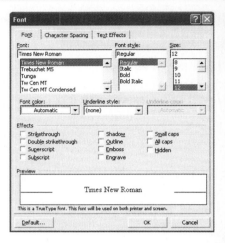

DRILL 1 CHARACTER EFFECTS

1. Key the text at the right applying the character effects shown.
2. Apply blue color to SMALL CAPS in line 1.
3. Apply double underline to the formula in line 3.
4. Create the folder **Module 7 Keys** and save the document as **52c-drill1**. Save all documents for Module 7 in this folder.

Apply SMALL CAPS to this text.
The symbol for water, H_2O, contains a subscript.
Formulas often use superscripts, such as $\underline{\underline{X^2 + Y^3}}$.
~~Strikethrough~~ is a useful effect in editing text.
Outline and shadow change the appearance of text.

help keywords

Insert a symbol;
Insert a special character

Symbols and Special Characters

Symbols and special characters not available on the keyboard can be inserted using the symbol function. Examples of symbols and special characters include:

Em dash —   En dash –   Copyright ©   Registered ®   Trademark™

To insert symbols or special characters:

1. Position the insertion point where the symbol or special character is to be inserted.
2. Click **Insert** on the menu, and then click **Symbol**.
3. Click the **Symbols** tab to insert symbols or the **Special Characters** tab to insert special characters.
4. For symbols, select a font such as Symbol, Wingdings, Wingdings2, or Wingdings3, and then select the desired symbol. For special characters, select the character desired.
5. Click **Insert** and then click **Close**.

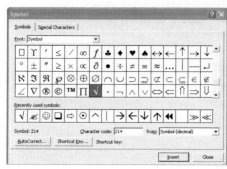

LESSON 17

4 and 9

17a
Key each line twice.

alphabet	1	Bob realized very quickly that jumping was excellent for us.
figures	2	Has each of the 18 clerks now corrected Item 501 on page 27?
shift keys	3	L. K. Coe, M.D., hopes Dr. Lopez can leave for Maine in May.
easy	4	The men paid their own firms for the eight big enamel signs.

NEW KEYS

17b 4 and 9
Key each line once SS.

4 Reach *up* with *left first* finger.

4

5 4 4f f4 4 4 4; if 4 furs; off 4 floors; gaff 4 fish; 4 flags

6 44th floor; half of 44; 4 walked 44 flights; 4 girls; 4 boys

7 I order exactly 44 bagels, 4 cakes, and 4 pies before 4 a.m.

9 Reach *up* with *right third* finger.

9

8 9 9l l9 9 9 9; fill 9 lugs; call 9 lads; Bill 9 lost; dial 9

9 also 9 oaks; roll 9 loaves; 9.9 degrees; sell 9 oaks; Hall 9

10 Just 9 couples, 9 men and 9 women, left at 9 on our Tour 99.

all figures learned

11 Memo 94 says 9 pads, 4 pens, and 4 ribbons were sent July 9.

12 Study Item 17 and Item 28 on page 40 and Item 59 on page 49.

13 Within 17 months he drove 85 miles, walked 29, and flew 490.

SKILLBUILDING

17c Textbook Keying
Key each line once.

14 My staff of *18* worked *11* hours a day from May *27* to June *12*.

15 There were *5* items tested by Inspector *7* at *4* p.m. on May *8*.

16 Please send her File *10* today at *8*; her access number is *97*.

17 Car *47* had its trial run. The qualifying speed was *198* mph.

18 The estimated score? *485*. Actual? *190*. Difference? *295*.

Edit Business Documents

- Build keying skill.
- Build editing skills.
- Edit letters.
- Edit memos and e-mail.
- Edit tables and reports.

LESSON 52   Skillbuilding, Editing, and Reference Tools

SKILLBUILDING

52a
Warmup
Key each line twice SS.

alphabet	1	Jim Daley gave us in that box the prize he won for his quick car.
figures	2	At 7 a.m., I open Rooms 18, 29, and 30; I lock Rooms 4, 5, and 6.
adjacent reaches	3	As Louis said, few questioned the points asserted by the porters.
easy	4	Did he vow to fight for the right to work as the Orlando auditor?

| 1 | 2 | 3 | 4 | 5 | 6 | 7 | 8 | 9 | 10 | 11 | 12 | 13 |

52b
Technique Builder
Key each line twice SS.

caps	5	James Carswell plans to visit Austin and New Orleans in December.
	6	Will Peter and Betsy go with Mark when he goes to Alaska in June?
	7	John Kenny wrote the book Innovation and Timing—Keys to Success.
double letters	8	Jeanne arranges meeting room space in Massey Hall for committees.
	9	Russell will attend to the bookkeeping issues tomorrow afternoon.
	10	Todd offered a free book with all assessment tools Lynette sells.
balanced hand	11	Jane, a neighbor and a proficient auditor, may amend their audit.
	12	Blanche and a neighbor may make an ornament for an antique chair.
	13	Claudia may visit the big island when they go to Orlando with us.

17d Technique Reinforcement

Key smoothly; strike the keys at a brisk, steady pace.

first finger

19 buy them gray vent guy brunt buy brunch much give huge vying
20 Hagen, after her July triumph at tennis, may try volleyball.
21 Verna urges us to buy yet another of her beautiful rag rugs.

second finger

22 keen idea; kick it back; ice breaker; decide the issue; cite
23 Did Dick ask Cecelia, his sister, if she decided to like me?
24 Suddenly, Micki's bike skidded on the Cedar Street ice rink.

third/fourth finger

25 low slow lax solo wax zip zap quips quiz zipper prior icicle
26 Paula has always allowed us to relax at La Paz and at Quito.
27 Please ask Zale to explain who explores most aquatic slopes.

17e Speed Builder

1. Key each paragraph in the Open Screen for a 1' writing.
2. Set the Timer for 2'. Take two 2' writings on all paragraphs. Reach for a speed within two words of 1' *gwam*.
3. Take a 3' writing on all paragraphs. Reach for a speed within four words of 1' *gwam*. Print.

all letters

	gwam	2'	3'
We consider nature to be limited to those things, such		6	4
as air or trees, that we humans do not or cannot make.		11	7
For most of us, nature just exists, just is. We don't		17	11
question it or, perhaps, realize how vital it is to us.		22	15
Do I need nature, and does nature need me? I'm really		28	19
part of nature; thus, what happens to it happens to me.		33	22

2' | 1 | 2 | 3 | 4 | 5 | 6 |
3' | 1 | | 2 | | 3 | | 4 |

17f Speed Builder

TECHNIQUE TIP

Keep hands quiet and fingers well curved over the keys. Do not allow your fingers to bounce.

1. In the Open screen, key the information below at the left margin.

Your name   ENTER
Current date   ENTER
Skillbuilders 1, Drill 2   ENTER ENTER

2. Key Drill 2, page 32 from your textbook. Concentrate as you practice on your own, working for good control. Save as **xx-17f**.

DRILL 6

OPPOSITE HAND REACHES

Key at a controlled rate; concentrate on the reaches.

y/t

1 yj my say may yes rye yarn eye lye yap any relay young berry
2 tf at it let the vat tap item town toast right little attire
3 Yesterday a young youth typed a cat story on the typewriter.

b/n

4 bf but job fibs orb bow able bear habit boast rabbit brother
5 nj not and one now fun next pony month notice runner quicken
6 A number of neighbors banked on bunking in the brown cabins.

g/h

7 gag go gee god rig gun log gong cog gig agog gage going gang
8 huh oh hen the hex ash her hash ah hush shah hutch hand ache
9 Hush; Greg hears rough sounds. Has Hugh laughed or coughed?

r/u

10 row or rid air rap par rye rear ark jar rip nor are right or
11 cut us auk out tutu sun husk but fun cub gun nut mud tug hug
12 Ryan is sure you should pour your food from an urn or cruet.

| 1 | 2 | 3 | 4 | 5 | 6 | 7 | 8 | 9 | 10 | 11 | 12 |

 all letters

Writing 27

gwam 3' | 5'

Most people think traveling is fun because they associate | 4 | 2
travel with exciting vacations. People who have to travel as | 8 | 5
part of their jobs have a very different view of travel. They | 12 | 7
are more prone to view business travel as a hassle than a plea- | 16 | 10
sure. Business travelers often have to work under less than | 21 | 12
ideal circumstances. While they are away from the office, regu- | 25 | 15
lar work tends to pile up; and they often return to find stacks | 29 | 17
of work waiting for them. Many business travelers learn to uti- | 33 | 20
lize wisely the waiting time that is a part of most travel. | 37 | 22

A successful business trip requires careful planning. The | 41 | 25
typical business traveler tends to think of a trip as a success | 45 | 27
if two conditions are met. The business goals must be achieved, | 50 | 30
and the trip must be totally free of headaches. The person mak- | 54 | 32
ing the trip has to worry about achieving the business goals, but | 58 | 35
a good travel agent can relieve the traveler of many of the wor- | 63 | 38
ries of making travel arrangements. A good checklist can help to | 67 | 40
ensure that all the personal items as well as business items | 71 | 43
needed for the trip will be handy when they are needed. | 75 | 45

gwam 3' | 1 | 2 | 3 | 4 |
     5' | 1 | 2 | 3 |

LESSON 18

3 and 6

WARMUP

18a
Key each line twice SS.

alphabet 1 Jim Kable won a second prize for his very quixotic drawings.

figures 2 If 57 of the 105 boys go on July 29, 48 of them will remain.

easy 3 With the usual bid, I paid for a quantity of big world maps.

| 1 | 2 | 3 | 4 | 5 | 6 | 7 | 8 | 9 | 10 | 11 | 12 |

NEW KEYS

18b 3 and 6
Key each line once SS.

3 Reach *up* with *left second* finger.

6 Reach *up* with *right first* finger.

3

4 3 3d d3 3 3; had 3 days; did 3 dives; led 3 dogs; add 3 dips

5 we 3 ride 3 cars; take 33 dials; read 3 copies; save 33 days

6 On July 3, 33 lights lit 33 stands holding 33 prize winners.

6

7 6 6j 6j 6 6; 6 jays; 6 jams; 6 jigs; 6 jibs; 6 jots; 6 jokes

8 only 6 high; on 66 units; reach 66 numbers; 6 yams or 6 jams

9 On May 6, Car 66 delivered 66 tons of No. 6 shale to Pier 6.

all figures learned

10 At 6 p.m., Channel 3 reported the August 6 score was 6 to 3.

11 Jean, do Items 28 and 6; Mika, 59 and 10; Kyle, 3, 4, and 7.

12 Cars 56 and 34 used Aisle 9; Cars 2 and 87 can use Aisle 10.

SKILLBUILDING

18c Keyboard Reinforcement
Key each line once; DS between groups of three.

TECHNIQUE TIP
Make the long reaches without returning to the home row between reaches.

long reaches

13 ce cede cedar wreck nu nu nut punt nuisance my my amy mystic

14 ny ny any many company mu mu mull lumber mulch br br furbish

15 The absence of receiving my umbrella disturbed the musician.

number review

16 set 0; push 4; Car 00; score 44; jot 04; age 40; Billet 4004

17 April 5; lock 5; set 66; fill 55; hit 65; pick 56; adds 5665

18 Her grades are 93, 87, and 100; his included 82, 96, and 54.

DRILL 5

IMPROVE CONCENTRATION

Set a right tab at 5.5" for the addresses. Key the Internet addresses in column 2 exactly as they are listed. Accuracy is critical.

 all letters

The paperless guide to New York City	http://www.mediabridge.com/nyc
A trip to outer space	http://spacelink.msfc.nasa.gov
Search engine	http://webcrawler.com
Government Printing Office access	http://www.access.gpo.gov/index.html
MarketPlace—corporate information	http://www.mktplace.com
Touchstone's PC-cillin virus scan	http://www.antivirus.com

Writing 26

gwam 3'

Many small businesses fail. Surprisingly, though, many 4
people are still willing to take a chance on starting one of 8
their own. A person who is willing to take the risks necessary 12
to manage a business in order to receive the potential rewards is 17
called an entrepeneur. In a sense, such individuals are pio- 21
neers who enjoy each step on the way to achieving objectives that 25
they have determined to be important. This type of person has 29
had a profound impact on shaping our economy and our quality of 34
life. 34

What does is take to start a business venture, and what 38
kinds of people make it work? Obviously, the desire to make 42
money and to be one's own boss are two basic incentives, but 40
these alone are not enough to guarantee success. Two qualifica- 50
tions common to most successful entrepeneurs, whatever field 54
they are in, are an attentiveness to detail and a knack for 58
solving day-to-day problems without losing sight of long-range 62
goals. 63

While there is a high risk in organizing any new business, 67
the entrepeneur who is successful is seldom someone who could be 71
considered a gambler. Most gamblers expect to have the odds 75
against them. On the other hand, a clever businessperson sees to 80
it that the odds are as good as possible by getting all of the 84
facts and planning carefully before going ahead. Luck helps, to 88
be sure, but a new business enterprise depends far more on good 92
ideas and detailed plans. 94

3' | 1 | 2 | 3 | 4 |
5' | 1 | 2 | 3 |

18d Textbook Keying

Key each line once; DS between 2-line groups; repeat.

word response: *think* and *key* words

19 he el id is go us it an me of he of to if ah or bye do so am

20 Did she enamel emblems on a big panel for the downtown sign?

stroke response: *think* and *key* each stroke

21 kin are hip read lymph was pop saw ink art oil gas up as mop

22 Barbara started the union wage earners tax in Texas in July.

combination response: vary speed but maintain rhythm

23 upon than eve lion when burley with they only them loin were

24 It was the opinion of my neighbor that we may work as usual.

18e Diagnostic Writing

Return to the Numeric Lesson menu. Click the **Diagnostic Writings** button. Key the paragraph as a 3' Diagnostic Writing.

Goals: 1', 17–23 *gwam*
2', 15–21 *gwam*
3', 14–20 *gwam*

 all letters

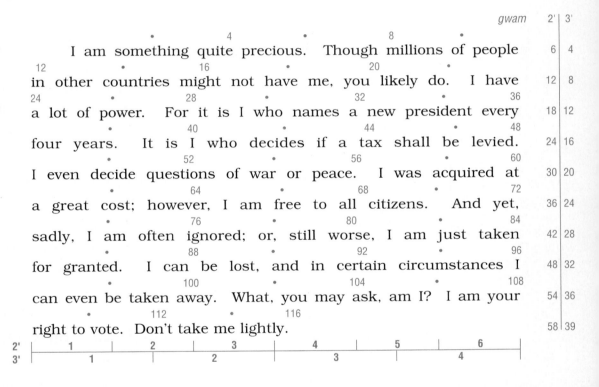

	gwam	2'	3'
I am something quite precious. Though millions of people		6	4
in other countries might not have me, you likely do. I have		12	8
a lot of power. For it is I who names a new president every		18	12
four years. It is I who decides if a tax shall be levied.		24	16
I even decide questions of war or peace. I was acquired at		30	20
a great cost; however, I am free to all citizens. And yet,		36	24
sadly, I am often ignored; or, still worse, I am just taken		42	28
for granted. I can be lost, and in certain circumstances I		48	32
can even be taken away. What, you may ask, am I? I am your		54	36
right to vote. Don't take me lightly.		58	39

2' | 1 | 2 | 3 | 4 | 5 | 6 |
3' | 1 | 2 | 3 | 4 |

COMMUNICATION

18f Composition

1. Go to the Open Screen.

2. Introduce yourself to your instructor by composing two paragraphs, each containing about three sentences. Use proper grammatical structure. Do not worry about keying errors at this time.

3. Save the document as **xx-profile**. It is not necessary to print the document. You will open and print it in a later lesson.

DRILL 4

IMPROVE RESPONSE PATTERNS

Key lines 5–16 once; DS between 4-line groups; work at a controlled rate; repeat drill.

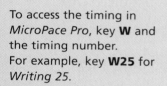

all letters

To access the timing in *MicroPace Pro*, key **W** and the timing number. For example, key **W25** for *Writing 25*.

direct reaches: reaches with the same finger; keep hands quiet

1 brand much cent numb cease bright music brief jump special carved
2 create mumps zany mystic curve mummy any checks brag brunch after
3 Bradley broke his left thumb after lunch on a great hunting trip.
4 After having mumps, Cecil once saw June excel in a funny musical.

adjacent reaches: keep fingers curved and upright

5 were junior sad yuletide trees polo very join safe property tweed
6 tree trio trickle tripod quit excess was free easy million option
7 Gwen and Sumio are going to be quite popular at the Western Club.
8 Fred said we were going to join the guys for polo this afternoon.

double letters: strike keys rapidly

9 dill seem pool attic miss carry dragged kidded layoff lapped buzz
10 commend accuse inner rubber cheer commission football jazz popper
11 Tammy called to see if she can borrow my accounting book at noon.
12 Lynnette will meet with the bookseller soon to discuss the issue.

Writing 25

gwam

	1'	5'

Working at home is not exactly a new phenomenon, but the concept is growing quite rapidly. For many years, people have worked at home. In most instances, they were self-employed and operated a business from their homes. Today, the people who work at home fit into a variety of categories. Some own their own businesses; others bring extra work home after the workday ends. A key change is the large group of people who are employed by huge organizations but who work out of home offices. These employees are in jobs that include sales, creative, technical, and a host of other categories.

The real change that has occurred is not so much the numbers of people who are working at home and the variety of jobs, but the complex tools that are now available for doing the job. Technology has truly made the difference. In many cases, clients and customers are not even aware that they are dealing with individuals working at home. Computers, printers, fax machines, telephone systems, and other office equipment enable the worker in the home to function in the same way as workers in a typical business office.

1'												
1	2	3	4	5	6	7	8	9	10	11	12	13
5'		1			2				3			

gwam 1' / 5' column values:
12 | 2 | 47
26 | 5 | 50
39 | 8 | 52
52 | 10 | 55
65 | 13 | 58
79 | 16 | 60
92 | 18 | 63
106 | 21 | 66
120 | 24 | 69
12 | 26 | 71
26 | 29 | 74
39 | 32 | 76
53 | 35 | 79
66 | 37 | 82
79 | 40 | 84
93 | 42 | 87
104 | 45 | 89

SKILL BUILDERS 4

MODULE 6 192

LESSON 19

$ and - (hyphen), Number Expression

WARMUP

19a
Key each line twice SS.

alphabet 1 Why did the judge quiz poor Victor about his blank tax form?

figures 2 J. Boyd, Ph.D., changed Items 10, 57, 36, and 48 on page 92.

3d row 3 To try the tea, we hope to tour the port prior to the party.

easy 4 Did he signal the authentic robot to do a turn to the right?

| 1 | 2 | 3 | 4 | 5 | 6 | 7 | 8 | 9 | 10 | 11 | 12 |

NEW KEYS

19b $ and -
Key each line once SS;
DS between 2-line groups.

- = hyphen
-- = dash
Do not space before or after a hyphen or a dash.

$ Shift; then reach *up* with *left first* finger.

- (hyphen) Reach *up* with *right fourth* finger.

$

5 $ $f f$ $ $; if $4; half $4; off $4; of $4; $4 fur; $4 flats

6 for $8; cost $9; log $3; grab $10; give Rolf $2; give Viv $4

7 Since she paid $45 for the item priced at $54, she saved $9.

- (hyphen)

8 - -; ;- - - -; up-to-date; co-op; father-in-law; four-square

9 pop-up foul; big-time job; snap-on bit; one- or two-hour ski

10 You need 6 signatures--half of the members--on the petition.

all symbols learned

11 I paid $10 for the low-cost disk; high-priced ones cost $40.

12 Le-An spent $20 for travel, $95 for books, and $38 for food.

13 Mr. Loft-Smit sold his boat for $467; he bought it for $176.

SKILLBUILDING

19c Keyboard Reinforcement
Key each line once; repeat the drill.

e/d 14 Edie discreetly decided to deduct expenses in making a deed.

w/e 15 Working women wear warm wool sweaters when weather dictates.

r/e 16 We heard very rude remarks regarding her recent termination.

s/d 17 This seal's sudden misdeeds destroyed several goods on land.

v/b 18 Beverley voted by giving a bold beverage to every brave boy.

NUMBER REACHES

Key each line at a comfortable rate; practice difficult lines.

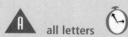 all letters ⏱

To access the timing in *MicroPace Pro*, key **W** and the timing number. For example, key **W24** for *Writing 24*.

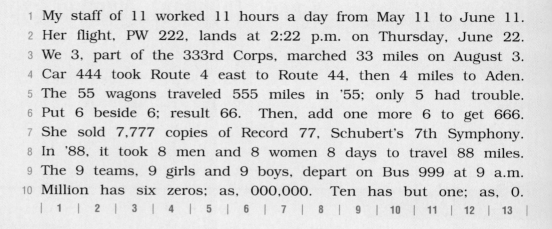

1 My staff of 11 worked 11 hours a day from May 11 to June 11.
2 Her flight, PW 222, lands at 2:22 p.m. on Thursday, June 22.
3 We 3, part of the 333rd Corps, marched 33 miles on August 3.
4 Car 444 took Route 4 east to Route 44, then 4 miles to Aden.
5 The 55 wagons traveled 555 miles in '55; only 5 had trouble.
6 Put 6 beside 6; result 66. Then, add one more 6 to get 666.
7 She sold 7,777 copies of Record 77, Schubert's 7th Symphony.
8 In '88, it took 8 men and 8 women 8 days to travel 88 miles.
9 The 9 teams, 9 girls and 9 boys, depart on Bus 999 at 9 a.m.
10 Million has six zeros; as, 000,000. Ten has but one; as, 0.

| 1 | 2 | 3 | 4 | 5 | 6 | 7 | 8 | 9 | 10 | 11 | 12 | 13 |

Writing 24

gwam 3' | 5'

Planning, organizing, and controlling are three of the | 4 | 2 | 65
functions that are familiar to all sorts of firms. Because these | 8 | 5 | 68
functions are basic to the managerial practices of a business, | 12 | 7 | 71
they form the very core of its daily operations. Good managerial | 17 | 10 | 73
procedures, of course, do not just occur by accident. They must | 21 | 13 | 76
be set into motion by people. Thus, a person who plans to enter | 25 | 15 | 78
the job market, especially in an office position, should study | 30 | 18 | 81
all of the elements of good management in order to apply those | 34 | 20 | 83
principles to her or his work. | 36 | 22 | 85

Leadership is another very important skill for a person | 40 | 24 | 87
to develop. Leaders are needed at all levels in a business to | 44 | 26 | 89
plan, organize, and control the operations of a firm. A person | 48 | 29 | 92
who is in a key position of leadership usually is expected to ini- | 52 | 31 | 95
tiate ideas as well as to carry out the goals of a business. | 57 | 34 | 97
Office workers who have developed the qualities of leadership are | 61 | 37 | 100
more apt to be promoted than those without such skills. While | 65 | 39 | 102
leadership may come naturally for some people, it can be learned | 70 | 42 | 105
as well as be improved with practice. | 72 | 43 | 106

Attitude is an extremely important personality trait that | 76 | 46 | 109
is a big contributor to success in one's day-to-day activities. | 80 | 48 | 111
Usually a person with a good attitude is open-minded to the ideas | 85 | 51 | 114
of others and is able to relate with others because he or she has | 89 | 53 | 117
an interest in people. Thus, one's attitude on the job often | 93 | 56 | 119
makes a great difference in whether work gets done and done | 97 | 58 | 122
right. Because teamwork is a part of many jobs, developing a | 101 | 61 | 124
good attitude toward work, people, and life seems logical. | 105 | 63 | 126

3' | 1 | 2 | 3 | 4
5' | 1 | 2 | 3

19d Speed Builder

Key each line once, working for fluid, consistent stroking. Repeat at a faster speed.

easy words

19 am it go bus dye jam irk six sod tic yam ugh spa vow aid dug
20 he or by air big elf dog end fit and lay sue toe wit own got
21 six foe pen firm also body auto form down city kept make fog.

easy phrases

22 it is|if the|and also|to me|the end|to us|if it|it is|to the
23 if it is|to the end|do you wish|to go to|for the end|to make
24 lay down|he or she|make me|by air|end of |by me|kept it|of me

easy sentences

25 Did the chap work to mend the torn right half of the ensign?
26 Blame me for their penchant for the antique chair and panel.
27 She bid by proxy for eighty bushels of a corn and rye blend.

TECHNIQUE TIP

- Key the easy words as "words" rather than stroke by stroke.
- Key each phrase (marked by a vertical line) without pauses between words.

COMMUNICATION

19e Number Expression

1. Study the rules and examples at the right.
2. Key the sample sentences 28–33.
3. Change figures to words as needed in sentences 34–36.

Spell out numbers:

1. **First word in a sentence.** Key numbers ten and lower as words unless they are part of a series of related numbers, any of which are over ten.

    Three of the four members were present.
    She wrote 12 stories and 2 plays in five years.

2. The **smaller of two adjacent numbers** as words.

    SolVir shipped six 24-ton engines.

3. **Isolated fractions and approximate numbers.** Key as words **large round numbers that can be expressed as one or two words.** Hyphenate fractions expressed as words.

    She completed one-fourth of the experiments.
    Val sent out three hundred invitations.

4. **Preceding "o'clock".**

    John's due at four o'clock. Pick him up at 4:15 p.m.

28 **Six** or **seven** older players were cut from the **37**-member team.
29 I have **2** of **14** coins I need to start my set. Kristen has **9.**
30 Of **nine 24**-ton engines ordered, we shipped **six** last Tuesday.
31 Shelly has read just **one-half** of about **forty-five** documents.
32 The **six** boys sent well over **two hundred** printed invitations.
33 **One** or **two** of us will be on duty from **two** until **six** o'clock.
34 The meeting begins promptly at 9. We plan 4 sessions.
35 The 3-person crew cleaned 6 stands, 12 tables, and 13 desks.
36 The 3d meeting is at 3 o'clock on Friday, February 2.

KEYBOARDING TECHNIQUE

Key each line twice, SS.

  all letters

1. Key three 1' writings on each ¶.
2. Key one 5' writing or two 3' writings. Proofread; circle errors; determine *gwam*.

Option: Practice as a guided writing.

			gwam
1/4'	1/2'	3/4'	1'
8	16	24	32
9	18	27	36
10	20	30	40
11	22	33	44
12	24	36	48
13	26	39	52
14	28	41	56
15	30	45	60
16	32	48	64
17	34	51	68
18	36	54	72

1st
1 Zam and six lazy men visited Cecil and Bunn at a bank convention.
2 Zane, much to the concern of Bev and six men, visited their zone.

2d
3 Jill said she wished that she had fed Dale's dog a lot less food.
4 Jake Hall sold the glass flask at a Dallas "half-off" glass sale.

3d
5 Did either Peter or Trey quip that reporters were out to get you?
6 Either Trey or Peter tried to work with a top-quality pewter toy.

4th
7 18465 97354 12093 87541 09378 34579 74629 45834 28174 11221 27211
8 02574 29765 39821 07623 17659 20495 39481 10374 32765 77545 22213

Writing 23

gwam   3' | 5'

Students, for decades, have secured part-time jobs to help   4 | 2 | 52
pay for college expenses. Today, more students are gainfully   8 | 5 | 54
employed while they are in college than ever before. Many of   12 | 7 | 57
them are employed because their financial situation requires that   17 | 10 | 59
they earn money. Earnings from jobs go to pay for tuition,   21 | 12 | 62
books, living costs, and other necessities. Some work so that   25 | 15 | 64
they can own cars or buy luxury items; others seek jobs to gain   29 | 17 | 67
skills or to build their vitas. These students are aware that   33 | 20 | 69
many organizations prefer to hire a person who has had some type   38 | 23 | 72
of work experience than one who has had none.   41 | 24 | 74

Students often ask if the work experience has to be in   44 | 27 | 76
exactly the same field. Obviously, the more closely related the   49 | 29 | 78
experience, the better it is. However, the old adage, anything   53 | 32 | 81
beats nothing, applies. Regardless of the types of jobs students   57 | 34 | 84
have, they can demonstrate that they get to work regularly and on   62 | 37 | 86
time, they have good human relations skills, they are organized   66 | 40 | 89
and can manage time effectively, and they produce good results.   70 | 42 | 91
All of these factors are very critical to employers. The bottom   75 | 45 | 94
line is that employers like to use what you have done in the past   79 | 47 | 97
as a predictor of what you will do in the future.   82 | 49 | 99

3' 1   2   3   4
5' 1   2   3

LESSON 20

and /

WARMUP

20a
Key each line twice SS (slowly, then faster).

alphabet 1 Freda Jencks will have money to buy six quite large topazes.
symbols 2 I bought 10 ribbons and 45 disks from Cable-Han Co. for $78.
home row 3 Dallas sold jade flasks; Sal has a glass flask full of salt.
easy 4 He may cycle down to the field by the giant oak and cut hay.

NEW KEYS

20b # and /
Key each line once SS.

= number sign, pounds

/ = diagonal, slash

LEFT FINGERS   4 \ 3 \ 2 \ 1 \ 1 \ 2 \ 3 \ 4   RIGHT FINGERS

Shift; then reach *up* with *left second* finger.

/ Reach *down* with *right fourth* finger.

#

5 # #e e# # # #; had #3 dial; did #3 drop; set #3 down; Bid #3
6 leave #82; sold #20; Lyric #16; bale #34; load #53; Optic #7
7 Notice #333 says to load Car #33 with 33# of #3 grade shale.

/

8 / /; :/ / / /; 1/2; 1/3; Mr./Mrs.; 1/5/94; 22 11/12; and/or;
9 to/from; /s/ William Smit; 2/10, n/30; his/her towels; 6 1/2
10 The numerals 1 5/8, 3 1/4, and 60 7/9 are "mixed fractions."

all symbols learned

11 Invoice #737 cites 15 2/3# of rye was shipped C.O.D. 4/6/95.
12 B-O-A Company's Check #50/5 for $87 paid for 15# of #3 wire.
13 Our Co-op List #20 states $40 for 16 1/2 crates of tomatoes.

SKILLBUILDING

gwam 30"

20c Keyboard Reinforcement
Key each line once; work for fluency.
Option: In the Open Screen, key 30" writings on both lines of a pair. Work to avoid pauses.

14 She did the key work at the height of the problem. 20
15 Form #726 is the title to the island; she owns it. 20

16 The rock is a form of fuel; he did enrich it with coal. 22
17 The corn-and-turkey dish is a blend of turkey and corn. 22

18 It is right to work to end the social problems of the world. 24
19 If I sign it on 3/19, the form can aid us to pay the 40 men. 24

Skill Builders 4

Save each drill as a separate file. Save as SB4-d1, etc. (Skill Builder 4, Drill 1).

DRILL 1

KEYSTROKING PATTERNS

Key each line twice SS.

3d row

1 it we or us opo pop you rut rip wit pea lea wet pit were quiet
2 pew tie toe per rep hope pour quip rope your pout tore rip quirk.

Home row

3 ha has kid lad led last wash lash gaff jade fads half sash haggle
4 as dad had add leg jug lads hall lass fast deal fall leafs dashes

1st row

5 ax ban man zinc clan bank calm lamb vain amaze bronze back buzzer
6 ax sax can bam zag cab mad fax vans buzz caves knack waxen banana

Standard Plan for Guided Writing Procedures

1. Take a 1' writing on paragraph 1. Note your *gwam*.
2. Add four words to your 1' *gwam* to determine your goal rate.
3. In the Open screen, set the timer for 1' and the Timer option to beep every 15" (*MicroPace Pro* or *Keyboarding Pro*).
4. From the table below, select from Column 4 the speed nearest your goal rate. Note the ¼' point at the left of that speed. Place a check mark at each ¼' goal.
5. Take two 1' guided writings on paragraphs 1 and 2 striving to meet your ¼' goal. Do not save.

A all letters

1. Key two 1' writings on each paragraph.
2. Key one 3' or one 5' writing.

Optional: Practice as a guided writing.

1/4'	1/2'	3/4'	*gwam* 1'
8	16	24	32
9	18	27	36
10	20	30	40
11	22	33	44
12	24	36	48
13	26	39	52
14	28	41	56
15	30	45	60
16	32	48	64
17	34	51	68
18	36	54	72

Writing 22

		gwam	3'	5'

Who is a professional? The word can be defined in many   4 | 2 | 32
ways. Some may think of a professional as someone who is in an   8 | 5 | 35
exempt job category in an organization. To others the word can   12 | 7 | 37
denote something quite different; being a professional denotes an   17 | 10 | 40
attitude that requires thinking of your position as a career, not   21 | 13 | 43
just a job. A professional exerts influence over her or his job   25 | 15 | 45
and takes pride in the work accomplished.   28 | 17 | 47

Many individuals who remain in the same positions for a long   32 | 19 | 49
time characterize themselves as being in dead-end positions.   36 | 22 | 52
Others who remain in positions for a long time consider them-   40 | 24 | 54
selves to be in a profession. A profession is a career to which   45 | 27 | 57
you are willing to devote a lifetime. How you view your pro-   49 | 29 | 59
fession is up to you.   50 | 30 | 60

3' | 1 2 3 4
5' | 1 2 3

COMMUNICATION

20d Number Usage Review

Key each line once. Decide whether the circled numbers should be keyed as figures or as words and make needed changes. Check your finished work with 19e, page 47.

```
20 Six or (7) older players were cut from the (37)-member team.
21 I have (2) of 14 coins I need to start my set.  Kristen has (9).
22 Of (9) 24-ton engines ordered, we shipped (6) last Tuesday.
23 Shelly has read just (1) half of about (45) documents.
24 The (6) boys sent well over (200) printed invitations.
25 (1) or (2) of us will be on duty from (2) until (6) o'clock.
```

SKILLBUILDING

20e Speed Builder

1. Go to the Open Screen.
2. Follow the procedures at the right for increasing your speed by taking guided writings.
3. Take a 3' writing without the guide on the complete writing.

all letters

			gwam
1/4'	1/2'	3/4'	1'
4	8	12	16
5	10	15	20
6	12	18	24
7	14	21	28
8	16	24	32
9	18	27	36
10	20	30	40

STANDARD PLAN for Guided Writing Procedures

1. In the Open Screen, take a 1' writing on paragraph 1. Note your *gwam*.
2. Add four words to your 1' *gwam* to determine your goal rate.
3. Set the Timer for 1'. Set the Timer option to beep every 15".
4. From the table below, select from column 4 the speed nearest your goal rate. Note the ¼' point at the left of that speed. Place a light check mark within the paragraphs at the ¼' points.
5. Take two 1' guided writings on paragraphs 1 and 2. Do not save.
6. Turn the beeper off.

	gwam 2'	3'	
Some of us think that the best way to get attention is	6	4	35
to try a new style, or to look quixotic, or to be different	12	8	39
somehow. Perhaps we are looking for nothing much more than	18	12	43
acceptance from others of ourselves just the way we now are.	24	16	47
There is no question about it; we all want to look our	29	19	50
best to impress other people. How we achieve this may mean	35	23	54
trying some of this and that; but our basic objective is to	41	27	58
take our raw materials, you and me, and build up from there.	47	31	62

2' | 1 | 2 | 3 | 4 | 5 | 6
3' | 1 | 2 | 3 | 4

DRILL 1
SUBJECT-VERB AGREEMENT

1. Review the rules and examples on the previous page.
2. Open **subjectverb1** from the data files. Save it as **subjectverb-drill1**.
3. Follow the specific directions provided in the data file.
4. Save again and print.

DRILL 2
SUBJECT-VERB AGREEMENT

1. Open **subjectverb2** from the data files. Save it as **subjectverb-drill2**.
2. Follow the specific directions provided in the data file.
3. Save and print.

DRILL 3

SUBJECT/VERB AND CAPITALIZATION

1. Key the ten sentences at the right, choosing the correct verb and applying correct capitalization.

2. Save as **subjectverb-drill3** and print.

1. both of the curies (was/were) nobel prize winners.
2. each of the directors in the sales department (has/have) given us approval.
3. mr. and mrs. thomas funderburk, jr. (was/were) married on november 23, 1936.
4. my sister and her college roommates (plan/plans) to tour london and paris this summer.
5. our new information manager (suggest/suggests) the following salutation when using an attention line: ladies and gentlemen.
6. the body language expert (place/places) his hand on his cheek as he says, "touch your hand to your chin."
7. the japanese child (enjoy/enjoys) the american food her hosts (serve/serves) her.
8. all of the candidates (was/were) invited to the debate at boston college.
9. the final exam (cover/covers) chapters 1-5.
10. turn south onto interstate 20; then take exit 56 to bossier city.

DRILL 4

EDITING SKILLS
Key the paragraph. Correct all errors in grammar and capitalization. Save as **editing-drill4**.

This past week I visited the facilities of the magnolia conference center in isle of palms, south carolina, as you requested. bob bremmerton, group manager, was my host for the visit.

magnolia offers many advantages for our leadership training conference. The prices are reasonable; the facilities is excellent; the location is suitable. In addition to the beachfront location, tennis and golf packages are part of the group price.

LESSON 21

% and !

WARMUP

21a
Key each line twice SS.

alphabet 1 Merry will have picked out a dozen quarts of jam for boxing.

fig/sym 2 Jane-Ann bought 16 7/8 yards of #240 cotton at $3.59 a yard.

1st row 3 Can't brave, zany Cave Club men/women next climb Mt. Zamban?

easy 4 Did she rush to cut six bushels of corn for the civic corps?

NEW KEYS

21b % and !
Key each line once SS.

% Shift; then reach *up* with *left first* finger.

% = percent sign: Use % with business forms or where space is restricted; otherwise, use the word "percent." Space twice after the exclamation point!

%

5 % %f f% % %; off 5%; if 5%; of 5% fund; half 5%; taxes of 5%

6 7% rent; 3% tariff; 9% F.O.B.; 15% greater; 28% base; up 46%

7 Give discounts of 5% on rods, 50% on lures, and 75% on line.

! reach *up* with the *left fourth* finger

8 ! !a a! ! ! !; Eureka! Ha! No! Pull 10! Extra! America!

9 Listen to the call! Now! Ready! Get set! Go! Good show!

10 I want it now, not next week! I am sure to lose 50% or $19.

all symbols

11 The ad offers a 10% discount, but this notice says 15% less!

12 He got the job! With Clark's Supermarket! Please call Mom!

13 Bill #92-44 arrived very late from Zyclone; it was paid 7/4.

SPACING TIP

■ Do not space between a figure and the % or $ signs.
■ Do not space before or after the dash.

all symbols

14 As of 6/28, Jeri owes $31 for dinner and $27 for cab fare.

15 Invoice #20--it was dated 3/4--billed $17 less 15% discount.

16 He deducted 2% instead of 6%, a clear saving of 6% vs. 7%.

combination response

17 Look at my dismal grade in English; but I guess I earned it.

21c Keyboard Reinforcement

Key each line once; work for fluency.

18 Kris started to blend a cocoa beverage for a shaken cowhand.

19 Jan may make a big profit if she owns the title to the land.

Communication Skills 3

Use a singular verb

1. With a **singular subject**. (The singular forms of *to be* include: am, is, was. Common errors with *to be* are: you was, we was, they was.)

> She monitors employee morale.
> You are a very energetic worker.
> A split keyboard is in great demand.

2. With most **indefinite pronouns**: *another, anybody, anything, everything, each, either, neither, one, everyone, anyone, nobody.*

> Each of the candidates has raised a considerable amount of money.
> Everyone is eager to read the author's newest novel.
> Neither of the boys is able to attend.

3. With singular subjects joined by *or/nor, either/or, neither/nor.*

> Neither your grammar nor punctuation is correct.
> Either Jody or Jan has your favorite CD.
> John or Connie has volunteered to chaperone the field trip.

4. With a **collective noun** (*family, choir, herd, faculty, jury, committee*) that acts as one unit.

> The jury has reached a decision.
> The council is in an emergency session.
> But:
> The faculty have their assignments. (Each has his/her own assignments.)

5. With words or phrases that express **periods of time, weights, measurements**, or **amounts of money**.

> Fifteen dollars is what he earned.
> Two-thirds of the money has been submitted to the treasurer.
> One hundred pounds is too much.

Use a plural verb

6. With a **plural subject**.

> The students sell computer supplies for their annual fundraiser.
> They are among the top-ranked teams in the nation.

7. With **compound (two or more) subjects** joined by *and*.

> Headaches and backaches are common worker complaints.
> Hard work and determination were two qualities listed by the references.

8. With *some, all, most, none, several, few, both, many*, and *any* when they refer to more than one of the items.

> All of my friends have seen the movie.
> Some of the teams have won two or more games.

21d Textbook Keying
Key each line once;
DS between groups; fingers
curved, hands quiet. Repeat if
time permits.

1st finger

20 by bar get fun van for inn art from gray hymn July true verb
21 brag human bring unfold hominy mighty report verify puny joy
22 You are brave to try bringing home the van in the bad storm.

2d finger

23 ace ink did cad keyed deep seed kind Dick died kink like kid
24 cease decease decades kick secret check decide kidney evaded
25 Dedre likes the idea of ending dinner with cake for dessert.

3d finger

26 oil sow six vex wax axe low old lox pool west loss wool slow
27 swallow swamp saw sew wood sax sexes loom stew excess school
28 Wes waxes floors and washes windows at low costs to schools.

4th finger

29 zap zip craze pop pup pan daze quote queen quiz pizza puzzle
30 zoo graze zipper panzer zebra quip partizan patronize appear
31 Czar Zane appears to be dazzled by the apple pizza and jazz.

21e Speed Runs
with Numbers

Take 1' writings; the last
number you key when you stop
is your approximate *gwam*.

1 and 2 and 3 and 4 and 5 and 6 and 7 and 8 and 9 and 10 and
11 and 12 and 13 and 14 and 15 and 16 and 17 and 18 and 19
and 20 and 21 and 22 and 23 and 24 and 25 and 26 and 27 and

21f Speed Check

Key a 1' and a 2' writing.
Option: Key a 3' writing.

 all letters

gwam 1' | 2'

	1'	2'
Teams are the basic unit of performance for a firm.	11	5	42
They are not the solution to all of the organizational needs.	23	12	48
They will not solve all of the problems, but it is known	35	17	54
that a team can perform at a higher rate than other groups.	47	23	60
It is one of the best ways to support the changes needed for	59	30	66
a firm. The team must have time in order to make	71	36	72
a quality working plan.	74	37	74

1'	1	2	3	4	5	6	7	8	9	10	11	12
2'		1		2		3		4		5		6

Module 6: Checkpoint

Answer the questions below to see if you have mastered the content of Module 6.

1. A vertical list of information within a table is referred to as a(n) _____.
2. To move to the next cell in a table, press the _____ key.
3. A quick way to select an entire table is by clicking the _____ .
4. To center a table horizontally on the page, use the _____ option.
5. Preformatted styles can be applied to tables by using the _____ feature.
6. A row can be added at the end of the table by clicking the insertion point in the last cell and pressing _____.
7. The Table feature that allows you to join cells is referred to as _____ Cells.
8. Increase row height by selecting the rows and clicking _____ on the Table menu.
9. Whole numbers are generally aligned at the _____ in columns.
10. Text is generally aligned at the _____ in columns.

Performance Assessment

Document 1
Create Table

1. Format the main and secondary headings. Increase row 1 height to 1" and apply 15% shading.
2. Right-align columns B and C.
3. Change row height of rows 2–9 to .3". Adjust column widths, and center the table horizontally and vertically.
4. Save as **checkpoint6-d1**. Print but do not close.

UNIVERSITY OF NEVADA		
College of Business		
Department	**Majors**	**Growth Rate**
Accounting	945	3.65%
Banking, Finance, and Insurance	1,021	2.17%
Communications	326	-2 .5%
Economics	453	1.4%
International Business	620	14.74%
Management Science	1,235	11.8%
Marketing	1,357	10.38%

Document 2
Edit Table

1. Save the table as **checkpoint6-d2**.
2. Add the row at the right in alphabetical order.

Information Technology   8,756   14.5%

LESSON 22 (and) and Backspace Key

WARMUP

22a
Key each line twice SS.

alphabet	1	Avoid lazy punches; expert fighters jab with a quick motion.
fig/sym	2	Be-Low's Bill #483/7 was $96.90, not $102--they took 5% off.
caps lock	3	Report titles may be shown in ALL CAPS; as, BOLD WORD POWER.
easy	4	Do they blame me for their dismal social and civic problems?

| 1 | 2 | 3 | 4 | 5 | 6 | 7 | 8 | 9 | 10 | 11 | 12 |

NEW KEYS

22b (and)
(parentheses)
Key each line once SS.

( ) = parentheses
Parentheses indicate offhand, aside, or explanatory messages.

(Shift; then reach *up* with the *right third* finger.

) Shift; then reach *up* with the *right fourth* finger.

5 ((l l((; (; Reach from l for the left parenthesis; as, ((.

6)); ;))); Reach from ; for the right parenthesis; as,)).

( )

7 Learn to use parentheses (plural) or parenthesis (singular).

8 The red (No. 34) and blue (No. 78) cars both won here (Rio).

9 We (Galen and I) dined (bagels) in our penthouse (the dorm).

all symbols learned

10 The jacket was $35 (thirty-five dollars)--the tie was extra.

11 Starting 10/29, you can sell Model #49 at a discount of 25%.

12 My size 8 1/2 shoe--a blue pump--was soiled (but not badly).

22c Textbook Keying
Key each line once, keeping eyes on copy.

13 Jana has one hard-to-get copy of her hot-off-the-press book.

14 An invoice said that "We give discounts of 10%, 5%, and 3%."

15 The company paid Bill 3/18 on 5/2/97 and Bill 3/1 on 3/6/97.

16 The catalog lists as out of stock Items #230, #710, and #13.

17 Elyn had $8; Sean, $9; and Cal, $7. The cash total was $24.

51c-d3
Table with Bullets

1. Key the table below. Make column A approximately 2" wide. Apply bullets to column B. Align bullets at the left; DS between bullets.
2. Bold column A. Align the text at the left.
3. Center the main heading in bold. Shade row 1 15%.
4. Select the entire table. Center the text vertically in the cells.
5. Set the row height for each of the rows as follows: row 1—.65", row 2—1.5", row 3—1.9", and row 4—1.4".
6. Center the table vertically. Save as **51c-d3**.

BENEFITS OF DSL SERVICE	
Improves productivity and eliminates frustration	• Always on; ends busy signals and dropped calls. • High-speed Internet access; greatly reduces wait time when uploading or downloading files.
Saves money	• Unlimited Internet access for one affordable flat rate. • One dedicated connection; no extra costs for network or multiple users. • No additional telephone company fees or usage charges.
Maximizes growth potential	• Increased bandwidth enables you to fully take advantage of the Internet. • Scalable enhanced services and applications that can accommodate change and growth with your business needs.

51c-d4
Insert Columns and Rows

1. Open **51c-d1** and insert the columns and rows as directed.
2. Key the data below in a new column B; then adjust column widths.

   Publisher
   Bodwin
   American
   TWSS
   Bodwin
   TWSS
   American

3. Insert a new row above Pommery Mountain and add the following information. Save as **51c-d4**. Print.

   The Lion and the Mouse   American   2003   63,500.00   9.95

SKILLBUILDING

22d BACKSPACE Key

Practice reaching to the BACK-SPACE key with your right little finger. Key the sentences, using the BACKSPACE key to correct errors.

22e Speed Check

1. Take two 1' timings on each paragraph.
2. Take a 3' timing on all paragraphs. Determine *gwam*.

Goal: 17 *gwam*

all letters

18 You should be interested in the special items on sale today.

19 If she is going with us, why don't we plan to leave now?

20 Do you desire to continue working on the memo in the future?

21 Did the firm or their neighbors own the autos with problems?

22 Juni, Vec, and Zeb had perfect grades on weekly query exams.

23 Jewel quickly explained to me the big fire hazards involved.

Most people will agree that we owe it to our children to pass the planet on to them in better condition than we found it. We must take extra steps just to make the quality of living better.

If we do not change our ways quickly and stop damaging our world, it will not be a good place to live. We can save the ozone and wildlife and stop polluting the air and water.

	1'	3'
10	4	28
22	7	32
34	12	36
38	13	37
11	16	41
12	21	45
35	25	49

```
1' | 1 | 2 | 3 | 4 | 5 | 6 | 7 | 8 | 9 | 10 | 11 | 12 |
3' |     1     |     2     |     3     |     4     |
```

COMMUNICATION

22f Number Expression

1. Study the rules and examples at the right.
2. In the Open Screen, key the information below at the left margin. Press ENTER as shown.

   Your name ENTER

   Current date ENTER

   Skillbuilders 1, Drill 6

   ENTER ENTER

3. Key the sample sentences 24–28. Backspace to correct errors.
4. Save the file as **xx-22f**.

Express as figures

1. **Money amounts** and **percentages, even when appoximate.** Spell out cents and percent except in statistical copy.

   The 16 percent discount saved me $145; Bill, 95 cents.

2. **Round numbers expressed in millions or higher with their word modifier.**

   Ms. Ti contributed $3 million.

3. **House numbers** (Except house number One) and street names over ten. If a street name is a number, separate it from the house number with a dash.

   1510 Easy Street   One West Ninth Avenue   1592-11th Street

4. **Date followed by a month.** A date preceding the month or standing alone is expressed in figures followed by "d" or "th."

   June 9, 2001   4th of July   March 3d

5. **Numbers used with nouns.**

   Volume 1   Chapter 6

24 Ask **Group 1** to read **Chapter 6** of **Book 11** (**Shelf 19, Room 5**).

25 All **six** of us live at **One Bay Road**, not at **126--56th Street**.

26 At **9 a.m.** the owners decided to close from **12 noon** to **1 p.m.**

27 Ms. Vik leaves **June 9**; she returns the **14th or 15th of July**.

28 The **16 percent** discount saves **$115**. A stamp costs **35 cents**.

51c-d1
Table with AutoFormat

1. Key the table below.
2. Center column B; right-align columns C and D.
3. Format the table and apply Table List 4 format.
4. Center the table vertically. Save as **51c-d1**. Print.

LARSON LEARNING

Book Title	Publications	Sales	Unit Price
Adventures of Sally Boyer	2003	478,769.00	9.95
Tale of Five Cities	2002	91,278.00	32.50
New York, New York	2003	32,829.00	28.75
Horrell Hill Adventures	2003	89,412.00	29.00
Pommery Mountain	2003	194,511.00	33.75
Tom Creek's Adventures	2002	105,750.00	27.50

51c-d2
Memo with Table

1. Key the memo.
2. Right-align column D and center columns B and C.
3. Save as **51c-d2**. Print.

TO: Brenda Cook | FROM: Mark Olson | SUBJECT: Sales Report

A comparison of the sales figures for 2003 and 2004 are shown below. Figures look pretty good for all the regions except the Northern region. I am concerned about the decrease in sales for the Northern region; this has always been a high-growth area.

Region	2003 Sales	2004 Sales	% of Change
East	53,256	72,002	+18.55%
North	41,899	37,576	−4.07%
West	62,965	64,211	+2.88%
South	27,894	29,031	+3.55%

Please research the cause in the drop of sales for the Northern area. Let's get together next week and discuss how we can improve Northern sales for next year.

& and : (colon), Proofreaders' marks

23a
Key each line twice SS.

alphabet	1	Roxy waved as she did quick flying jumps on the trapeze bar.
symbols	2	Ryan's--with an A-1 rating--sold Item #146 (for $10) on 2/7.
space bar	3	Mr. Fyn may go to Cape Cod on the bus, or he may go by auto.
easy	4	Susie is busy; may she halt the social work for the auditor?

| 1 | 2 | 3 | 4 | 5 | 6 | 7 | 8 | 9 | 10 | 11 | 12 |

NEW KEYS

23b & and : (colon)
Key each line once SS.

& Shift; then reach *up* with *right first* finger.

: (colon) Left shift; then press key with *right fourth* finger.

& = ampersand: The ampersand is used only as part of company names.
Colon: Space twice after a colon except when used within a number for time.

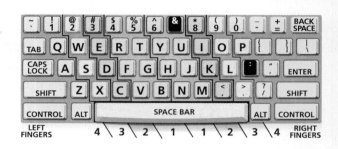

& (ampersand)
5 & &j j& & & &; J & J; Haraj & Jay; Moroj & Jax; Torj & Jones
6 Nehru & Unger; Mumm & Just; Mann & Hart; Arch & Jones; M & J
7 Rhye & Knox represent us; Steb & Doy, Firm A; R & J, Firm B.

: (colon)
8 : :; :; : : :; as: for example: notice: To: From: Date:
9 in stock: 8:30; 7:45; Age: Experience: Read: Send: See:
10 Space twice after a colon, thus: To: No.: Time: Carload:

all symbols learned
11 Consider these companies: J & R, Brand & Kay, Uper & Davis.
12 Memo #88-89 reads as follows: "Deduct 15% of $300, or $45."
13 Bill 32(5)--it got here quite late--from M & N was paid 7/3.

23c Keyboard Reinforcement
Key each line twice; work for fluency.

double letters
14 Di Bennett was puzzled by drivers exceeding the speed limit.
15 Bill needs the office address; he will cut the grass at ten.
16 Todd saw the green car veer off the street near a tall tree.

figures and symbols
17 Invoice #84 for $672.91, plus $4.38 tax, was due on 5/19/02.
18 Do read Section 4, pages 60-74 and Section 9, pages 198-225.
19 Enter the following: (a) name, (b) address, and (c) tax ID.

LESSON 51 Table Assessment

SKILLBUILDING

51a
Warmup
Key each line twice SS.

alphabet 1 Jacob Kazlowski and five experienced rugby players quit the team.

figures 2 E-mail account #82-4 is the account for telephone (714) 555-0108.

double letters 3 Anne will meet with the committee at noon to discuss a new issue.

easy 4 The men may pay my neighbor for the work he did in the cornfield.

| 1 | 2 | 3 | 4 | 5 | 6 | 7 | 8 | 9 | 10 | 11 | 12 | 13 |

51b
Timed Writing
Take two 3' timings. Strive to key with control and fluency.

  all letters

gwam 3' | 5'

	3'	5'
Whether any company can succeed depends on how well it fits	4	2
into the economic system. Success rests on certain key factors	8	5
that are put in line by a management team that has set goals for	13	8
the company and has enough good judgment to recognize how best to	17	10
reach these goals. Because of competition, only the best-organized	21	13
companies get to the top.	23	14
A commercial enterprise is formed for a specific purpose:	27	16
that purpose is usually to equip others, or consumers, with	31	19
whatever they cannot equip themselves. Unless there is only one	36	21
provider, a consumer will search for a company that returns the	40	24
most value in terms of price; and a relationship with such a	43	27
company, once set up, can endure for many years.	47	28
Thus our system assures that the businesses that manage to	51	31
survive are those that have been able to combine successfully an	56	33
excellent product with a low price and the best service—all in a	60	36
place that is convenient for the buyers. With no intrusion from	64	39
outside forces, the buyer and the seller benefit both themselves	69	41
and each other.	70	42

3' | 1 | 2 | 3 | 4 |
5' | 1 | 2 | 3 |

APPLICATIONS

51c
Assessment

 Continue

 Check

With CheckPro: When you complete a document, proofread it, check the spelling, and preview for placement. When you are completely satisfied with the document, click the **Continue** button to move to the next document. You will not be able to return and edit a document once you continue to the next document. Click the **Check** button when you are ready to error-check the test. Review and/or print the document analysis results.

Without CheckPro: On the signal to begin, key the documents in sequence. When time has been called, proofread all documents again and identify errors.

SKILLBUILDING

23d Textbook Keying
Key each line once; work for fluency.

20 Jane may work with an auditing firm if she is paid to do so.
21 Pam and eight girls may go to the lake to work with the dog.
22 Clancy and Claudia did all the work to fix the sign problem.
23 Did Lea visit the Orlando land of enchantment or a neighbor?
24 Ana and Blanche made a map for a neighbor to go to the city.
25 Sidney may go to the lake to fish with worms from the docks.
26 Did the firm or the neighbors own the auto with the problem?

| 1 | 2 | 3 | 4 | 5 | 6 | 7 | 8 | 9 | 10 | 11 | 12 |

23e Speed Check
Key two 1' timed writings on each paragraph; then two 3' writings on both paragraphs; compute *gwam*.

Goals: 1', 20–27 *gwam*
3', 17–24 *gwam*

all letters

gwam 1' | 3'

Is how you judge my work important?   It is, of course;   11 | 4 | 26
I hope you recognize some basic merit in it.   We all expect   23 | 8 | 30
to get credit for good work that we conclude.   32 | 11 | 33

I want approval for stands I take, things I write, and   11 | 14 | 36
work I complete.   My efforts, by my work, show a picture of   23 | 18 | 41
me; thus, through my work, I am my own unique creation.   34 | 22 | 44

1' | 1 | 2 | 3 | 4 | 5 | 6 | 7 | 8 | 9 | 10 | 11 | 12 |
3' | 1 | 2 | 3 | 4 |

COMMUNICATION

23f Edit Text
1. Read the information about proofreaders' marks.
2. In the Open Screen, key your name, class, and 23f at the left margin. Then key lines 27–32, making the revisions as you key. Use the BACKSPACE key to correct errors.
3. Save as **xx-23f** and print.

Proofreaders' marks are used to identify mistakes in typed or printed text. Learn to apply these commonly used standard proofreaders' marks.

Symbol	Meaning	Symbol	Meaning
——	Italic	sp (circled)	Spell out
～～～	Bold	¶	Paragraph
Cap or ≡	Capitalize	#	Add horizontal space
∧	Insert	/ or lc	Lowerca
𝒶	Delete	⌒	Close up space
⊏	Move to left	～	Transpose
⊐	Move to right	stet	Leave as originally written

27 We miss 50% in life's rewards by refusing to new try things.

28 do it now--today--then tomorrow's load will be 100%% lighter.

29 Satisfying work--whether it pays $40 or $400-is the pay off.

30 Avoid mistakes: confusing a #3 has cost thousands.

31 Pleased most with a first-rate job is the person who did it.

32 My wife and/or me mother will except the certifi cate for me.

1. Key the report in unbound format.
2. DS before and after the table. Apply **Table List 7** format to the table.
3. Save as **50b-d4**.

MALICIOUS INTRUDERS

We previously only worried about getting a virus by booting the computer from an infected floppy disk or by downloading and running programs from a BBS, a computer bulletin board system. Today, the majority of the viruses are obtained through the Internet. Downloading files from the Internet or opening e-mail containing a virus is the primary means by which malware spreads.

"Malware" is defined as getting your system infected by malicious software. Malware is usually classified according to two traits: where it hides and how it spreads. The table below will help you understand the categories of malicious software.

Type	Description
Boot sector viruses	This virus is obtained from booting an infected floppy disk.
File infectors	This virus modifies the programs you use, inserting code that runs when you execute programs.
Macro viruses	This is a file infector that hides inside macros. The virus is activated when the macro is opened.
Worm	This malware propagates from machine to machine without human intervention.

Load antivirus software on your computer to help screen out viruses. You will also want to carefully scrutinize all e-mail attachments and download programs from trusted sources only. Protect your computer, files, and software from dangerous intruders.

LESSON 24 — Other Symbols

WARMUP

24a

Key each line twice SS.

alphabet 1 Pfc. Jim Kings covered each of the lazy boxers with a quilt.
figures 2 Do problems 6 to 29 on page 175 before class at 8:30, May 4.
" 3 They read the poems "September Rain" and "The Lower Branch."
easy 4 When did the busy girls fix the tight cowl of the ruby gown?
| 1 | 2 | 3 | 4 | 5 | 6 | 7 | 8 | 9 | 10 | 11 | 12 |

NEW KEYS

24b Textbook Keying

Key each pair of lines once SS;
DS between 2-line groups.

Become familiar with
these symbols:

@ at
< less than
> greater than
* asterisk
+ plus sign (use a
   hyphen for minus
   and x for "times")
= equals
[ ] left and right
     bracket

@   shift; reach *up* with *left third* finger to @
5 @ @s s@ @ @; 24 @ .15; 22 @ .35; sold 2 @ .87; were 12 @ .95
6 You may contact Luke @: LJP@rx.com or fax @ (602) 555-0101.

<   shift; reach *down* with *right second* finger to <
>   shift; reach *down* with *right third* finger to >
7 Can you prove "a > b"? If 28 > 5, then 5a < x. Is a < > b?
8 E-mail Al ajj@crewl.com and Matt mrw10@scxs.com by 9:30 p.m.

*   shift; reach *up* with *right second* finger to *
9 * *k k8* * *; aurelis*; May 7*; both sides*; 250 km.**; aka*
10 Note each *; one * refers to page 29; ** refers to page 307.

+   shift; reach *up* with *right fourth* finger to +
11 + ;+ +; + + +; 2 + 2; A+ or B+; 70+ F. degrees; +xy over +y;
12 The question was 8 + 7 + 51; it should have been 8 + 7 + 15.

=   reach *up* with *right fourth* finger to =
13 = =; = = =; = 4; If 14x = 28, x = 2; if 8x = 16, then x = 2.
14 Change this solution (where it says "= by") to = bx or = BX.

[ ]   reach *up* with *right fourth* finger to [and]
15 Mr. Wing was named. [That's John J. Wing, ex-senator. Ed.]
16 We [Joseph and I] will be in Suite #349; call us @ 555-0102.

50b-d2
Memo with Table

1. Key the following memo to **Robert May**, from **Marcia Lewis**. The subject is **Purchase Order 5122**.
2. Center the data in column A, right-align column C, apply 15% shading to row 1, adjust the column widths, and center the table horizontally.
3. DS after the table, and add your reference initials. Save it as **50b-d2**.

The items that you requested on Purchase Order 5122 are in stock and will be shipped from our warehouse today. The shipment will be transported via Romulus Delivery System and is expected to arrive at your location in five days. ↓2

Item Number	Description	Unit Price
329	Lordusky locking cabinet	212.00
331	Anchorage heavy duty locking cabinet	265.00
387	Lordusky locking cabinet (unassembled)	175.00

↓2

50b-d3
Letter with Table

1. Key the following letter in modified block format. Supply all necessary letter parts. All column heads in the table should fit on one line.
2. Apply the **Table Contemporary** format to the table. Right-align numbers in column D. Save as **50b-d3**.

Ms. Beatrice Snow | Collection Manager | Precision Office Products | 2679 Orchard Lake Road | Farmington Hills, MI 48297-5534

Thank you for allowing International Financial Systems to assist you in managing your delinquent accounts. We provide you with the fastest interface to International Systems Collection Services. The activity report for last month is shown below.

Client Number	Last Name	First Name	Current Balance
1487	Jones	Alice	1,576.00
1679	Kim	Lisa	954.35
1822	Batavia	Roger	1,034.21
1905	Vokavich	Kramer	832.09

Please verify the accuracy of the names transmitted by your billing office. If you find any transmission errors, please contact Joseph Kerning at (888) 555-0134 immediately.

Sincerely | Sandra McCulley | Information Systems Specialist

SKILLBUILDING

double letters	17	feel pass mill good miss seem moons cliffs pools green spell
	18	Assets are being offered in a stuffy room to two associates.
balanced hand	19	is if of to it go do to is do so if to to the it sign vie to
	20	Pamela Fox may wish to go to town with Blanche if she works.
one hand	21	date face ere bat lip sew lion rear brag fact join eggs ever
	22	get fewer on; after we look; as we agree; add debt; act fast
combination	23	was for|in the case of|they were|to down|mend it|but pony is
	24	They were to be down in the fastest sleigh if you are right.

| 1 | 2 | 3 | 4 | 5 | 6 | 7 | 8 | 9 | 10 | 11 | 12 |

24c Rhythm Builder

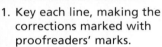

In the Open Screen, key each line twice; DS between 2-line groups.

24d Edited Copy

1. Key each line, making the corrections marked with proofreaders' marks.
2. Correct errors using the BACKSPACE key.
3. Save as **xx-24d**.

25 Ask Group 1 to read Chater 6 of Book 11 (Shelf 19, Room 5).

26 All 6 of us live at One Bay road, not at 126-56th Street.

27 AT 9 a.m. the owners decided to close form 12 noon to 1 p.m.

28 Ms. Vik leaves June 9; she returns the 14 or 15 of July.

29 The 16 per cent discount saves $115. A stamp costs 35 cents.

30 Elin gave $300,000,000; our gift was only 75 cents.

gwam 1' 3'

24e Speed Check

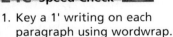

1. Key a 1' writing on each paragraph using wordwrap.
2. Key two 3' writings on both paragraphs. Save the timings if desired (**xx24e-t1** and **xx24e-t2**).

Why don't we like change very much? Do you think that just maybe we want to be lazy; to dodge new things; and, as much as possible, not to make hard decisions?

We know change can and does extend new areas for us to enjoy, areas we might never have known existed; and to stay away from all change could curtail our quality of life.

11	4	26
23	8	30
32	11	33
11	14	36
24	18	40
34	22	44

1' | 1 | 2 | 3 | 4 | 5 | 6 | 7 | 8 | 9 | 10 | 11 | 12 |
3' | 1 | 2 | 3 | 4 |

COMMUNICATION

24f Composition Revision

1. In the Open Screen, open the file **xx-profile** that you created in Lesson 18.
2. Position the insertion point at the end of the last paragraph. Press ENTER twice.
3. Key an additional paragraph that begins with the following sentence:
   Thank you for allowing me to introduce myself.
4. Finish the paragraph by adding two or more sentences that describe your progress and satisfaction with keyboarding.
5. Correct any mistakes you have made. Click **Save** to resave the document. Print.
6. Mark any mistakes you missed with proofreaders' marks. Revise the document, save, and reprint. Submit to your instructor.

50a
Warmup
Key each pair of
lines twice at
a controlled rate.

1st and 2d fingers
1 Mickey teaches golf three times this month to young children.
2 Jenny might meet her husband at the new stadium before the match.

3d and 4th fingers
3 Wallace was so puzzled over the sizable proposal due in six days.
4 Paula will wash, wax, and polish Polly's old, aqua car quite soon.

direct reach
5 Kilgore, located in a low-lying area, was destroyed by the flood.
6 Dennie framed the ball to help the Jupiter pitcher earn a strike.

| 1 | 2 | 3 | 4 | 5 | 6 | 7 | 8 | 9 | 10 | 11 | 12 | 13 |

50b-d1
Table Report

The table structure can be used to create an attractive report. Create the report using a 2-column, 5-row table. Print the report without borders to achieve this look.

1. Key the title at about 2". Change the width of column A to approximately 2" and bold the text. Wrap the text in Column B. Do not change the row height.

2. After keying the table, insert a blank row after each row except the last.

3. Remove the table borders (**Format**, **Borders and Shading**, **Borders** tab, *Setting*: **None**, *Apply to:* **Table**, **OK**). Save as **50b-d1**. Print.

NOTEBOOK SECURITY GUIDELINES

Choose an easy-to-use security system.	Select a security system that is easy to use. If the security system is difficult to use and requires complicated steps, users will either not use it or look for ways to defeat it.
Assign someone to be in charge of notebook security.	One or more persons in the company should be responsible for monitoring the hardware and software on notebook computers. This person needs to be in charge of disseminating security rules and making sure that the rules are followed.
Apply several levels of security.	Different levels of security should be applied to different levels of employees. A CEO or an engineer working in the company's R & D department may be working with data that will require a higher level of security than someone in the art department. Don't bog down the artist with the high level of security needed for the CEO.
Most laptop/notebook thefts are opportunistic.	Train users to be alert and to keep an eye on their computers at all times. Remind them to use extra caution when passing through airports and staying in hotels.
Hold users responsible for their computers.	Encourage users to take precautions, and punish those who are careless by taking away laptop privileges.

Assessment

25a
Key each line twice SS.

alphabet 1 My wife helped fix a frozen lock on Jacque's vegetable bins.
figures 2 Sherm moved from 823 West 150th Street to 9472--67th Street.
double letters 3 Will Scott attempt to sell his bookkeeping books to Elliott?
easy 4 It is a shame he used the endowment for a visit to the city.
| 1 | 2 | 3 | 4 | 5 | 6 | 7 | 8 | 9 | 10 | 11 | 12 |

25b Reach Review
Key each line once; repeat.

TECHNIQUE TIP
Keep arms and hands quiet as you practice the long reaches.

n/y 5 deny many canny tiny nymph puny any puny zany penny pony yen
6 Jenny Nyles saw many, many tiny nymphs flying near her pony.

b/r 7 bran barb brim curb brat garb bray verb brag garb bribe herb
8 Barb Barber can bring a bit of bran and herbs for her bread.

c/e 9 cede neck nice deck dice heck rice peck vice erect mice echo
10 Can Cecil erect a decent cedar deck? He erects nice condos.

n/u 11 nun gnu bun nut pun numb sun nude tuna nub fun null unit gun
12 Eunice had enough ground nuts at lunch; Uncle Launce is fun.

25c Speed Check
Key two 3' writings.
Strive for accuracy.
Goal: 3', 19–27 *gwam*

all letters

gwam 3'

The term careers can mean many different things to   3 | 51
different people. As you know, a career is much more than a   8 | 55
job. It is the kind of work that a person has through life.   12 | 59
It includes the jobs a person has over time. It also involves 16 | 63
how the work life affects the other parts of our life. There 20 | 67
are as many types of careers as there are people.   23 | 71

Almost all people have a career of some kind. A career   27 | 74
can help us to reach unique goals, such as to make a living   31 | 79
or to help others. The kind of career you have will affect   35 | 83
your life in many ways. For example, it can determine where   39 | 87
you live, the money you make, and how you feel about yourself. 44 | 91
A good choice can thus help you realize the life you want.   47 | 95

3' | 1 | 2 | 3 | 4 |

49d-d2
Insert Column and Row; Merge Cells

1. Save **49d-d1** as **49d-d2**.
2. Click the insertion point in cell B1 and insert a column to the right.
3. Add the following text left-aligned in the column. Resave and print.

   Division
   Commercial
   Space Shuttle
   Military
   Commercial

4. Insert a blank row above row 1. Merge the cells in the new row 1.
5. Cut the title SAFETY AWARDS and paste it in row 1. Apply 15% shading. Save as **49d-d2b**; print.

49d-d3
Insert and Delete Rows

1. Save **49d-d2** as **49d-d3**.
2. Insert a row after Lorianna Mendez, and add the following information.

   Robert Ruiz, Research, Military, 2,250

3. Insert a row at the end of the table, and add the following information:

   Franklin Cousins, Security, Space Shuttle, 500

4. Delete the row for William Mohammed. Resave and print.

49d-d4
Table with Merge Cells

1. Create a 6-column, 10-row table. Merge the cells in rows 1 and 2 as needed.
2. Center the table vertically. Save as **49d-d4**; print.

CANADA GEOGRAPHICAL INFORMATION					
Key Islands		Key Mountains		Key Lakes	
Island	**Sq. Miles**	**Mountain**	**Height**	**Lake**	**Sq. Miles**
Baffin	195,928	Logan	19,524	Superior	31,700
Victoria	83,897	St. Elias	18,008	Huron	23,000
Ellesmere	75,767	Lucania	17,147	Great Bear	12,095
Newfoundland	42,031	Fairweather	15,300	Great Slave	11,030
Banks	27,038	Waddington	13,104	Erie	9,910
Devon	21,331	Robson	12,972	Winnipeg	9,416
Melville	16,274	Columbia	12,294	Ontario	7,540

SKILLBUILDING

25d Textbook Keying

Key each line once; DS between groups; repeat.

Key with precision and without hesitation.

```
13  is if he do rub ant go and am pan do rut us aid ox ape by is
14  it is|an end|it may|to pay|and so|aid us|he got|or own|to go
15  Did the girl make the ornament with fur, duck down, or hair?

16  us owl rug box bob to man so bit or big pen of jay me age it
17  it|it is|time to go|show them how|plan to go|one of the aims
18  It is a shame they use the autobus for a visit to the field.
    |  1  |  2  |  3  |  4  |  5  |  6  |  7  |  8  |  9  |  10  |  11  |  12  |
```

25e Figure Check

In the Open Screen, key two 1' writings and two 3' writings at a controlled speed.

all letters/figures

Goal: 3', 16–24 gwam

```
                                                           gwam   3'
                    •          4          •          8          •
        Do I read the stock market pages in the news?  Yes; and    4 | 35
    12            •         16         •         20         •
at about 9 or 10 a.m. each morning, I know lots of excited    8 | 39
    24            •         28         •         32         •
people are quick to join me.  In fact, many of us zip right   12 | 43
    36            •         40         •         44         •
to the 3d or 4th part of the paper to see if the prices of    16 | 47
    48            •         52         •         56         •
our stocks have gone up or down.  Now, those of us who are    19 | 51
    60            •         64         •         68         •
"speculators" like to "buy at 52 and sell at 60"; while the   23 | 55
    72            •         76         •         80         •
"investors" among us are more interested in a dividend we     27 | 59
    84            •         88         •         92         •
may get, say 7 or 8 percent, than in the price of a stock.    31 | 62
3' |     1     |     2     |     3     |     4     |
```

COMMUNICATION

25f Edited Copy

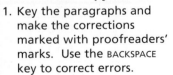

1. Key the paragraphs and make the corrections marked with proofreaders' marks. Use the BACKSPACE key to correct errors.
2. Check all number expressions and correct any mistakes that may exist.
3. Save as **xx-25f**.

Last week the healthy heart foundation relased the findings of a study that showed exercise diet and if individuals don't smoke are the major controllable factors that led to a healthy heart. Factors such as heredity can not be controlled. The study included 25 to 65 year-old males as well as females.

The study also showed that just taking a walk benefits our health. Those who walked an average of 2 to 3 hours a week were more then 30 percent less likely to have problems than those who did no exercise.

Insert and Delete Columns and Rows

Columns can be added to the left or right of existing columns. Rows can be added above or below existing rows. A row also can be added at the end of the table by clicking the insertion point in the last cell and pressing TAB.

To insert rows or columns in a table:

1. Click the insertion point where the new row or column is to be inserted. If several rows or columns are to be inserted, select the number you want to insert.
2. Choose **Insert** from the Table menu.
3. Choose **Rows Above** or **Rows Below** to insert rows. Choose **Columns to the Left** or **Columns to the Right** to insert columns.

To delete rows or columns in a table:

1. Click the insertion point in the row or column to be deleted. If you want to delete more than one row or column, you must first select them.
2. Choose **Delete** from the Table menu, and then choose **Rows or Columns**.

DRILL 2   **INSERT AND DELETE ROWS AND COLUMNS**

1. Open **49c-drill1**. Insert the information at the right so that the employees' names are in alphabetical order.

2. Delete the row containing Janice Goodman.

3. Save as **49c-drill2a**; print.

4. Delete row 1, and then place the cursor in cell B1 and insert a column to the right.

5. Key the text at the right in the new column. Left-align the text in the column. Center the text vertically in the cells.

6. Save as **49c-drill2b** and print.

| Ed Baker | Associate | 87321 | 9.3 |
| Susan Torres | Manager | 5611 | 9.8 |

Office

Wilshire

Toledo

Lake Forest

Tampa

Seattle

APPLICATIONS

49d-d1
Create Table

1. Key the table below; right-align column C. Center vertically on the page.
2. Save as **49d-d1** and print.

SAFETY AWARDS

Award Winners	Department	Amount
Lorianna Mendez	Accounting	2,000
William Mohammed	Marketing	800
Marjorie Adams	Engineering	1,500
Charles Drake	Purchasing	1,000

Skill Builders 2

 Use the Option Screen for Skill Builders 2. Save each drill as a separate file.

DRILL 1

OPPOSITE HAND REACHES

Key at a controlled rate; concentrate on the reaches.

i/e

1 ik is fit it sit laid site like insist still wise coil light
2 ed he ear the fed egg led elf lake jade heat feet hear where
3 lie kite item five aide either quite linear imagine brighter
4 Imagine the aide eating the pears before the grieving tiger.

w/o

5 ws we way was few went wit law with weed were week gnaw when
6 ol on go hot old lot joy odd comb open tool upon money union
7 bow owl word wood worm worse tower brown toward wrote weapon
8 The workers lowered the brown swords toward the wood weapon.

DRILL 2

PROOFREADERS' MARKS

Key each sentence. DS after each sentence. Make all the editing (handwritten) corrections. Print. Go on to Drill 3.

≡ Capitalize
/ Change letter
⊂ Close up space
⅄ Delete
∧ Insert
ℓ𝒸 Lowercase
Space
𝖓 Transpose

1. When a writer create the preliminary version of a document, they are concentrating on conveying the intended ideas.
2. This version of a preliminary document is called a rough.
3. After the draft is created, the Writer edits refines the copy.
4. Sometimes proofreader's marks are used to edit the draft.
6. The changes will them be make to the original. editing
7. After the changes have been made, then the Writer reads the copy.
8. Editing and proofreading requires alot of time and effort.
9. An attitude of excellence is required to produce error-free message.

DRILL 3

PROOFREADING

Compare your printout to this paragraph. How did you do? Then key the paragraph for fluency. Concentrate on keying as accurately as possible.

When a writer creates the preliminary version of a document, he or she is concentrating on conveying ideas. This preliminary version is called a rough draft. After the draft is created, the writer edits or refines the copy. Proofreaders' marks are used to edit the rough draft. The editing changes will be made to the original. Then the writer reads the copy again. Editing requires a lot of time and effort. An attitude of excellence is required to produce an error-free message.

SKILLBUILDING

49a
Warmup
Key each line twice at a controlled rate.

<table>
<tr><td>adjacent key</td><td>1</td><td>her err ire are cash free said riot lion soil join went wean news</td></tr>
<tr><td></td><td>2</td><td>sat coil riot were renew forth weed trade power grope owner score</td></tr>
<tr><td>one hand</td><td>3</td><td>him bear joy age kiln loup casts noun loop facet moon deter edges</td></tr>
<tr><td></td><td>4</td><td>get hilly are fear imply save phony taste union versa yummy wedge</td></tr>
<tr><td>balanced hand</td><td>5</td><td>oak pay hen quay rush such burp urus vial works yamen amble blame</td></tr>
<tr><td></td><td>6</td><td>cot duty goal envy make focus handy ivory lapel oriel prowl queue</td></tr>
</table>

| 1 | 2 | 3 | 4 | 5 | 6 | 7 | 8 | 9 | 10 | 11 | 12 | 13 |

49b
Timed Writing
Take two 2' timings; count errors. Take two more 2' timings. Try to reduce errors with each timing.

  all letters

	gwam	2'
Little things do contribute a lot to success in keying.	6	53
Take our work attitude, for example. It's a little thing; yet,	12	59
it can make quite a lot of difference. Demonstrating patience	18	66
with a job or a problem, rather than pressing much too hard for a	25	72
desired payoff, often brings better results than we expected.	31	79
Other "little things," such as wrist and finger position, how we	38	85
sit, size and location of copy, and lights, have meaning for	44	91
any person who wants to key well.	47	94

2' | 1 | 2 | 3 | 4 | 5 | 6 |

NEW FUNCTIONS

49c

help keywords
cell

Merge Cells

Cells can be joined horizontally or vertically by selecting the cells and then choosing the **Merge Cells** command on the Table menu or the Tables and Borders toolbar. Frequently, main and secondary headings are included in the table by merging cells in row 1 and centering the headings in the row.

To merge cells:

Select the cells to be merged. Choose **Merge Cells** from the Table menu, or click the **Merge Cells** button on the Tables and Borders toolbar.

DRILL 1   MERGE CELLS

1. Create a four-column, six-row table.

2. Select row **1** and merge the cells.

3. Key the table. Center and bold the headings.

4. Center-align column B. Right-align columns C and D.

5. Save as **49c-drill1**. Print.

EMPLOYEE RATINGS			
Employee	**Position**	**Identification**	**Rating**
Janice Goodman	Manager	3495075	8.7
Dinh Lee	Manager	732	9.1
Ralph Marshall	Associate	486028776	9.5
Frank Wiley	Associate	9376	7.6

ASSESS SKILL GROWTH:

These writings are available as Diagnostic Writings in *Keyboarding Pro*. Access Diagnostic Writings from the Numeric & Skill menu.

OPEN SCREEN OPTION:

1. Key 1' writings on each paragraph of a timing. Note that paragraphs within a timing increase by two words.

   Goal: to complete each paragraph.

2. Key a 3' timing on the entire writing.

E all letters

To access writings on *MicroPace Pro*, key **W** and the timing number. For example, key **W8** for *Writing 8*.

gwam

	1'	3'

Writing 8

Any of us whose target is to achieve success in our professional   13   4
lives will understand that we must learn how to work in harmony   26   8
with others whose paths may cross ours daily.   35   12

We will, unquestionably, work for, with, and beside people, just   13   16
as they will work for, with, and beside us. We will judge them,   26   20
as most certainly they are going to be judging us.   38   24

A lot of people realize the need for solid working relations and   13   28
have a rule that treats others as they, themselves, expect to be   26   33
treated. This seems to be a sound, practical idea for them.   40   37

Writing 9

I spoke with one company visitor recently; and she was very much   13   4
impressed, she said, with the large amount of work she had noted   26   9
being finished by one of our front office workers.   36   12

I told her how we had just last week recognized this very person   13   16
for what he had done, for output, naturally, but also because of   26   21
its excellence. We know this person has that "magic touch."   38   25

This "magic touch" is the ability to do a fair amount of work in   13   29
a fair amount of time. It involves a desire to become ever more   26   34
efficient without losing quality--the "touch" all workers should   39   38
have.   40   38

Writing 10

Isn't it great just to untangle and relax after you have keyed a   13   4
completed document? Complete, or just done? No document is   25   8
quite complete until it has left you and passed to the next step.   38   13

There are desirable things that must happen to a document before   13   17
you surrender it. It must be read carefully, first of all, for   26   22
meaning to find words that look right but aren't. Read word for   39   26
word.   40   26

Check all figures and exact data, like a date or time, with your   13   31
principal copy. Make sure format details are right. Only then,   26   35
print or remove the work and scrutinize to see how it might look   39   39
to a recipient.   42   40

1'	1	2	3	4	5	6	7	8	9	10	11	12	13
3'		1			2			3			4		

APPLICATIONS

1. Follow the Table Format Guides on page 175 when keying the tables.
2. Center each table vertically on the page.
3. Save and print.

48d-d1
Table with Shading

48d-d2
Table with Indented Lines

48d-d3
Table with Adjusted Column Width

1. Key the table. Adjust column width so that each entry fits on one line.
2. Apply 20% shading to row 1. Center the table on the page.

MAJOR SPORTS TEAMS

City	Baseball	Basketball	Football	Hockey
Detroit	Tigers	Pistons	Lions	Red Wings
Chicago	Cubs—White Sox	Bulls	Bears	Black Hawks
New York	Yanks—Mets	Knicks—Mets	Giants—Jets	Rangers
Boston	Red Sox	Celtics	Patriots	Bruins
San Francisco	Giants	Warriors	49'ers	Seals

1. Key the table below; press CTRL + TAB to indent lines. Adjust column width so each entry fits on one line.
2. Apply 20% shading to row 1; apply 10% shading to rows 2 and 5.

EFFECTS OF CRONIX ON PATIENTS

Body Systems	Cronix + Aspirin	Placebo + Aspirin
Central nervous system		
Headache	867	402
Dizziness	1,084	839
Gastrointestinal system disorders		
Abdominal pain	317	130
Dyspepsia	62	1,017
Diarrhea	64	9

1. Key the table below; adjust column width so all items fit on one line.
2. Apply 15% shading to row 1.

FREQUENTLY PRESCRIBED MEDICATIONS

Brand Name	Generic Name	Treatment
Actifed	Tripolidene-Pseudoephedrine	Decongestant
E-Mycin	Erythromycin	Antibiotic
Lanoxin	Digoxin	Abnormal heart rhythm or CHF
Prostep	Nicotine patch	Smoking addiction
Prozac	Fluoxetine	Depression

Writing 11

gwam 3'

•	4	•	8	•	12

Anyone who expects some day to find an excellent job should   4 | 34

begin now to learn the value of accuracy. To be worth anything,   8 | 38

completed work must be correct, without question. Naturally, we   13 | 43

realize that the human aspect of the work equation always raises   17 | 47

the prospect of errors; but we should understand that those same   20 | 51

errors can be found and fixed. Every completed job should carry   26 | 56

at least one stamp; the stamp of pride in work that is exemplary.   30 | 60

Writing 12

No question about it: Many personal problems we face today   4 | 34

arise from the fact that we earthlings have never been very wise   8 | 38

consumers. We haven't consumed our natural resources well; as a   13 | 43

result, we have jeopardized much of our environment. We excused   17 | 47

our behavior because we thought that our stock of most resources   20 | 51

had no limit. So, finally, we are beginning to realize just how   26 | 56

indiscreet we were; and we are taking steps to rebuild our world.   30 | 60

Writing 13

When I see people in top jobs, I know I'm seeing people who   4 | 34

sell. I'm not just referring to employees who labor in a retail   8 | 38

outlet; I mean those people who put extra effort into convincing   13 | 43

others to recognize their best qualities. They, themselves, are   17 | 47

the commodity they sell; and their optimum tools are appearance,   20 | 51

language, and personality. They look great, they talk and write   26 | 56

well; and, with candid self-confidence, they meet you eye to eye.   30 | 60

3' | 1 | 2 | 3 | 4 |

Tables and Borders Toolbar

You can change the appearance of tables by adding shading, borders, patterns, and color. You can use Table AutoFormat to apply a preformatted design to the table, or display the Tables and Borders toolbar, which provides you with many formatting options. To display this toolbar, click **View** on the menu; then click **Toolbars**, **Tables and Borders**.

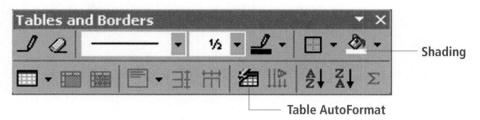

Shading

Table AutoFormat

Shading Cells

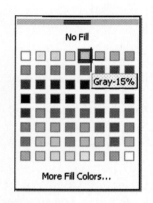

Shading can be applied to cells for emphasis. Normally, shading is applied to emphasize headings, totals, or divisions and sections of a table.

To add shading to cells:

1. Select the cells to be shaded, and click the **Shading** button on the Tables and Borders toolbar.

2. Click the down arrow, and choose a color or shade of gray. For class assignments, choose 15% gray (row 1, item 5).

Option: Choose **Borders and Shading** on the Format menu. Click on the **Shading** tab. Under Style, click the down arrow to change *Clear* to 15%; then click **OK**.

DRILL 3   SHADING

1. Open **48b-drill1**.
2. Apply 15% shading to row 1.
3. Save as **48b-drill3a** and print.

4. Open **48b-drill2a**.
5. Apply 20% shading to row 1.
6. Save as **48b-drill3b** and print.

DOCUMENT DESIGN

48c

Table Format Guides

1. Position the table (or main heading) at about 2", or center the table vertically on the page.

2. **Headings:** Center, bold, use 12-point font, and key the main heading in all caps. Key the secondary heading a DS below the main heading in bold, centered and 12-point font; capitalize main words. Center and bold all column headings.

3. Adjust column widths attractively, and center the table horizontally.

4. Increase the row height to .3" and center text vertically in the cell.

5. Align text within cells at the left. Align numbers at the right. Align decimal numbers of varying lengths at the decimal point.

6. When a table appears within a document, DS before and after the table.

To access writings on *MicroPace Pro*, key **W** and the timing number. For example, key **W14** for *Writing 14*.

Writing 14

	gwam
	1' 3'

What do you expect when you travel to a foreign country? Quite a few people realize that one of the real joys of traveling is to get a brief glimpse of how others think, work, and live.

The best way to enjoy a different culture is to learn as much about it as you can before you leave home. Then you can concentrate on being a good guest rather than trying to find local people who can meet your needs.

gwam 1' / 3':
12 / 4
23 / 8
36 / 12
40 / 12
11 / 16
24 / 20
36 / 24
44 / 27

Writing 15

	gwam
	1' 3'

What do you enjoy doing in your free time? Health experts tell us that far too many people choose to be lazy rather than to be active. The result of that decision shows up in our weight.

Working to control what we weigh is not easy, and seldom can it be done quickly. However, it is quite important if our weight exceeds what it should be. Part of the problem results from the amount and type of food we eat.

If we want to look fit, we should include exercise as a substantial part of our weight loss plan. Walking at least thirty minutes each day at a very fast rate can make a big difference both in our appearance and in the way we feel.

gwam 1' / 3':
12 / 4
24 / 8
36 / 12
37 / 13
12 / 16
24 / 21
37 / 25
44 / 27
11 / 31
23 / 35
35 / 39
47 / 42

Writing 16

	gwam
	1' 3'

Doing what we like to do is quite important; however, liking what we have to do is equally important. As you ponder both of these concepts, you may feel that they are the same, but they are not the same.

If we could do only those things that we prefer to do, the chances are that we would do them exceptionally well. Generally, we will take more pride in doing those things we like doing, and we will not quit until we get them done right.

We realize, though, that we cannot restrict the things that we must do just to those that we want to do. Therefore, we need to build an interest in and an appreciation of all the tasks that we must do in our positions.

gwam 1' / 3':
10 / 4
23 / 8
36 / 12
41 / 14
12 / 18
25 / 22
37 / 26
47 / 29
11 / 33
23 / 37
36 / 41
44 / 44

1' | 1 | 2 | 3 | 4 | 5 | 6 | 7 | 8 | 9 | 10 | 11 | 12 |
3' | 1 | | 2 | | 3 | | 4 |

Adjust Column Widths

help keywords
column; resize

Tables extend from margin to margin when they are created, regardless of the width of the data in the columns. Some tables, however, would be more attractive and easier to read if the columns were narrower. Column widths can be changed manually using the mouse or automatically using AutoFit. Using the mouse enables you to adjust the widths as you like. Once you change the width of a table, you will need to center it horizontally.

Column marker

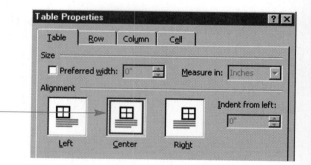

To adjust column widths using the mouse:

1. Point to the column border between the first and second columns in the table.

2. When the pointer changes to ↔, drag the border to the left to make the column narrower or to the right to make the column wider.

3. Adjust the column widths attractively. Leave approximately 0.5" to .75" between the longest line and the border. Use the Horizontal Ruler as a guide.

4. You can display the width of the columns by pointing to a column marker on the ruler, holding down the ALT key, and clicking the left mouse button.

To center a table horizontally:

1. With the insertion point in the table, choose **Table Properties** from the Table menu.

2. Click the **Table tab**, if necessary.

3. Choose the **Center** option in the Alignment box, and click **OK**.

DRILL 1 — CHANGE ROW HEIGHT, CENTER TEXT IN CELL, AND ADJUST COLUMN WIDTH

1. Open **46c-d1**.

2. Select the table. (Do not select the title or any ¶ markers outside the table.)

3. Change the row height to .3" and center the text vertically in the cell.

4. Use the mouse to manually adjust the column width of each column. Leave approximately 0.5" of blank space to the right of the longest line in each column.

5. Center the table horizontally.

6. Save as **48b-drill1** and print.

DRILL 2 — CHANGE ROW HEIGHT, CENTER TEXT IN CELL, AND ADJUST COLUMN WIDTH

1. Open **46c-d2**. Change the row height to .3" and center the text vertically in the cell. Adjust the column width and center the table horizontally. Save as **48b-drill2a**.

2. Open **46c-d3** and apply the directions in step 1. Save as **48b-drill2b**.

3. Open **46c-d4** and apply the directions in step 1. Save as **48b-drill2c**.

Writing 17

gwam   1' 3'

Many people like to say just how lucky a person is when   11   4 29
he or she succeeds in doing something well.   Does luck play a   24   8 33
large role in success?   In some cases, it might have a small   36 12 37
effect.   37 13 38

Being in the right place at the right time may help, but   11 16 41
hard work may help far more than luck.   Those who just wait for   24 20 46
luck should not expect quick results and should realize luck   36 24 50
may never come.   39 26 51

Writing 18

gwam   1' 3'

New golfers must learn to zero in on just a few social   11   4 39
rules.   Do not talk, stand close, or move around when another   23   8 44
person is hitting.   Be ready to play when it is your turn.   35 12 47

Take practice swings in an area away from other people.   11 15 51
Let the group behind you play through if your group is slow.   24 20 55
Do not rest on your club on the green when waiting your turn.   36 23 59

Set your other clubs down off the green.   Leave the green   12 27 63
quickly when done; update your card on the next tee.   Be sure   24 31 67
to leave the course in good condition.   Always have a good time.   37 36 72

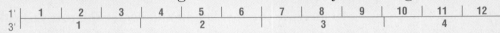

Writing 19

gwam   1' 3'

Do you know how to use time wisely?   If you do, then its   11   4 51
proper use can help you organize and run a business better.   24   8 55
If you find that your daily problems tend to keep you from   35 12 59
planning properly, then perhaps you are not using time well.   48 16 63
You may find that you spend too much time on tasks that are   60 20 67
not important.   Plan your work to save valuable time.   70 24 70

A firm that does not plan is liable to run into trouble.   12 27 74
A small firm may have trouble planning.   It is important   23 31 78
to know just where the firm is headed.   A firm may have a   35 35 82
fear of learning things it would rather not know.   To say   46 39 86
that planning is easy would be absurd.   It requires lots of   58 43 90
thinking and planning to meet the expected needs of the firm.   70 47 94

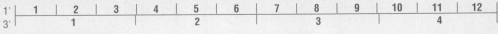

LESSON 48   Format Tables

SKILLBUILDING

48a
Warmup
Key each line twice SS.

direct reaches
1 June and my brother, Bradly, received advice from junior umpires.
2 My bright brother received minimum reward for serving many years.

adjacent reaches
3 Clio and Trey were sad that very few voters were there last week.
4 Western attire was very popular at the massive auction last week.

double letters
5 Tommie Bennett will go to a meeting in Dallas tomorrow afternoon.
6 Lee will meet Joanne at the swimming pool after accounting class.

NEW FUNCTIONS

48b

Change Row Height

The tables that were created in Lesson 46 can be made more attractive and easier to read by inserting some blank space above and below the text; this can be done by increasing the row height. Center the text vertically in the cell after increasing the row height.

Default row height

This illustrates	A table created
Using default	Row height

Increased row height

This illustrates	A table created
With increased	Row height

To increase the row height and center the text vertically in the cell:

1. Create and key the table. Turn on Show/Hide.

2. Select only the table; be careful not to select any ¶ markers outside the table. Select **Table Properties** from the Table menu.

3. Click the **Row** tab. Click the **Specify Height** checkbox. Use the spin arrows to select a row height. (See Figure 1.)

4. Click the **Cell** tab. Choose **Center Alignment** so the text will display in the middle of the cell. (See Figure 2.) Click **OK**.

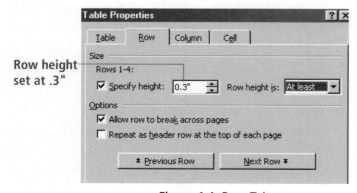

Row height set at .3"

Figure 1-1 Row Tab

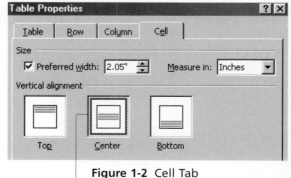

Figure 1-2 Cell Tab

Center alignment

Writings 20 and 21 are available as Diagnostic Writings.

To access writings on *MicroPace Pro*, key **W** and the timing number. For example, key **W20** for *Writing 20*.

Writing 20

	3'	5'

If asked, most people will agree that some people have far more creative skills than others, and they will also say that these skills are in great demand by most organizations. A follow-up question is in order. Are you born with creative skills or can you develop them? No easy answer to that question exists, but it is worth spending a bit of time pondering.

If creative skills can be developed, then the next issue is how can you develop these skills. One way is to approach each task with a determination to solve the problem and a refusal to accept failure. If the normal way of doing a job does not work, just keep trying things never tried before until you reach a good solution. This is called thinking outside the box.

3'	5'
4	2 | 21
8	5 | 34
12	7 | 37
17	10 | 39
21	13 | 42
24	15 | 44
28	17 | 46
32	19 | 49
37	22 | 51
41	25 | 54
45	27 | 56
49	29 | 58

```
3' |    1    |    2    |    3    |    4    |
5' |    1    |    2    |    3    |
```

Writing 21

	1'	3'

Figures are not as easy to key as many of the words we use. Balanced-hand figures such as 16, 27, 38, 49, and 50, although fairly easy, are slower to key because each one requires longer reaches and uses more time per stroke.

Figures such as 12, 45, 67, and 90 are even more difficult because they are next to one another and each uses just a single hand to key. Because of their size, bigger numbers such as 178, 349, and 1,220 create extra speed losses.

1'	3'
12	4 | 36
25	8 | 40
37	12 | 44
45	16 | 46
12	20 | 50
25	25 | 54
39	29 | 59
45	32 | 61

```
1' | 1 | 2 | 3 | 4 | 5 | 6 | 7 | 8 | 9 | 10 | 11 | 12 | 13 |
3' |   1   |     2     |     3     |     4     |
```

DRILL 5

SKILL TRANSFER

1. Set the timer for 2'. Take a 2' writing on paragraph 1. Do not save.
2. Set the timer for 2'. Take a 2' writing on paragraph 2. Do not save.
3. Take 2 or more 2' writings on the slower paragraph. Do not save.

	1'	2'

Few people attain financial success without some kind of planning. People who realize the value of prudent spending and saving are those who set up a budget. A budget helps individuals determine just how much they can spend and how much they can save so that they will not squander their money recklessly.

Keeping records is a ~~crucial~~ *vital* part of ~~a~~ *ing* budget. ~~Complete~~ *A detailed* records *of all* of income and expenses *ditures* over a period of ~~a number of~~ *serveral* months ~~can~~ *will* help ~~to~~ determine what bills, *like utilities* ~~as water~~ or rent, are *fixed* ~~static~~ and which are flexible. To get the most out of your income, *focus* ~~pay~~ attention *on* ~~to~~ the items that you can ~~modify.~~ *be changed*

1'	2'
11	6
24	12
36	18
49	24
61	31
12	6
24	12
37	18
49	25
61	30

```
1' | 1 | 2 | 3 | 4 | 5 | 6 | 7 | 8 | 9 | 10 | 11 | 12 |
2' |   1   |   2   |   3   |   4   |   5   |   6   |
```

47d-d2
Table with AutoFormat

1. Key and format the table. Position the main heading at about 2".
2. Right-align columns B, C, and D.
3. Apply **Table 3D Effects 2** style.
4. Save as **47d-d2**. Print.

words

ESTIMATES ON KITCHEN CABINETRY 6

Kitchen Component	VSP Kitchens	Designs by Pat	Euro Image	
Cabinetry	$34,475	$22,100	$38,350	24
Granite countertops	8.150	7,950	10,275	32
Halogen lighting	1,450	1,600	1,800	39
Appliances (allowance)	12,000	12,000	12,000	48
Total	$56,075	$43,650	$62,425	54

(header row words: 18)

47d-d3
Table with AutoFormat

1. Key the table. Right-align column C.
2. Apply the **Table List 8** style.
3. Center the table vertically on the page.
4. Save as **47d-d3**. Print.

words

CANADIAN PROVINCES 4

Province	Capital	Population	
Alberta	Edmonton	2,375,300	15
British Columbia	Victoria	2,889,200	22
Manitoba	Winnipeg	1,071,250	28
New Brunswick	Fredericton	710,450	34
Newfoundland	St. John's	568,350	41
Northwest Territories	Yellowknife	52,250	49
Nova Scotia	Halifax	873,200	55
Ontario	Toronto	9,113,500	60
Prince Edward Island	Charlottetown	126,650	68
Quebec	Quebec	6,540,300	73
Saskatchewan	Regina	1,010,200	79
Yukon	Whitehorse	23,500	84

(header row words: 9)

Internet Activities 1

Open Web Browser

Know your Browser

Knowing your browser includes opening the browser, opening a Web site, and getting familiar with the browser toolbar. You will also learn to set a bookmark at a favorite Web site.

Word users can quickly access the Internet while in *Word* by using the Web toolbar.

1. Display the Web toolbar by right-clicking on any toolbar and then choosing **Web** from the list of choices.

2. Open your Web browser by clicking the **Start Page** button on the Web toolbar. The Web page you have designated as your Home or Start Page displays.

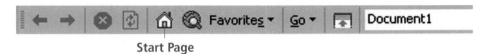

Start Page

DRILL 1

1. Begin a new *Word* document.
2. Display the Web toolbar.
3. Click the **Start Page** button to open your Web browser.

Open Web Site

With the Web browser open, click **Open** or **Open Page** from the File menu (or click the **Open** button if it is available on your browser's toolbar). Key the Web address (e.g., http://www.weather.com) and click **Open**. The Web site displays.

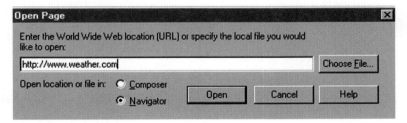

Shortcut: Click inside the Location or Address entry box, key the Web address, and press ENTER.

A **Web address** or site—commonly called the *URL* or *Uniform Resource Locator*—is composed of one or more domains separated by periods: http://www.house.gov/.

As you move from left to right in the address, each domain is larger than the previous one. In the Web address above, *gov* (United States government) is larger than *house* (House of Representatives). Other domains include educational institutions (.edu), commercial organizations (.com), military sites (.mil), and other organizations (.org).

A Web address may also include a directory path and filenames separated by slashes. In the address, the Web document named *index* provides various resources for students and faculty using Lessons 1–60 of the 15th edition of College Keyboarding. http://www.collegekeyboarding.com/fifteenth/lessons1-60/index.html

NEW FUNCTIONS

47c

Table AutoFormat

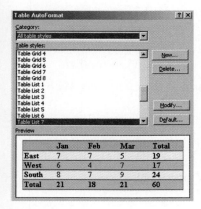

AutoFormat enables you to apply one of *Word*'s many preformatted styles to tables. You can view those styles in the Preview box. Choose a style based on the information in the table. For example, a style with shading in the last row is well suited to a table with totals.

To use AutoFormat:

1. Create the table and key the table data without formats.
2. Click the insertion point in the table, and then click the **AutoFormat** button on the Tables and Borders toolbar.
3. In the Table AutoFormat dialog box, check to see that All table styles is displayed in the Category list box; then choose a style from the Table styles list box.
4. Click **Apply** to apply the style, and return to the table.

Option: Choose Table AutoFormat from the Table menu. Continue with Step 3 above.

DRILL 1   AUTOFORMAT

1. Open **46b-drill2**.
2. Apply the Table List 4 format.

3. Save the document as **47c-drill1**.
4. Print.

APPLICATIONS

47d-d1
Table with Center Page

1. Key the table below and center it vertically on the page.
2. Save as **47d-d1**. Print.

MAJOR METROPOLITAN AREAS OF CANADA

City	Province	Population	
			7
Toronto	Ontario	3,427,250	12
			17
Montreal	Quebec	2,921,375	22
Vancouver	British Columbia	1,380,750	30
Ottawa	Ontario	819,275	34
Winnipeg	Manitoba	625,325	40
Quebec	Quebec	603,275	44
Hamilton	Ontario	557,250	49

DRILL 2

Open the following Web sites. Identify the high-level domain for each site.

1. http://www.weather.com _____
2. http://fbla-pbl.org _____
3. http://www.army.mil _____
4. http://www.senate.gov _____

DRILL 3

Open the following Web sites and identify the filenames.

1. http://www.cnn.com/TRAVEL/ _____
2. http://sports.espn.go.com/ncaa/index _____
3. http://www.usps.com/buy/welcome.htm _____

Explore the Browser's Toolbar

The browser's toolbar is very valuable when surfing the Internet. Become familiar with your browser's toolbar by studying the screen. Browsers may vary slightly.

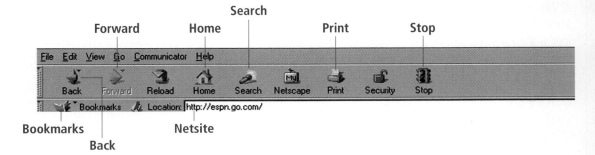

Netsite entry box	Displays the active URL or Web site address.
Back	Moves to Web sites or pages visited since opening the browser.
Forward	Moves forward to sites visited prior to using the Back button. (The Forward button is ghosted if the Back button has not been used.)
Print	Prints a Web page.
Home	Returns to the Web page designated as the Home or Start Page.
Stop	Stops computer's search for a Web site.
Search	Opens one of the Internet search engines.
Bookmarks	Moves to the list of Web sites marked for easy access.

DRILL 4

1. Open the following Web sites:
   a. http://nike.com
   b. http://realage.com
   c. http://mapquest.com
   d. A site of your choice
2. Click the **Back** button twice. The_____Web site displays.
3. Click the **Forward** button once. The_____Web site displays.
4. Print the active Web page.

SKILLBUILDING

47a
Warmup
Key each line twice.

alphabet	1	Dixie Vaughn acquired that prize job with a firm just like yours.
figures	2	By May 15 do this: Call Ext. 4390; order 472 clips and 168 pens.
easy/figures	3	The 29 girls kept 38 bushels of corn and 59 bushels of rich yams.
easy	4	The members paid half of the endowment, and their firm paid half.

| 1 | 2 | 3 | 4 | 5 | 6 | 7 | 8 | 9 | 10 | 11 | 12 | 13 |

47b
Timed Writings
Key a 3' or a 5' timing at your
control rate.

   all letters

gwam   3' | 5'

	3'	5'
You may be familiar with the expression that we live in an	4	2
information age now. People interpret this expression in a host of	8	5
diverse ways, but most people agree on two key things. The first	13	8
thing is that a huge amount of information exists today; some even	17	10
think we suffer from information overload. The second thing is that	22	13
technology has changed the way we access that huge pool of data.	26	16
Some people are quick to point out that a big difference exists	30	18
between the quantity and the quality of information. It is very	35	21
critical to recognize that anyone who has access can simply post	39	23
information on the Internet. No test exists to screen for junk	43	26
before something is posted. Some of the data may be helpful and	48	29
valid. However, much of it must be analyzed quite carefully to	52	31
judge if it is valid.	53	32
Just how do you judge if the data you have accessed is valid?	58	35
Some of the same techniques that can be used with print media can be	62	37
applied with electronic media. A good way to assess material is to	67	40
examine its source carefully. What do you know about the people who	71	42
provided this information? Is the provider ethical and qualified	75	45
to post that information? If you cannot unearth the answer to this	80	48
question, you should be wary of trusting it.	83	50

3'	1	2	3	4
5'	1	2	3	

Bookmark a Favorite Web Site

When readers put a book aside, they insert a bookmark to mark the place. Internet users also add bookmarks to mark their favorite Web sites or sites of interest for browsing later.

To add a bookmark:

1. Open the desired Web site.

2. Click **Bookmarks** and then **Add Bookmark**. (Browsers may vary on location and name of Bookmark button.)

To use a bookmark:

1. Click **Bookmarks** (or **Communicator**, **Favorites**, or **Window Bookmarks**).

2. Select the desired bookmark. Click or double-click, depending on your browser. The desired Web site displays.

DRILL 5

1. Open these favorite Web sites and bookmark them on your browser.
   a. http://www.weather.com
   b. http://www.cnn.com
   c. http://ask.com
   d. Key the Web address of a city you would like to visit (destin.com)

2. Use the bookmarks to go to the following Web sites to find answers to the questions shown.
   a. The Weather Channel—What is today's temperature in your city? _____
   b. CNN—What is today's top news story? _____
   c. Ask Jeeves. Ask a question; then find the answer. _____
   d. City Web site you bookmarked—Find one attraction in the city to visit. _____

Activity 2

Set up E-mail Addresses

Electronic mail

Electronic mail or **e-mail** refers to electronic messages sent by one computer user to another computer user. To be able to send or receive e-mail, you must have an e-mail address, an e-mail program, and access to the Internet or an intranet (in-house network).

Many search engines such as Excite, Google, Lycos, Hotbot, and others provide free e-mail via their Web sites. These e-mail programs allow users to set up an e-mail address and then send and retrieve e-mail messages. To set up an account and obtain an e-mail address, the user must (1) agree to the terms of agreement, (2) complete an online registration form, and (3) compose an e-mail name and password.

DRILL 1

1. Click the Search button on the browser's toolbar. Click a search engine that offers free e-mail.

2. Click **Free E-mail** or **Mail**. (Terms will vary.)

3. Read the Terms of Agreement and accept.

4. Enter an e-mail name. This name will be the login-name portion of your e-mail address.

5. Enter a password for your e-mail account. For security reasons, do not share your password, do not leave it where others can use it, and avoid choosing pet names or birth dates.

6. Review the entire registration form and submit it. You will be notified immediately that your e-mail account has been established. (If your e-mail name is already in use by someone else, you may be instructed to choose a different name before your account can be established.)

46c-d3
Table

1. Create a 3-column, 4-row table. Key the text in the table.
2. Place the cursor in cell C4; press the TAB key to create another blank row. Key the last row.
3. Center table vertically on the page. Save as **46c-d3**.

POMMERY SPRINGS PROJECT STATUS   *Center and Bold*

Job	Description	Date Completed
Road work	Building and grading	February 10, 200-
Drain	Adding french drain	February 25, 200-
Lot prep *aration*	Clearing and leveling	March 12, 200-

Pond   *Adding silt fence*   *March 15, 200-*   (*add row*)

46c-d4
Table

1. Position the main heading at about 2". Center main heading in all caps and bold. Key the secondary heading in title case, bold, and center.
2. Center column heads. Save as **46c-d4**. Print.

OFFICIAL BIRDS AND FLOWERS
For Selected States

State	Official Bird	Official Flower
Alaska	Willow ptarmigan	Forget-me-not
Arkansas	Mockingbird	Apple blossom
California	California valley quail	Golden poppy
Connecticut	American robin	Mountain laurel
Delaware	Blue hen chicken	Peach blossom
Georgia	Brown thrasher	Cherokee rose
Idaho	Mountain bluebird	Syringe
Illinois	Cardinal	Native violet
Louisiana	Eastern brown pelican	Magnolia
Maryland	Baltimore oriole	Black-eyed Susan
Massachusetts	Chickadee	Mayflower
Nebraska	Western meadowlark	Goldenrod
New Jersey	Eastern goldfinch	Purple violet
New Mexico	Roadrunner	Yucca
North Carolina	Cardinal	Dogwood

Send E-mail Message

To send an e-mail message, you must have the address of the computer user you want to write. Business cards, letterheads, directories, etc., now include e-mail addresses. Often a telephone call is helpful in obtaining e-mail addresses. An e-mail address includes the user's login name followed by @ and the domain (sthomas@yahoo.com)

Creating an e-mail message is quite similar to preparing a memo. The e-mail header includes TO, FROM, and SUBJECT. Key the e-mail address of the recipient on the TO line, and compose a subject line that concisely describes the theme of your message. Your e-mail address will automatically display on the FROM line.

DRILL 2

1. Open the search engine used to set up your e-mail account. Click **E-mail** or **Mail**. (Terms will vary.)

2. Enter your e-mail name and password when prompted.

E-mail Message 1

3. Enter the e-mail address of your instructor or another student. Compose a brief message describing the city you would like to visit. Mention one of the city's attractions (from Activity 1, Drill 5). Include a descriptive subject line. Send the message.

E-mail Message 2

4. Enter your e-mail address. The subject is **Journal Entry for March 29, 200-**. Compose a message to show your reflections on how keyboarding is useful to you. Share your progress in the course and your plan for improving this week. Send the message.

Respond to Messages

Replying to e-mail messages

Reading one's e-mail messages and responding promptly are important rules of netiquette (etiquette for the Internet). However, avoid responding too quickly to sensitive situations.

Forwarding e-mail messages

Received e-mail messages are often shared or forwarded to other e-mail users. Be sure to seek permission from the sender of the message before forwarding it to others.

DRILL 3

1. Open your e-mail account if it is not open.

2. Read your e-mail messages and respond immediately and appropriately to any e-mail messages received from your instructor or fellow students. Click **Reply** to answer the message.

3. Forward the e-mail message titled *Journal Entry for March 29, 200-* to your instructor.

4. Delete all read messages.

Attach a Document to an E-mail Message

Electronic files can be attached to an e-mail message and sent to another computer electronically. Recipients of attached documents can transfer these documents to their computers and then open them for use.

DRILL 4

1. Open your e-mail account if it is not open.

2. Create an e-mail message to your instructor that states your homework is attached. The subject line should include the specific homework assignment (**xx-profile**, for example).

3. Attach the file by clicking **Attach**. Use the browser to locate the homework assignment. (E-mail programs may vary.)

4. Send the e-mail message with the attached file.

APPLICATIONS

46c-d1
Table

1. Position the main heading at about 2". Key the heading using center alignment and bold; press ENTER twice. Change the alignment to left, and turn bold off.
2. Create the table using the Table button and key the information in the cells.
3. Select row 1. Bold and center-align the column headings. Center-align cells C2–C7.
4. Save the document as **46c-d1**.

KEY CONTACTS FOR BUILDING PROJECT

Contact	Title	Telephone Number
Lara G. Elkins	Architect	(420) 555-0167
James C. Weatherwax	Contractor	(317) 555-0190
Peggy R. Lancaster	Site Supervisor	(513) 555-0164
Joanna B. Breckenridge	Interior Designer	(624) 555-0137
Marshall C. Dinkins	Kitchen Consultant	(502) 555-0126
Charles Wong	Engineer	(812) 555-0171

46c-d2
Table

1. Key the heading using center alignment and bold; press ENTER twice. Change the alignment to left, and turn bold off.
2. Create the table using the Insert command on the Table menu and key the information in the cells.
3. Select row 1. Bold and center-align the column headings. Center-align cells A2–A6. Right-align cells C2–C6.
4. Key the note DS below the table.
5. Center the table vertically on the page. Save the document as **46c-d2**.

TIP

Text is keyed left aligned, unless all the items are the same length (column A); then it can be center-aligned.

Numbers are right-aligned (column C).

PERSONAL COMPUTER ACCESSORIES

Stock Number	Description	Units Available
JGC2144	4mm Transporter	5,745,000
JGC9516	DLT/TK 20-pack Transporter	19,034,100
TMA3252	Mobile Base Storage System	3,972,155
CDS4971	Casa Multimedia Storage	9,734,250
LGT8920	Optical Keyboard and Mouse	10,457

Note: Inventory as of December 31, 200-

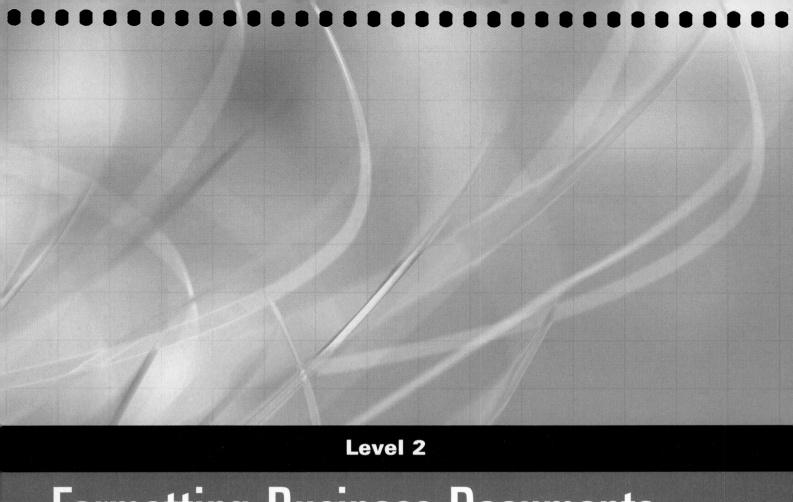

Level 2

Formatting Business Documents

OBJECTIVES

KEYBOARDING
To key about 40 *wam* with good accuracy.

DOCUMENT DESIGN SKILLS
To format accurately business letters, memos, reports, and tables.
To apply basic design skills to newsletters and announcements.

WORD PROCESSING SKILLS
To learn the basic word processing competencies.
To create, edit, and format documents efficiently.

COMMUNICATION SKILLS
To apply proofreaders' marks and revise text.
To compose simple e-mails and other documents.

Format Table, Rows, Columns, or Cells

If you wish to apply a format such as bold, alignment, or italics to the table, you must first select the table. Likewise, to format a specific row, column, or cell, you must select the table parts and then apply the format. Editing features such as delete and undo work in the usual manner. Follow these steps to select various parts of the table:

To select	Move the insertion point:
Entire table	Over the table and click the table move handle in the upper left of the table. (Option: **Table menu, Select, Table**). To move the table, drag the table move handle to a new location.
Column	To the top of the column until a solid down arrow appears; click the left mouse button.
Row	To the left area just outside the table until the pointer turns to an open arrow (◁), then click the left mouse button.

Note: You can also select rows and columns by selecting a cell, column, or row, and dragging across or down.

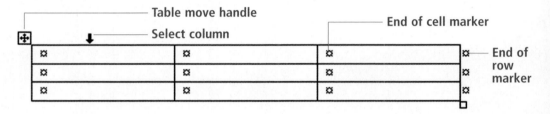

DRILL 2   CREATE TABLES

1. Center-align and key the main heading in bold; press ENTER twice.

2. Change the alignment to left and turn bold off.

3. Create a three-column, four-row table.

4. Key the table shown below; press TAB to move from cell to cell.

5. Select row 1; then bold and center-align the column headings. Row 1 is called the **header row** because it identifies the content in each column.

6. Create the folder **Module 6 keys** and save the table as **46b-drill2** in this folder.

COLLEGE SPORTS PROGRAM

Fall Events	Winter Events	Spring Events
Football	Basketball	Golf
Soccer	Gymnastics	Baseball
Volleyball	Swimming	Softball

Word Processing Basics

- Create documents.
- Save, preview, and print documents; use Help.
- Create and modify character and paragraph formats.
- Edit documents and apply communication skills.
- Build keyboarding skills.

LESSON 26 Create Documents

NEW FUNCTIONS

26a

Start Word

You are about to learn one of the leading word processing packages available today. At the same time, you will continue to develop your keyboarding skill. You will use *Microsoft Word*® to create and format professional-looking documents. *Word* will make keying documents such as letters, tables, and reports easy and fun.

When you first start *Word*, the screen appears with two windows. The left area is a blank document screen where you can enter text. The right area is called the **Task Pane**. The Task Pane provides options for opening current and and new files.

Study the illustration of the opening *Word* screen to learn the various parts of the screen.

CheckPro: If you are using *CheckPro*, it will launch or open *Microsoft Word* automatically when you choose the first activity to be done in *Word*. See instruction on page 79.

You can create tables using the Table menu or the Table button on the Standard toolbar. Either method produces the same results. Position the insertion point where you want the table to appear in the document before you begin.

To create a table using the Table menu:

1. From the Table menu, choose **Insert**; then **Table**. The Insert Table dialog box displays. The default setting of AutoFit is set to create a table with a fixed width. The columns will be of equal width and spread across the writing line.

2. Click the up or down arrows to specify the number of rows and columns. Click **OK**. The table displays.

Notice that column widths are indicated by column markers on the Ruler.

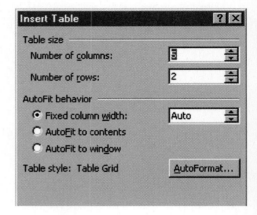

To create a table using the Insert Table button:

1. Click the **Insert Table** button on the Standard toolbar. A drop-down grid displays.

2. Click the left mouse button, and drag the pointer across to highlight the number of columns in the table and down to highlight the number of rows in the table. The table displays when you release the left mouse button.

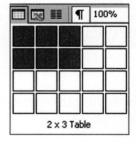

Move Within a Table

When a table is created, the insertion point is in cell A1. To move within a table, use the TAB key or simply click within a cell using the mouse. Refer to this table as you learn to enter text in a table:

Press	Movement
TAB	To move to the next cell. If the insertion point is in the last cell, pressing TAB will add a new row.
SHIFT + TAB	To move to the previous cell.
ENTER	To increase the height of the row. If you press ENTER by mistake, press BACKSPACE to delete the line.

DRILL 1   **CREATE TABLES**

1. Create a two-column, five-row table using the Table menu.

2. Turn on **Show/Hide** and notice the marker at the end of each cell and each row. Hold down the ALT key, and click on one of the column markers on the ruler. Notice that the width of the column is displayed in inches (2.93").

3. Close the table without saving it.

4. Create a four-column, four-row table using the Table button on the Standard toolbar.

5. Move to cell B3. Move to cell B2.

6. Move to cell A1 and press ENTER.

7. Move to cell D4 and press TAB.

8. Close the table without saving it.

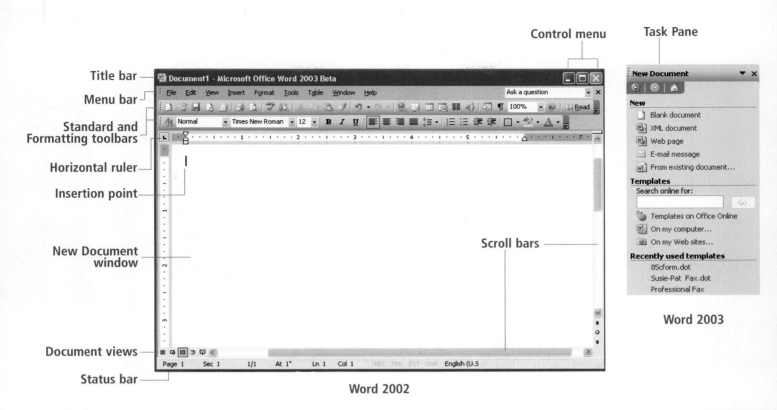

Word 2002

Word 2003

Word 2003 standard toolbar

Start Reading button

Title bar	Displays the names of the application and document that are currently open.
Control menu	Buttons that size (enlarge or shrink) and close a window. Buttons include Minimize, Restore, and Close.
Menu bar	Displays drop-down menus from which commands can be selected.
Standard and Formatting toolbars	Display buttons that provide access to common commands. The name of each button displays when you point to it.
Horizontal ruler	Displays the margins, tabs, and indents.
New Document window	A blank area on the screen where you can enter text.
Task Pane	Displays options for opening files and creating new documents.
Insertion point	Blinking vertical line that shows where the text you key will appear. Moving the pointer with the mouse does not move the insertion point until you click the mouse.
Document views	Display documents in four views: Normal, Print Layout, Outline, and Web Layout.
Scroll bars	Enable you to move rapidly through documents.
Status bar	Displays information about the document such as page number and position of the insertion point.
Taskbar	Displays the Start button and whatever programs are currently running.

Table Basics

- Create tables.
- Format tables using the Tables toolbar and AutoFormat.
- Edit table and cell structure.
- Build keying speed and accuracy.

LESSON 46   Create Tables

46a
Warmup
Key each line twice.

alphabetic	1	Jim Ryan was able to liquefy frozen oxygen; he kept it very cold.
figures	2	Flight 483 left Troy at 9:57 a.m., arriving in Reno at 12:06 p.m.
direct reaches	3	My brother served as an umpire on that bright June day, no doubt.
easy	4	Ana's sorority works with vigor for the goals of the civic corps.

| 1 | 2 | 3 | 4 | 5 | 6 | 7 | 8 | 9 | 10 | 11 | 12 | 13 |

NEW FUNCTIONS

46b

help keywords
tables; create a table

Create Tables

Tables consist of columns and rows of data—either alphabetic, numeric, or both.

Column: Vertical list of information labeled alphabetically from left to right.

Row: Horizontal list of information labeled numerically from top to bottom.

Cell: An intersection of a column and a row. Each cell has its own address consisting of the column letter and the row number (cell A1).

Use Show/Hide to display end-of-cell marks in each cell and end-of-row marks at the end of each row. End-of-cell and end-of-row markers are useful when editing tables. Use Print Layout View to display the table move handle in the upper left of the table and the Sizing handle in the lower right of the table.

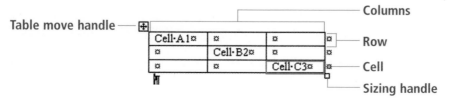

Wordwrap and Entering Text

When you key text, it is entered at the insertion point (the blinking vertical bar). When a line is full, the text automatically moves to the next line. This feature is called **wordwrap.** To begin a new paragraph, press ENTER. To indent the first line of a paragraph to the first default tab, press the TAB key.

To change or edit text, you must move the insertion point around within the document. You can move to different parts of the document by using the mouse or the keyboard. To use the mouse, move the I-beam pointer to the desired position and click the left mouse button. You can also use the arrow keys on the keyboard to move the insertion point to a different position.

DRILL 1   ENTER TEXT

1. Click the **Start** button at the bottom of the screen. Point to **All Programs**; then click **Microsoft Word**.

2. If the opening *Word* screen does not fill your entire screen, click the **Maximize** button.

3. Key the text that follows using wordwrap. Press ENTER twice only at the ends of paragraphs to DS between paragraphs. Ignore any red and green wavy lines that may appear under text as you key.

4. Using the mouse, move the insertion point immediately before the *S* at the beginning of the document.

5. Key your name. Press ENTER four times. Notice that paragraph 1 moves down four lines.

6. Keep the document on the screen for the next drill.

Use wordwrap.

Serendipity, a new homework research tool from Information Technology Company, is available to subscribers of the major online services via the World Wide Web. **(Press** ENTER **two times.)**

Offered as a subscription service aimed at college students, Serendipity is a collection of tens of thousands of articles from major encyclopedias, reference books, magazines, pamphlets, and Internet sources combined into a single searchable database. **(Press** ENTER **two times.)**

Serendipity puts an electronic library right at students' fingertips. The program offers two browse-and-search capabilities. Users can find articles by entering questions in simple question format or browse the database by pointing and clicking on key words that identify related articles. For more information, call 800-555-0174 or address e-mail to lab@serendipity.com.

Menu Bar Commands

The commands available in *Word* are listed in menus located on the menu bar at the top of your screen. The names of the menus indicate the type of commands they contain. You can execute all commands using the proper menu. When you click an item on the menu bar, a menu cascades or pulls down and displays the available commands. Note that common shortcuts including toolbar buttons and keyboard commands are provided when appropriate. The File menu that follows illustrates the main characteristics of pull-down menus.

DRILL 2

**PROOFREADING
AND EDITING**

Key the drill making all
necessary corrections. Save
as **proofreading-drill2**.

First impressions does count, and you never get a second
chance to make a good first impression. This statement applys
too both documents and people. The minute you walk in to a
room you are judged by you appearance, your facial expressions,
and the way you present your self. As soon as a document is
opened, it is judged by it's appearance and the way it is
presented. First impressions are often lasting impressions
therefore you should strive to make a positive first impression for
yourself and for the documents you prepare. Learn to manage
your image and the image of your documents.

DRILL 3

**PROOFREADING
FOR CONSISTENCY**

1. Open the data file **linger** from the Communication Skills folder.

2. Proofread the letter for consistency in usage, facts, and format (block letter style). Verify
   information against the price list below. Make corrections. Use today's date for the
   letter and your name for the writer's. Save the letter as **proofreading-drill3**.

COMPUTERS AND PRINTERS		
Product	**Manufacturer**	**Price**
Workstation 2010	**Chimera**	**$2,779**
550MHz processor, 19" monitor, 64GB RAM, 9.1GB hard drive, 7 x 24 dedicated workstation, 40X variable CD-ROM drive		
Vista XBT	**Chimera**	**2,299**
550MHz processor, 19" monitor, 128MB RAM, 9.1GB hard drive, Concord 2000 Office Suite, 40X variable CD-ROM drive		
Amina Optima	**Finn**	**2,199**
366MHz processor, 15" XGA active matrix display, 64MB RAM, 6.4GB hard drive, latest Capstone Office Suite, 20X variable CD-ROM/floppy drive		
Winger Laser Printer	**Primat**	**399**
600 dpi, 125-sheet input tray, 8 ppm		
Ink Jet Color Printer	**Primat**	**299**
Up to 600 dpi, 100-sheet input tray, 6 ppm, up to 16 million colors		
AZ Printer/Copier/Scanner	**Ventura**	**499**
600 dpi, 150-sheet input tray, 8 ppm, scans directly to e-mail, integrated desktop software for organizing scanned documents, OCR software for text editing		

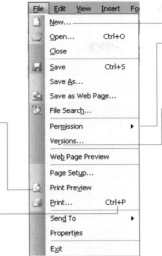

Ellipsis (...): indicates dialog box will display.

Arrow: indicates additional commands are available.

Bold: indicates the command can be used.

Dimmed command: indicates the command cannot be used.

Underlined letter: activates a command when keyed.

Files: List of files most recently opened.

Bottom chevrons ⌄: indicates additional commands are available.

Toolbar button: indicates button to click to activate a command.

Keyboard shortcut: activates a command when keys are pressed.

Toolbar Commands

Frequently used commands also can be accessed using the buttons on the Standard and Formatting toolbars. Whenever you use *Word*, make sure that both toolbars are displayed, with the Standard toolbar on top of the Formatting toolbar. If either toolbar is missing or other toolbars display, change the display following these steps. ✳ See Discover box at left.

Chevrons

To display or hide a toolbar:

1. Position the mouse pointer over any toolbar and click the right mouse button; a shortcut menu appears listing all of the toolbars that are available. (*Option:* Click **View** on the menu bar; then click **Toolbars**.)

2. Click to the left of **Standard** or **Formatting**, placing a check mark next to its name. The toolbar displays. If toolbars other than the Standard or Formatting toolbars are displayed, click the toolbar name to remove the checkmark and hide the toolbar.

3. To display the Task Pane, click **Task Pane** on the View menu: To close it, click the **Close** button at the upper-right corner of the Task Pane.

DRILL 2   COMMANDS

1. Check that the Standard and Formatting toolbars are the only ones that are displayed and that they each display on a separate row.

2. Point to several buttons on the Standard and Formatting toolbars. Notice the name of each button as it displays.

3. Click **File** on the menu bar. Point to the arrow at the bottom of the File menu, and click the left mouse button to display additional commands. If there is no arrow at the bottom of the File menu, then your entire menu is already displayed.

4. Click **Edit** on the menu bar. Note that *Cut* is dimmed. A dimmed command is not available; making it available requires another action.

5. Click **File** on the menu bar again. Note that the Save As command is followed by an ellipsis (...). Click **Save As** to display the Save As dialog box. Click **Cancel** to close the Save As dialog box.

6. Click each of the different View buttons on the status bar. Notice that a button is highlighted when that view is active. Return to Normal view. ▤

Communication Skills 2

Proofreading Guides

The final and important step in producing a document is proofreading. Error-free documents send the message the organization is detail-oriented and competent. Apply these procedures when producing any document.

1. Check spelling using the Spelling feature.

2. Proofread the document on the screen. Be alert for words that are spelled correctly but are misused, such as *you/your*, *in/on*, *of/on*, *the/then*, etc.

3. Check the document for necessary parts for correctness; be sure special features are present if needed—for example, in a letter, check for the enclosure or copy notation.

4. View the document on screen to check placement. Save and print.

These additional steps will make you a better proofreader:

5. Try to allow some time between writing a document and proofreading it.

6. If you are reading a document that has been keyed from a written draft, place the two documents next to each other and use guides to proofread the keyed document line by line against the original.

7. Proofread numbers aloud or with another person.

Proofreading for consistency is another important part of preparing documents. Consistency in style or tone, usage, facts, and format conveys an impression of care and attention to detail that reflects well on the writer and his or her organization. In contrast, lack of consistency gives an impression of carelessness and inattention to detail. Lack of consistency also makes documents more difficult to read and understand.

Proofreading statistical copy is extremely important. As you proofread, double-check numbers whenever possible. For example, verify dates against a calendar and check computations with a calculator. Remember these tips for proofreading numbers.

- Read numbers in groups. For example, the telephone number 618-555-0123 can be read in three parts: **six-one-eight, five five-five, zero-one-two-three**.

- Read numbers aloud.

- Proofread numbers with a partner.

DRILL 1

PROOFREADING

1. Open the data file **proof-it** from the Communication Skills folder and print it. Use proofreaders' marks to mark corrections. The letter contains ten mistakes; two in formatting, two in capitalization, two in number use, and four in spelling or keying.

2. Revise the letter, format it correctly, and save it as **proofreading-drill1**.

Save/Save As

Saving a document preserves it so that it can be used again. If a document is not saved, it will be lost once the computer is shut down. It is a good idea to save a document before printing. The first time you save a document, you must give it a filename. Filenames should accurately describe the document. In this course, use the exercise number as the filename (for example, **26b-drill4**).

The Save As command on the File menu is used to save a new document or to rename an existing document. The Save As dialog box contains a Save In list box, a File Name list box, and a Files of Type list box. The Save As dialog box may either be blank or display a list of files that have already been saved.

Word makes it easy to create a new folder when a file is saved. A folder would be created for storing related files. The Create New Folder button is located near the top of the Save As dialog box.

To save a new document:

1. Click the **Save** button on the Standard toolbar. (*Option:* Click **File** on the menu; then click **Save As**.) The Save As dialog box displays.

2. If necessary, change the folder or drive in the Save In box. Use the down arrow to locate the desired drive.

3. To save the document in a new folder, click the **Create New Folder** button at the top of the dialog box. Key the folder name (for example, **Module 3**).

4. Key the filename in the File Name text box.

5. Click the **Save** button or press ENTER. *Word* automatically adds the file extension **.doc** to the filename. This extension identifies the document as a *Word* document.

Word 2003

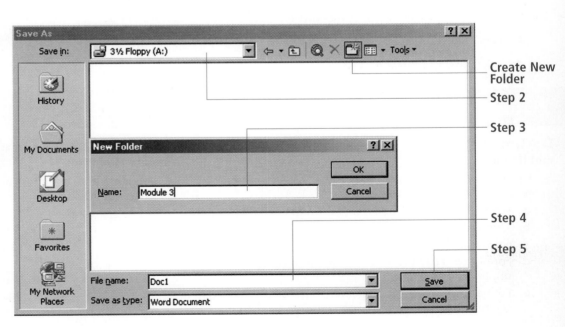

Word 2002

Module 5: Checkpoint

Answer the questions below to see if you have mastered the content of Module 5.

Part A:

1. Margins for unbound reports are _____ side margins, _____ top margin (first page), _____ top margin (second page), and _____ bottom margin.

2. To set margins, choose _____ from the _____ menu.

3. Use ____ -point font for main headings. Use _____-point for side headings.

4. The _____ format displays the first line of text at the left margin and indents all other lines to the first tab.

5. To prevent a side heading from printing at the bottom of a page, apply _____.

6. To number the pages of a multipage report, choose _____ from the _____ menu.

7. Page numbers are positioned at the _____.

8. Long quotatons are _____-spaced and indented _____" from the left margin.

Part B: Study each format below. Circle the correct format.

9. Which of the following illustrates a hanging indent format?

   A Bruce, Lawrence A. The Report Guide: Selected Form and Style. Boise:
         State of Idaho Press, 2000.

   B   Bruce, Lawrence A. The Report Guide: Selected Form and Style. Boise:
   State of Idaho Press, 2000.

10. Which of the following illustrates correct formatting of main heading?

   A ELECTRONIC MAIL USAGE

   B Electronic Mail Usage

Performance Assessment

Document 1
Edit Report

1. Open **checkpoint5** from the data files. Make the edits below and save as **checkpoint5-d1**.
   a. Position the main heading and format it correctly.
   b. Format the side headings correctly.
   c. Format the report as a DS, unbound report.
   d. Format correctly the two long quotations that are displayed in red font.
   e. Format the references in hanging indent format. Begin references on a separate page. Position the first line correctly.
   f. Insert page numbers. Suppress the number on the first page.

Document 2
Prepare Title Page

1. Prepare a title page for **checkpoint5-d1**. Save as **checkpoint5-d2**.

   Prepared for
   Mr. Derrick Novorot, President
   Altman Corporation
   388 North Washington Street
   Starkville, MS 39759

   Prepared by
   Your Name, Communication Consultant
   Your Street Address
   Your City, State ZIP Code

1. The document you keyed in Drill 1 should be displayed. If you are saving your files to a disk, insert a disk into Drive A or save to another location as directed by your instructor.

2. Click the **Save** button. The Save As dialog box displays.

3. Click the arrow in the Save In list box to locate the drive you will use. Point to Drive A to highlight it; then click the left mouse button to select it.

4. Click the **Create New Folder** button. The New Folder dialog box displays. Key the name **Module 3 Keys** in the text box; then click **OK**.

5. With the insertion point in the File Name text box, key **26a-drill3** as the filename.

6. Check to see that the default (*Word Document*) is displayed in the Files of Type list box. If not, click the down arrow and select **Word Document**.

7. Click the **Save** button or press ENTER to close the dialog box and return to the document window.

8. Keep the document on the screen for the next drill.

Print Preview

Print Preview enables you to see how a document will look when it is printed. Use Print Preview to check the layout of your document, such as margins, line spacing, and tabs, before printing.

To preview a document:

1. Click **Print Preview** on the Standard toolbar. A full-page version of the document displays. Print Preview displays the page where the insertion point is located.

2. Click **Close** to return to the document screen.

In Print Preview, a special toolbar displays with additional options for viewing the document. For example, when you click on the Magnifier button, the mouse pointer changes to a magnifying glass. When you click the magnifying glass on the page, you can see a portion of the document at 100%. Change the zoom percentage to view the document at a different size.

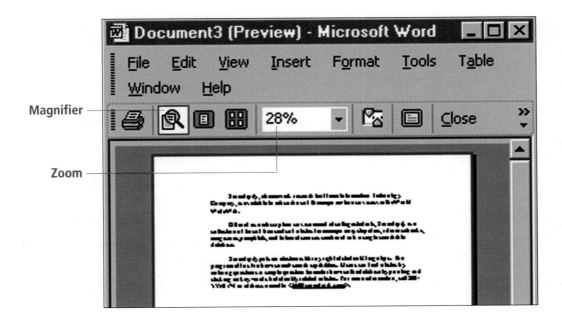

Magnifier

Zoom

Copyright Laws

To avoid copyright infringement, the Internet user must be knowledgeable about copyright law. Two important laws include The Copyright Law of 1976 and the Digital Millennium Copyright Act, which was enacted in 1998 to update the copyright law for the digital age. Zielinski (1999, 40) explains that under the Copyright Law of 1976:

Copyright is automatic when an original work is first 'fixed' in a tangible medium of expression. That means material is protected by copyright at the point when it is first printed, captured on film, drawn, or saved to hard drive or disk. . . . The farsighted statute covers fixed works 'now known or later developed'.

Insert the file copyright here.

REFERENCES

Lee, John E. "Technology Aids in Stopping Copyright Offenders." *Hopper* *Business Journal*, Fall 2000: http://www.hpj.edu/technologyaids.htm (26 December 2000).

Zielinski, Dave. "Are You a Copyright Criminal?" *Presentations*, Vol. 13, No. 6, June 1999, 36-46.

45c-d2
Unbound Report

1. Open **present** from the data files. Save it as **45c-d2**.
2. Convert this leftbound report to an unbound report.
3. Format main and side headings correctly. Position the main heading on the correct line.
4. Number the pages at the top right; suppress page number on the first page.
5. Be alert to a widow line on page 1.

45c-d3
Title Page for Leftbound Report

1. Prepare a title page for the leftbound report prepared in **45c-d1**.
2. The report is prepared for **Webb & Morse Company Employees** by **Your Name, Information Technology Manager**.
3. Save the document as **45c-d3**.

Print

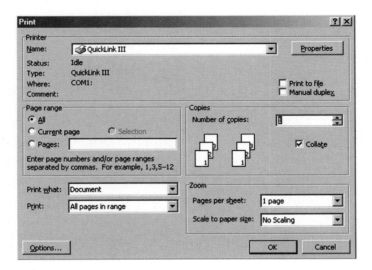 You can print a document by clicking Print on the File menu or by clicking the Print button on the Standard toolbar. Clicking the Print button immediately prints the document using all of the default settings. To view or change the default settings, click **Print** on the File menu or use the keyboard shortcut CTRL + P to display the Print dialog box.

DRILL 4   PREVIEW AND PRINT

1. The document **26a-drill3** should be displayed on your screen.

2. Click the **Print Preview** button to view your document.

3. Change the magnification to **75%**; then change it to **Whole Page**.

4. Click the **Close** button to return to Normal view.

5. Check to be sure that your printer is turned on and has paper.

6. Click **File** on the menu bar, and then click **Print**. Compare your dialog box with the one above. Your printer name may differ, but other choices should be the same. Verify that you will print one copy, and then click **OK**.

Close

 **Close** clears the screen of the document and removes it from memory. You will be prompted to save the document before closing if you have not saved it or to save your changes if you have made any to the document since the previous save. It is necessary to close each document that is open.

To close a document, do one of the following:

- Click **File** on the menu bar; then click **Close**.
- Click the **Close** button at the right side of the Menu bar.

1. Key this leftbound report DS. Align bulleted items with the other paragraphs.
2. Number the pages at the top right; suppress the page number on the first page.
3. Insert the file **copyright** from the data files where indicated in the report.
4. Key the references on a separate references page at the end of the report.
5. Save the report as **45c-d1**.

words

COPYRIGHT LAW IN THE INTERNET AGE

7

Copyright owners continue to face copyright challenges as   19
technology advances more rapidly than ever before. History shows us that   34
copyright infringements occur at the introduction of each new invention or   49
emerging technology. Examples include the phonograph and tape recorder   63
and mimeograph and copy machines. Today, the Internet age provides   76
Internet users the ease of copying and distributing electronic files via the   92
Internet.   94

Copyright owners of content published on the Web, photographers   107
who view their photographs on Web pages, and recording artists whose   121
music is downloaded from the Internet are only a few examples of   134
copyright issues resulting from the Internet age. Compounding the issue   148
is that many Internet users may not be aware they are violating copyright   163
law (Zielinski, 1999, 38). The following list shows actions taken daily that   179
are considered copyright infringements: 187

- Copying content from a Web page and pasting it into documents.   200

- Reproducing multiple copies of a journal article that were   214
  printed from an online journal.   219

- Distributing presentation handouts that contain cartoon   233
  characters or other graphics copied from a Web page.   241

- Presenting originally designed electronic presentations that   255
  contain graphics, sound and video clips, and/or photographs   269
  copied from a Web page.   271

- Duplicating and distributing copies of music downloaded from   284
  the Web.   286

New

When all documents have been closed, *Word* displays a blank screen. To create a new document, click the **New Blank Document** button on the Standard toolbar.

Open

Any documents that have been saved can be opened and used again. When you open a file, a dialog box displays the names of folders or files within a folder. You can also select files saved on a disk.

To open a document:

1. Click the **File** menu. If the document name is shown in the list of files, click it to open the document. If it is not listed, click **Open** to display the Open dialog box. (*Option*: Click the **Open** button on the toolbar.)

2. In the Look In box, click the down arrow; then click the drive where your files are stored (Drive A).

3. If necessary, double-click the folder name to display the filenames. Click the desired filename; then click **Open**.

Exit

Exit saves all documents that are on the screen and then quits the software. When you exit *Word*, you close both the document and the program window. You will be prompted to save before exiting if you have not already saved the document or if you have made changes to it since last saving. Click the **Close** button in the title bar (top bar) to exit *Word*.

DRILL 5   CLOSE AND OPEN A DOCUMENT

1. Close the file **26a-drill3** that you saved in Drill 3.

2. Click **New Blank Document** on the Standard toolbar.

3. Close the blank document.

4. Click **Open** on the Standard toolbar, and open the file **26a-drill3**.

5. Click **Save As** on the File menu. In the Save As dialog box, save the file again as **26a-drill5**. Leave the document on the screen for the next drill.

LESSON 45   Assessment

SKILLBUILDING

45a
Warmup
Key each line twice SS.

one-hand sentences
1 In regard to desert oil wastes, Jill referred only minimum cases.
2 Carra agrees you'll get a reward only as you join nonunion races.
3 Few beavers, as far as I'm aware, feast on cedar trees in Kokomo.
4 Johnny, after a few stewed eggs, ate a plump, pink onion at noon.
5 A plump, aged monk served a few million beggars a milky beverage.

| 1 | 2 | 3 | 4 | 5 | 6 | 7 | 8 | 9 | 10 | 11 | 12 | 13 |

45b
Timed Writings
Key one 3' timing and one 5' timing.

  all letters

	gwam	3'	5'

How is a hobby different from a business? A very common way to describe the difference between the hobby and the business is that the hobby is done for fun, and the business is done as work which enables people to earn their living. Does that mean that people do not have fun at work or that people do not work with their hobbies? Many people would not agree with that description.

Some people begin work on a hobby just for fun, but then they realize it has the potential to be a business. They soon find out that others enjoy the hobby as well and would expect to pay for the products or services the hobby requires. Many quite successful businesses begin as hobbies. Some of them are small, and some grow to be large operations.

gwam 3' | 5'
4 | 2 | 32
8 | 5 | 35
13 | 8 | 38
17 | 10 | 40
22 | 13 | 43
26 | 15 | 45
30 | 18 | 48
34 | 21 | 51
39 | 23 | 53
43 | 26 | 56
48 | 29 | 59
49 | 30 | 60

3' | 1 | 2 | 3 | 4
5' | 1 | 2 | 3

APPLICATIONS

45c
Assessment

 Continue

 Check

With CheckPro: *CheckPro* will keep track of the time it takes you to complete the entire production test and compute your speed and accuracy rate on each document and summarize the results. When you complete a document, proofread it, check the spelling, and preview for placement. When you are completely satisfied with the document, click the **Continue** button to move to the next document. You will not be able to return and edit a document once you continue to the next document. Click the **Check** button when you are ready to error-check the test. Review and/or print the document analysis results.

Without CheckPro: On the signal to begin, key the documents in sequence. When time has been called, proofread all documents again; identify errors, and determine *g-pwam*.

$$g\text{-}pwam = \frac{\text{total words keyed}}{25'}$$

You may choose to use *CheckPro* for Lesson 26. To complete exercises in *CheckPro*, follow these steps:

1. Open *CheckPro* and choose Lesson 26.

2. Select the exercise to be completed from the Lesson menu. Whenever the exercise is to be completed in *Word*, *CheckPro* automatically opens *Word*.

3. Key the document as directed in your textbook.

4. When you are finished with the document, click the check mark button on the *CheckPro* toolbar in the upper-right corner. *CheckPro* will automatically check your document for speed and accuracy and save your document.

5. If you wish to save a document without checking it for accuracy, click the **Back** button. You will be able to open the document at a later time.

APPLICATIONS

26b-d1
Create a
New Document

1. Start *Microsoft Word*.

2. Key the paragraphs using wordwrap. Press ENTER twice between paragraphs to create a double space

3. Save the document as **26b-d1**. Print; then close the document.

In Lesson 26, I have learned the basic operations of my word processing software. Today I opened the word processor, created a new document, saved the document, printed the document, closed the document, and exited the software. This new document that I am creating will be named 26b-d1. I will save it so that I can use it in the next lesson to open an existing document.

(Press ENTER two times)

Learning basic word processing functions at the same time I improve my keyboarding skills is easy and fun. The toolbar functions provide a quick way to apply functions.

26b-d2
Create a
New Document

1. In a new document, key the text below using wordwrap. Press TAB to indent the first line of each paragraph. Double-space (DS) between paragraphs.

2. Save the document as **26b-d2** and print. Close the document. Then exit *Word*.

As the man says, "I have some good news and some bad news." Let me give you the bad news first. **(Press ENTER two times)**

Due to a badly pulled muscle, I have had to withdraw from the Eastern Racquetball Tournament. As you know, I have been looking forward to the tournament for a long time, and I had begun to hope that I might even win it. I've been working hard.

That's the bad news. The good news is that I have been chosen to help officiate, so I'll be coming to Newport News anyway. In fact, I'll arrive there a day earlier than I had originally planned.

So, put the racquet away, but get out the backgammon board. I'm determined to win something on this trip!

Set DS; Press ENTER 3 times

About 2"

PLANNING A SUCCESSFUL PRESENTATION

Presenters realize the need to prepare for a successful presentation. Two areas of extensive preparation are the development of a thorough audience analysis and a well-defined presentation purpose.

Audience Analysis

1.5" The presenter must conduct a thorough audience analysis before developing the presentation. The profile of the audience includes the following demographics.[1]   1.25"

Align bullet
with paragraphs

- Age and gender
- Education
- Ethnic group
- Marital status
- Geographic location
- Group membership

Interviews with program planners and organization leaders will provide insight into the needs, desires, and expectations of the audience. This information makes the difference in preparing a presentation that is well received by the audience.

Purpose of the Presentation

After analyzing the audience profile, the presenter has a clear focus on the needs of the audience and then writes a well-defined purpose of the presentation. With a clear focus, the presenter confidently conducts research and organizes a presentation that is on target. The presenter remembers to state the purpose in the introduction of the presentation to assist the audience in understanding the well-defined direction of the presentation.

12 point font ⟶ _____

[1]Susie Phelan, *Presentations*. (Indianapolis: King Press, 2002), p. 38.

NEW FUNCTIONS

27a

Navigate in a Document

The document window displays only a portion of a page at one time. The keyboard, mouse, and scroll bars can be used to move quickly through a document to view it. To move to the end of a document, press CTRL + END. To move to the beginning of a document, press CTRL + HOME.

Scroll Bars

To move through the document using the mouse, use the scroll bars. The vertical scroll bar enables you to move up and down through a document. The horizontal scroll bar enables you to move left and right across a line. Scrolling does not change the position of the insertion point, only your view of the document.

To scroll	Click
Up or down	Scroll bar and drag or click Up and Down arrows
Up one screen	Above the scroll box
Down one screen	Below the scroll box
To a specific page	Drag the vertical scroll box and watch for page number
Left or right	Scroll bar and drag or click arrows

Select Text

To make any formatting changes to existing text, you must first select the text you want to change. Selected text is highlighted in black. An easy way to select text is to click at the beginning of the text and drag the mouse over the text. You can also double-click a word to select it or triple-click within a paragraph to select the whole paragraph. To deselect text, click anywhere outside of the selected text.

DRILL 1   **NAVIGATE AND SELECT TEXT**

1. Open the file you created in Lesson 26, **26b-d1.**

2. Move to the end of the document (CTRL + END).

3. Move to the top of the document (CTRL + HOME).

4. Select the first sentence; then deselect it.

5. Scroll down to the last sentence and select the word **.Microsoft**. toolbar

6. Move to the top of the document (CTRL + HOME), and key your name followed by a DS.

7. Save the document as **27a-drill1**; then close it.

DOCUMENT DESIGN

44e

Leftbound report

The binding on a report usually takes about 0.5" inch of space. Therefore, when a report is bound on the left, set the left margin to 1.5" for all pages.

The same right, top, and bottom margins are used for both unbound and leftbound reports.

APPLICATIONS

44f-d1
Leftbound Report

1. Key the leftbound report on page 158. Save the report as **44f-d1**.
2. To create the bulleted list, key the items; then select the items and apply bullets.
3. With the items selected, click the **Increase Indent** button to align the bullets with the paragraph indent.

44f-d2
Title Page

1. Create a title page for the leftbound report prepared in Document 1. Set the left margin at 1.5".
2. Prepare the title page for **John E. Swartsfager, Marketing Director**, by you as the **Information Technology Manager**.
3. Save the document as **44f-d2**.

44f-d3
Leftbound Report

1. Open **39e-d2** and format the document as a leftbound report.
2. Insert page numbers. Do not print page number on first page.
3. Add the last paragraph shown below, and save the document as **44f-d3**.

Summary

Remember to plan your page layout with the three basic elements of effective page design. Always include sufficient white space to give an uncluttered appearance. Learn to add bold when emphasis is needed, and do consider your audience when choosing typestyles. Finally, use typestyles to add variety to your layout, but remember, no more than two typestyles in a document.

44f-d4
Leftbound Report

1. Reformat report **43e-d2** as an unbound report.
2. Change the numbered list to a bulleted list.
3. Preview the document for correct pagination; then save it as **44f-d4**.

Character Formats

Character formats apply to letters, numbers, and punctuation marks and include such things as bold, underline, italic, fonts, and font sizes. The Formatting toolbar provides an efficient way to apply character formats. Formatting toolbar buttons also make it easy to align text.

Font style   Font size

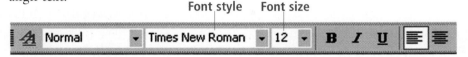

To apply character formats as you key:

1. Click the appropriate format button, and key the text to be formatted.
2. When you finish keying the formatted text, click the same button again to turn off the format. Notice that a format button is highlighted when the feature is on.

To apply character formats to existing text:

1. Select the text.
2. Click the appropriate format button.

Font Size and Styles

Word's default font is 12-point Times New Roman. Font size is measured in points. One vertical inch equals 72 points. Most text is keyed in a 10-, 11-, or 12-point font, although a larger font may be used to emphasize headings. *Word* has a variety of font styles available.

To change font size:

1. Select the text to be changed.
2. Click the **Font Size** down arrow.
3. Scroll through the list of available sizes, and click the desired font size.

To change font style:

1. Select the text to be changed.
2. Click the **Font** down arrow.
3. Scroll through the list of available styles, and click the desired style.

TIP

You can also change font size and formats by choosing **Format** on the menu bar, and then choosing **Fonts** to display the Font dialog box.

DRILL 1   FOOTNOTES

1. Key the paragraph in Drill 2 DS, and add the three footnotes.
2. Format footnotes in 12 point and DS between them.

3. Include all three sources on a separate references page in proper reference format. Select the title *References* and format it in 14 pt., bold, centered.
4. Save as **44d-drill1** and print.

DRILL 2   DELETE FOOTNOTES

1. Open **44d-drill1**. Delete the second footnote. Update the references page.

2. Save as **44d-drill2** and print.

Payton Devaul set the school record for points in a game—50.[1] He holds six statewide records. This makes him one of the top ten athletes in the school's history.[2] He expects to receive a basketball scholarship at an outstanding university.[3]

Footnotes

Book ⸻ [1]Marshall Baker, *High School Athletic Records.* (Seattle: Sports Press, 2001), p. 41.

Online Journal ⸻ [2]Lori Guo, "Top Ten Athletes," *The Sports Journal*, Spring 2001, http://www.tsj.edu/athletes/topten.htm, 25 June 2001.

E-mail ⸻ [3]Payton Devaul, pdevaul@mail.com. "Basketball Scholarship." E-mail to Kirk Stennis, kstennis@umt.edu, 15 April 2001.

References

Baker, Marshall. *High School Athletic Records.* Seattle: Sports Press, 2001.

Devaul, Payton. pdevaul@mail.com. "Basketball Scholarship." E-mail to Kirk Stennis, kstennis@umt.edu. 15 April 2001.

Guo, Lori. "Top Ten Athletes." *The Sports Journal*, Spring 2001. http://www.tsj.edu/athletes/topten.htm (25 June 2001).

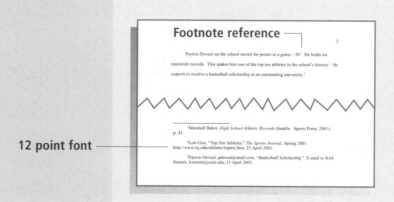

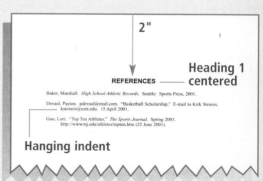

DRILL 2　　CHARACTER STYLES

1. Open a new blank document.

2. Key your name, and press ENTER.

3. Key the document name **27a-drill2**, and press ENTER four times.

4. Key the first three sentences that follow, applying the formats as you key. Press ENTER after each sentence.

5. Key the last three sentences in normal style; then select the sentence and apply the formats.

6. Save the document as **27a-drill2**.

This sentence is keyed in bold. (Press ENTER.)

This sentence is keyed in italic.

This sentence is underlined. (Press ENTER two times.)

This sentence is keyed in bold and italic and underlined.

This sentence is keyed in 14-point Times New Roman.

This sentence is keyed in 12-point Arial.

Paragraph Formats

Paragraph formats apply to an entire paragraph and can be applied before or after a paragraph has been keyed. Each time you press ENTER, *Word* inserts a paragraph mark and starts a new paragraph. Thus, a paragraph may consist of a single line followed by a hard return (¶ mark) or several lines that wrap and are followed by a hard return. In order to apply paragraph formats such as line spacing or alignment, you must be able to see where paragraphs begin and end. Show/Hide displays hard returns as a paragraph mark (¶).

Show/Hide

¶　Click the **Show/Hide** button on the Standard toolbar to display all nonprinting characters such as paragraph markers (¶) and spaces (··). The Show/Hide button appears highlighted or depressed when it is active. To turn nonprinting characters off, click the **Show/Hide** button again.

Alignment

Alignment refers to the way in which the text lines up. Text can be aligned at the left, center, right, or justified (lined up with both margins). Use the Alignment buttons on the Formatting toolbar to quickly align paragraphs.

To align existing text:

1. Place the insertion point in the paragraph to be changed. If more than one paragraph is affected, select the paragraphs to be aligned.

2. Click the appropriate **Align** button.

To align text as you key:

1. Click the appropriate **Align** button.

2. Key the text. This alignment will remain in effect until you click the button again.

NEW FUNCTIONS
44d

help keywords
insert footnote

Footnotes

References cited in a report are often indicated within the text by a superscript number (... story.[1]) and a corresponding footnote with full information at the bottom of the same page where the reference was cited.

Word automatically numbers footnotes sequentially with Arabic numerals (1, 2, 3), positions them at the left margin, and applies 10-point type. After keying footnotes, select them and apply 12-point type to be consistent with the report text. Indent the first line of a footnote 0.5" from the left margin. Footnotes are automatically SS; however, DS between footnotes.

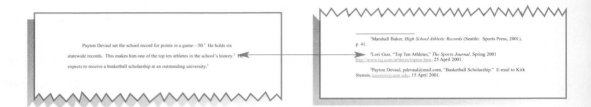

To insert and edit footnotes:

1. Switch to Normal view and position the insertion point where you want to insert the footnote reference.

2. On the menu, click **Insert**, **Reference**, and then **Footnote**. The Footnote and Endnote dialog box displays.

3. Be sure Footnotes is selected and Bottom of page (the default location) is displayed. Then click **Insert**.

4. The reference number and the insertion point appear in the Footnote Pane.

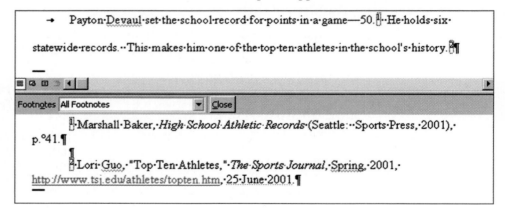

5. Move the insertion point before the reference number, and press TAB to indent it. Then move the insertion point beyond the number and key the footnote in 12-point font. (Note the default font is 10 point.) Click **Close** to return to the document text. (*Note*: If you are in Print Layout View, click anywhere above the footnote divider line to return to the document.)

6. To edit a footnote, double-click on the reference number in the text. Edit the footnote text in the Footnote Pane.

7. To delete a footnote, select the reference number in the text and press DELETE.

DRILL 3   ALIGNMENT

1. Open a new blank document, and center **USING ALIGNMENTS** in 14 point and bold. Strike ENTER twice to create a DS.

2. Change to left alignment and 12 point to key the first paragraph. Apply wordwrap within a paragraph. Press ENTER twice between paragraphs to create a DS.

3. Apply the formatting and alignment as shown in the following document.

4. Save the document as **27a-drill3,** and print a copy. Leave the document on the screen for the next drill.

USING ALIGNMENTS

Left alignment is used for this first paragraph. When left alignment is used, each line in the paragraph begins at the same position on the left side. The right margin will be uneven.

Center alignment (ENTER)
Center titles and short lines.(ENTER)
Use for invitations, announcements, and other documents. (ENTER) (ENTER)

Right alignment is used for this third paragraph. When right alignment is used, each line in the paragraph ends at the same position on the right side. The left side will be uneven.

Justify is used for this fourth paragraph. When justification is used, all lines (except the last line of a paragraph) begin and end at the same position at the left and right margins. Extra spaces are automatically inserted to achieve this look.

Line Spacing

Word's default line spacing is single. When paragraphs are single spaced, the first line of the paragraph normally is not indented. However, a blank line is inserted between paragraphs to distinguish them and to improve readability. Double spacing leaves a blank line between each keyed line. Therefore, it is necessary to indent the first line of each double-spaced paragraph to indicate the beginning of the paragraph. To indent the first line of a paragraph, press the TAB key. The default indention is 0.5".

To change line spacing:

1. Position the insertion point in the paragraph in which you want to change the line spacing. If more than one paragraph is to be changed, select all the paragraphs.

2. Click **Format** on the menu bar; then click **Paragraph**.

3. Select the **Indents and Spacing** tab.

4. Click the arrow in the Line Spacing box; then click **Double.** Click **OK**.

Line spacing can also be changed using the Formatting toolbar. Place the cursor in the paragraph in which the spacing will be changed. Click the **Line Spacing** button; click the Down arrow; then click the desired line spacing. If the Line Spacing button is not displayed, click the chevrons at the right of the toolbar (>>) to display additional formatting options.

LESSON 44

Leftbound Report with Footnotes

SKILLBUILDING

44a
Warmup
Key each line twice SS.

alphabetic	1	Jim Ryan was able to liquefy frozen oxygen; he kept it very cold.
double letters	2	Aaron took accounting lessons at a community college last summer.
one-hand	3	Link agrees you'll get a reward only as you join nonunion racers.
easy	4	Hand Bob a bit of cocoa, a pan of cod, an apricot, and six clams.

| 1 | 2 | 3 | 4 | 5 | 6 | 7 | 8 | 9 | 10 | 11 | 12 | 13 |

44b
Timed Writings
Key a 3' and a 5' writing.

  all letters

gwam 3' | 5'

The kinds of leisure activities you choose constitute 4 | 2 | 62
your life style and, to a great extent, reflect your personality. 8 | 5 | 65
For example, if your daily activities are people oriented, you 12 | 7 | 67
may balance this by spending your free time alone. On the other 17 | 10 | 70
hand, if you would rather be with people most of the time, your 21 | 13 | 72
socialization needs may be very high. At the other end of the 25 | 15 | 75
scale are people who are engaged in machine-oriented work and 29 | 18 | 77
also enjoy spending leisure time alone. These people tend to be 33 | 20 | 80
rather quiet and reserved. 35 | 21 | 81

3' | 1 | 2 | 3 | 4
5' | 1 | 2 | 3

44c
Troublesome Pairs
Key each line once; repeat if time permits.

d	5	do did dad sad faded daddy madder diddle deduced hydrated dredged
k	6	keys sake kicked karat kayak karate knock knuckle knick kilometer
d/k	7	The ten tired and dizzy kids thought the doorknob was the donkey.
w	8	we were who away whew snow windward waterway window webworm award
o	9	on to too onto solo oleo soil cook looked location emotion hollow
w/o	10	Those who know their own power and are committed will follow through.
b	11	be bib sub bear book bribe fiber bombard blueberry babble baboons
v	12	vet vat van viva have over avoid vapor valve seven vanish vanilla
b/v	13	Bo gave a very big beverage and seven coins to everybody bowling.
r	14	or rear rare roar saturate reassure rather northern surge quarrel
u	15	yours undue unity useful unique unusual value wound youth succumb
r/u	16	The truth of the matter is that only Ruth can run a rummage sale.

| 1 | 2 | 3 | 4 | 5 | 6 | 7 | 8 | 9 | 10 | 11 | 12 | 13 |

TECHNIQUE TIP
Keep hands and arms still as you reach up to the third row and down to the first row.

DRILL 4 LINE SPACING

1. Document **27a-drill3** should be on your screen.
2. Click in the first paragraph and change the line spacing to double.
3. Click on **Center Alignment** in the second paragraph. Change the line spacing to 1.5. Note that the spacing change affects only paragraph 2—the paragraph where the insertion point is located.
4. Click in the third paragraph and change the line spacing to multiple. Save the document as **27a-drill4** and close it.

APPLICATIONS

27b-d1
Character Formats

1. Key the heading and the sentences in Group A applying the character formats shown as you key. DS between sentences.
2. Key the heading and the sentences in Group B, then select and apply the formats shown. DS between sentences.
3. Select all sentences in Group A and change the font to Arial 11 point. Select all sentences in Group B and apply a 14-point script font.
4. Save the document as **27b-d1**. Print the document.

Group A

I read a very inspirational book, <u>Turning Dreams into Reality</u>.

Use **Skill Builder** in *Keyboarding Pro* frequently to improve your skills.

Please meet the team at *Gate 4* of *Terminal A* at the airport **no later than 9:15 a.m.**

Group B

The Broadway play *Marching to My Own Drummer* lasted **three** hours.

We owe a total of <u>$1,597.26</u> for flights, hotel, and tickets.

Please make your check payable to ***LaShanda C. Bullock*** and deliver it Friday <u>morning</u>.

REFERENCES

494

Gilreath, Erica. "Dressing Casually with Power." 504
http://www.dresscasual.com (23 March 2001). 513

Monaghan, Susan. "Business Dress Codes May Be Shifting." *Business* 527
Executive, April 2000, 34–35. 533

Sutphin, Rachel. "Your Business Wardrobe Decisions Are Important 546
Decisions." *Business Management Journal*, January 2000, 10–12. 559

Tartt, Kelsey. "Companies Support Business Casual Dress." 571
Management Success, June 1995, 23–25. 578

43e-d3
Title Page

1. Prepare a title page for the unbound report completed in **43e-d2**. Assume the report is prepared for Donovan National Bank by you as Image Consultant. Use the current date.
2. Use bold and 14 point for all lines. Center the page vertically.
3. Save as **43e-d3**.

43e-d4
Proofread Report

1. Open **Report4** from the data files and print.
2. Proofread the report for consistency in the formatting of reports. Mark any errors you locate on the printed report. As an editor, you will want to use the proofreaders' marks shown on page 55 to mark the corrections. In the upper-right corner, write the following: **Your Name, Editor**.
3. Exchange reports with a classmate. Then make the corrections indicated on your classmate's edited report. If you do not agree with his/her edits, discuss the questioned items and reach an agreement. Make the final edits.
4. At the end of the corrected report, key the following:
   a. **Corrections made by: Your Name**
   b. **1st Editor: Your Classmate's Name**
5. Save as **43e-d4** and print. Submit the report you marked in step 2 and the report you corrected in step 3. (Team Goal: Correct all the errors.)

SKILLBUILDING

43f

Use the remaining class time to build your skills using the Skill Builder module within *Keyboarding Pro*.

27b-d2
Paragraph Formats

1. Center and bold the title, Commitment; apply Arial 14-point font.
2. Single-space the paragraphs and use wordwrap. Double-space between paragraphs. Do not indent paragraphs. Align paragraphs at the left.
3. Preview the paragraphs and print the document.
4. Change the format on all paragraphs to left alignment, double-spacing, and indented paragraphs.
5. Use right-alignment and single-spacing to add your name and the date on separate lines a double space below the last paragraph.
6. Save the document as **27b-d2**. Print the document.

Commitment

Commitment simply means that you will follow up on promises you make and do what you said you would do. The concept of commitment is a prerequisite for building credibility. It is extremely difficult to believe in or trust individuals who do not do what they committed to do. Many people think commitments are not valid unless they are written commitments. However, verbal commitments are just as important and should be honored in the same way that written commitments are honored.

On rare occasions, circumstances may make it impossible for you to honor a commitment. If it is impossible for you to keep a commitment, notify the individual to whom the commitment was made as quickly as possible. Explain why you cannot meet the commitment and try to give the individual as much time as possible so that other arrangements can be made. Letting people down at the last minute puts them in an awkward position

Your name
Today's date

SKILLBUILDING

27c
Skill Builder, Lesson A

Use the remaining class time to build your skills using the Skill Builder module within *Keyboarding Pro*. Complete these lessons as time permits.

1. Open *Keyboarding Pro*. Log on in the usual manner.
2. Click **Edit** on the menu bar and then **Preferences**. On the Preferences dialog box under Skill Builder, click the radio button for **Speed** and then **OK**. (You must choose your preference before entering Skill Builder.)
3. Open the Skill Builder module, and select Lesson A.
4. Beginning with Keyboard Mastery, complete as much of the lesson as time permits.
5. Exit the software. Remove your storage disk. Store your materials as directed.

words

TRENDS FOR BUSINESS DRESS

5

Casual dress in the workplace has become widely accepted. According to a national study conducted by Schoenholtz & Associates in 1995, a majority of the companies surveyed allowed employees to dress casually one day a week, usually Fridays (Tartt, 1995, 23). The trend continued to climb as shown by the 1997 survey by Schoenholtz & Associates. Fifty-eight percent of office workers surveyed were allowed to dress casually for work every day, and 92 percent of the offices allowed employees to dress casually occasionally (Sutphin, 2000, 10).

19
33
47
62
76
91
106
114

Decline in Trend

118

The trend to dress casually that started in the early 1990s may be shifting, states Susan Monaghan (2000, 34):

131
140

Although a large number of companies are allowing casual attire every day or only on Fridays, a current survey revealed a decline of 10 percent in 1999 when compared to the same survey conducted in 1998. Some experts predict the new trend for business dress codes will be a dress up day every week.

152
165
177
181
190

What accounts for this decline in companies permitting casual dress? Several reasons may include:

203
210

1. Confusion of what business casual is with employees slipping into dressing too casually (work jeans, faded tee-shirts, old sneakers, and improperly fitting clothing).

223
236
245

2. Casual dress does not portray the adopted corporate image of the company.

258
260

3. Employees are realizing that promotion decisions are affected by a professional appearance.

274
279

Guidelines for Business Dress

285

Companies are employing image consultants to teach employees what is appropriate business casual and to plan the best business attire to project the corporate image. Erica Gilreath (2000), the author of *Casual Dress*, a guidebook on business casual, provides excellent advice on how to dress casually and still command the power needed for business success. She presents the following advice to professionals:

297
316
327
342
357
367

- Do not wear any clothing that is designed for recreational or sports activities, e.g., cargo pants or pants with elastic waist.

381
393

- Invest the time in pressing khakis and shirts or pay the price for professional dry cleaning. Wrinkled clothing does not enhance one's credibility.

407
421
424

- Do not wear sneakers.

428

- Be sure clothing fits properly. Avoid baggy clothes or clothes that are too tight.

443
446

In summary, energetic employees working to climb the corporate ladder will need to plan their dress carefully. If business casual is appropriate, it's best to consult the experts on business casual to ensure a professional image.

458
472
488
492

NEW FUNCTIONS

28a

Spelling and Grammar

When you key, *Word* places a red wavy line under misspelled words and a green wavy line under potential grammar errors. Clicking the right mouse button in a marked word displays a shortcut menu with suggested replacement words that you can use to correct the error.

The Spelling and Grammar Status button on the status bar also informs you if there is an error in the document.

 To manually check a document, click the Spelling and Grammar button on the Standard toolbar to start the checking process.

When *Word* locates a possible error, the Spelling and Grammar dialog box displays. You can change words marked as errors or ignore them. You can click the **Add** button to add correct words not recognized by *Word* to the dictionary. If you choose Ignore All and Change All, the marked words will either be ignored or changed throughout the entire document.

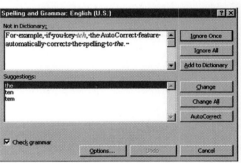

AutoCorrect

As you key, common errors are automatically corrected. For example, if you key *teh*, the AutoCorrect feature automatically corrects the spelling to *the*. When this feature is enabled, *Word* automatically replaces errors using the spell checker's main dictionary. You can customize or add words to the software's dictionary by accessing AutoCorrect Options on the Tools menu. Additional AutoCorrect options enable you to format text and automatically insert repetitive text as you key.

DRILL 1 · SPELLING AND GRAMMAR AND AUTOCORRECT

1. On the Tools menu, select **AutoCorrect Options**. Note the available options, and then scroll through the list of replacement words (you can add additional words).

2. Key the following sentences exactly as they are shown; include the misspellings and abbreviations. Note that many errors are automatically corrected as you key.

3. In the last sentence, press ENTER to accept the AutoCorrect entry at the beginning of the sentence.

4. Right-click on the words marked with a wavy red line, and correct the errors.

5. Proofread the lines to find two unmarked errors.

6. Save the document as **28a-drill1**. Print and close the document.

i beleive a lot of dissatisfied customers will not return.

a seperate committee was formed to deal with the new issues.

please includ a self-addressed stampted envelope with you letter.

To Whom It May Concern: If you don't receive a repsonse to you e-mail messige, call Robbins and Assocaites at 555-0106.

DOCUMENT DESIGN

43d

References Page

References cited in the report are listed at the end of the report in alphabetical order by authors' last names. The reference list may be titled REFERENCES or BIB-LIOGRAPHY. Become familiar with the three types of references listed below:

1. A book reference includes the name of the author (last name first), work (italicized), city of publication, publisher, and copyright date.

2. A magazine reference shows the name of the author (last name first), article (in quotation marks), magazine title (italicized), date of publication, and page references.

3. A reference retrieved electronically includes the author (inverted), article (in quotation marks), publication (italicized), publication information, Internet address, and date the document was retrieved or accessed (in parentheses).

Begin the list of references on a new page by inserting a manual page break at the end of the report. Use the same margins as the first page of a report, and number the page at the top right of the page. The main heading (REFERENCES or BIBLIOG-RAPHY) should be approximately 2" from the top of the page. References should be SS in hanging indent format; DS between references.

APPLICATIONS

43e-d1
References Page

1. Open **42e-d1**. Save it as **43e-d1**.

2. Position the insertion point at the end of the report. Press CTRL + ENTER to begin a new page. Key **REFERENCES** approximately 2" from the top of the page.

3. Key the references in hanging indent style. (*Hint:* Try the shortcut, CTRL + T.)

Lehman, C. M., and Dufrene, D. D. *Business Communication.* 13th ed. Cincinnati: South-Western/Thomson Learning, 2002.

Publication Manual of the American Psychological Association. 4th ed. Washington, D.C.: American Psychological Association, 2001.

43e-d2
Unbound Report

1. Key the following unbound report DS. SS the long quote, and indent it 0.5".

2. Number the pages at the top right; suppress page number on the first page.

3. Key the references on a references page at the end of the report.

4. Switch to Print Layout view to verify the page numbers and ensure there are no widows or orphans.

5. Save the report as **43e-d2**.

Undo/Redo

 To reverse the most recent action you have taken (such as inserting or deleting text, formatting in bold or underline, changing line spacing, etc.), click the **Undo** button. To reverse several actions, click the Down arrow beside Undo to display a list of recent actions. Then click the action you wish to reverse. Note, however, that all actions you performed prior to the action you select also will be reversed. Commands such as Save and Print cannot be undone this way.

Redo reverses the last Undo and can be applied several times to redo the past several actions. Click on the Down arrow beside Redo to view all actions that can be redone.

DRILL 2   UNDO/REDO

1. Key the following paragraph SS.

2. Bold and underline **Undo/Redo** in the first sentence.

3. Apply bold and italic to **Undo** in the second sentence and to **Redo** in the last sentence.

4. Change line spacing to DS.

5. Undo the underline in the first sentence.

6. Undo the double-spacing in the paragraph.

7. Redo the underline in the first sentence.

8. Undo the bold in the last sentence.

9. Redo the spacing to DS in the paragraph.

10. Save the document as **28a-drill2**.

Keying and formatting changes can be reversed easily by using the Undo/Redo function. If you make a change, one click of the Undo button can reverse the change. If you undo a change and decide that you really want to keep the change as it was originally made, you can go back to the original change by clicking the Redo button.

Help

Help provides you with quick access to information about commands, features, and screen elements. To access it, click **Help** on the menu bar, and then click **Microsoft Word Help**. This option includes Contents, Answer Wizard, and Index.

Contents displays a list of topics you can click on to display helpful information.

Answer Wizard enables you to ask a question. When you click **Search,** the Wizard displays a list of topics pertaining to your answer. Click on a topic to display additional information.

Index enables you to key a word or select a keyword to display a list of topics pertaining to the keyword. Click **Search** and then click on the topic to display the information in the right window.

Click outside the Help window to remove the window from the screen.

You can also access Help by clicking the Microsoft Word Help button or by keying a question in the Ask a Question box.

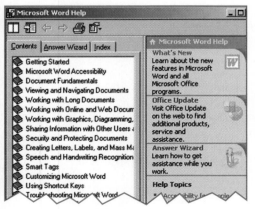

Word 2002

LESSON 43 — Two-Page Report with References

SKILLBUILDING

43a
Warmup
Key each line twice SS.

alphabetic 1 Melva Bragg required exactly a dozen jackets for the winter trip.

figures 2 The 1903 copy of my book had 5 parts, 48 chapters, and 672 pages.

direct reach 3 Olga, the French goalie, defended well against the frazzled team.

easy 4 Rodney and a neighbor may go to the dock with us to work for Ken.

| 1 | 2 | 3 | 4 | 5 | 6 | 7 | 8 | 9 | 10 | 11 | 12 | 13 |

43b
Timed Writings
Key one 3' timing; then key one 5' timing.

 all letters

	gwam	3'	5'

Subtle differences exist among role models, mentors, and sponsors. A role model is a person you can emulate, or one who provides a good example to follow. A mentor is one who will advise, coach, or guide you when you need information about your job or your organization. A sponsor is a person who will support you or recommend you for a position or a new responsibility.

4 2 32
8 5 35
12 7 37
16 10 40
21 12 42
25 15 45

One person may fill all three roles, or several people may serve as role models, mentors, or sponsors. These individuals usually have higher ranks than you do, which means they will be able to get information that you and your peers may not have. Frequently, a mentor will share information with you that will enable you to make good decisions about your career.

30 18 48
34 20 50
38 23 53
42 25 55
46 28 58
50 30 60

3' | 1 | 2 | 3 | 4 |
5' | 1 | 2 | 3 |

FUNCTION REVIEW

43c

Bullets, Page Break, Hanging Indent

In formatting a two-page report, you may need to use the Bullets and Page Break features. When formatting the references in a two-page report, you will also need to use the Hanging Indent feature.

DRILL 1   REVIEW BULLETS, PAGE BREAK, HANGING INDENT

1. Open **page break** from the data files.

2. Format the last three paragraphs as numbered bullets.

3. Insert a hard page break to begin REFERENCES on a new page. Position insertion point at about 2.1" for references page.

4. Format references as a hanging indent.

5. Save as **43c-drill1**.

DRILL 3   HELP

1. Click **Help** on the menu, then click **Microsoft Word Help.**
2. Click the **Contents** tab and note topics available.
3. Click the **Answer Wizard** tab and key: **Print a document.** Note the information provided.
4. Click the **Index** tab; key: **Print** in Box 1, Type Keywords or choose **Print** in Box 2, Choose Keywords. From the list of topics, choose **Print a document.**

5. Close Help.
6. Click the **Microsoft Word Help** button. Note that Help is accessed from the button in the same way it is accessed from the Help menu.
7. Key **Print a document** in the Ask A Question box; then click the **Print a document** option. Note that you access the same information in Help.

Edit Text

Once text is keyed, it often needs to be corrected or changed. The Insert and Delete functions are used to edit text.

To insert text: Click or move the insertion point where the new text is to appear and key the text. Existing text moves to the right.

To delete text: Select the text and press DELETE.

DRILL 4   INSERT AND DELETE

1. Open the document **26a-drill3.**
2. Edit the document as shown.
3. Change the line spacing to double. If necessary, delete any extra hard returns between paragraphs.

4. Tab to indent the first line of each paragraph.
5. Save the document as **28a-drill4** and print it.
6. Close the document.

Serendipity, a ~~new homework~~ research tool from Information Technology Company, is available to subscribers of ~~the major~~ online services via the World Wide Web.

Offered as a subscription service aimed at ~~college~~ students, Serendipity is a collection of tens of thousands of articles from ~~major~~ encyclopedias, reference books, magazines, pamphlets, and Internet sources combined into a single searchable database. *with just a computer and a modem*

Serendipity puts an electronic library right at students' fingertips. The program offers two browse-and-search capabilities. Users can find articles by entering questions in simple question format or browse the database by pointing and clicking on key words that identify related articles. For more information, call 800-555-0174 or address e-mail to lab@serendipity.com. *on just about any subject*

- All ideas of others must be cited so that credit is given appropriately.

- The reader will need to be able to locate the material using the information included in the reference citation.

- Format rules apply to ideas stated as direct quotations and ideas that are paraphrased.

- A thorough list of references adds integrity to the report and to the report writer.

Good writers learn quickly how to evaluate the many printed and electronic references that may have been located to support the theme of the report being written. Those references judged acceptable are then cited in the report. Writers of the *Publication Manual of the American Psychological Association* (1994, 174-175) share these simple procedures for preparing a reference list that correlates with the references cited in the report body:

Long quotation —

Note that a reference list cites works that specifically support a particular article. In contrast, a bibliography cites works for background or for further reading. . . . References cited in text must appear in the references list; conversely, each entry in the reference list must be cited in text.

Using a Style Manual

Three popular style manuals are the *MLA Handbook, The Chicago Manual of Style*, and the *Publication Manual of the American Psychological Association.* After selecting a style, carefully study the acceptable formats for citing books, magazines, newspapers, brochures, online journals, e-mail messages, and other sources. Visit Web sites such as http://www.wisc.edu/writing/Handbook/DocChicago.html, http://www.mla.org, and http://www.apastyle.org/elecref.html for assistance in understanding these styles.

With the availability and volume of excellent electronic resources, writers are including a number of electronic citations along with printed journals, books, and newspapers. Electronic citations may include online journal articles or abstracts, articles on CD-ROM, e-mail messages, discussion list messages, etc. To format references for documents retrieved electronically, Lehman and Dufrene (2002, B-9) offer the following guidelines:

Long quotation —

The various referencing styles are fairly standardized as to the elements included when citing documents retrieved electronically. . . . Include the following items: author (if given), date of publication, title of article and/or name of publication, electronic medium (such as online or CD-ROM), volume, series, page, path (Uniform Resource Locator or Internet address), and date you retrieved or accessed the resource.

42e-d2
Title Page

Prepare a title page for report **42e-d1**. Save the document as **42e-d2**.

APPLICATIONS

28b-d1
Rough Draft

1. Key the following paragraphs DS, and make the revisions shown.
2. Save the document as **28b-d1**. Print the document.

The World Wide Web (www) and Internet Usenet News groups are electronic fan clubs that offers users a ways to exchange views and information on just about any topic imaginable with people all around the world.

World Wide Web screens contain text, graphic, and pictures *, and often audio and video*. Simple pointing and clicking on the pictures and links (underlined words) bring users to new pages or sites of information.

28b-d2
Revise a Document

1. Open the document **28a-drill4**.   Select the entire document using the mouse, and change the font to Arial 12 point.
2. Center-align and bold your name.
3. Change the line spacing to 1.5.
4. Italicize Information Technology Company.
5. Undo center-align of your name.
6. Right-align your name.
7. Preview the document, print a copy, save as **28b-d2**, and close it.

SKILLBUILDING

28c
Key each line twice SS; DS between two-line groups.

one hand
1 A few treats were served as reserve seats were set up on a stage.
2 In my opinion, a few trees on a hilly acre created a vast estate.

balanced hand
3 Pam and Jake did go to visit the big island and may fish for cod.
4 Ken may visit the men he met at the ancient chapel on the island.

1/2 fingers
5 Kimberly tried to grab the bar, but she missed and hurt her hand.
6 My name is Frankie, but I prefer to be called Fran by my friends.

3/4 fingers
7 Zola and Polly saw us play polo at Maxwell Plaza; we won a prize.
8 Zack quickly swam past all six boys at a zoo pool on Saxony Land.

Internal Citations

Internal citations are an easy and practical method of documentation. The last name of the author(s), the publication date, and the page number(s) of the cited material are shown in parentheses within the body of the report (Crawford, 2002, 134). This information cues a reader to the name Crawford in the reference list included at the end of the report. When the author's name is used in the text to introduce the quotation, only the year of publication and the page numbers appear in parentheses: "Crawford (2002, 134) said that . . . ."

Short, direct quotations of three lines or fewer are enclosed within quotation marks. Long quotations of four lines or more are indented 0.5" from the left margin and SS. A DS or one blank line comes before and after the long quotation. The first line is indented an additional 0.5" if the quotation is the beginning of a paragraph.

If a portion of the text that is referenced is omitted, use an ellipsis (. . .) to show the omission. An ellipsis is three periods, each preceded and followed by a space. If a period occurs at the end of a sentence, include the period or punctuation.

deserves more attention that it gets. "Successful businesses have long known the

importance of good verbal communication." (Catlette, 2000, 29).

Short Quotation

Probably no successful enterprise exists that does not rely for its success upon the ability

of its members to communicate:

> Make no mistake; both written and verbal communication are the stuff upon which success is built . . . . Both forms deserve careful study by any business that wants to grow. Successful businesspeople must read, write, speak, and listen with skill. (Schaefer, 1999, 28)

Long Quotation

APPLICATIONS

42e-d1
Two-Page Report with Long Quotations

1. Key the unbound report that follows.
2. Press ENTER to position the main heading at about 2". SS the two-line main heading as shown. DS the report.
3. Insert page number to display at the right; suppress page number on the first page.
4. Check for side headings alone at the bottom of the page.
5. Save the report as **42e-d1**.

COMPLETE AND ACCURATE DOCUMENTATION ESSENTIAL FOR EFFECTIVE REPORTS

Preparing a thorough and convincing report requires excellent research, organization, and composition skills as well as extensive knowledge of documenting referenced materials. The purpose of this report is to present the importance of documenting a report with credible references and the techniques for creating accurate citations.

Documenting with References

For a report to be credible and accepted by its readers, a thorough review of related literature is essential. This background information is an important part of the report and provides believability of the writer and of the report. When sharing this literature in the body of the report, the report writer understands the following basic principles of report documentation:

●●●

LESSON 29	**Formatting Essentials**

29a

Center Page

The **Center Page** command centers a document vertically on the page. Should extra hard returns (¶) appear at the beginning or end of a document, these are also considered to be part of the document. Be careful to delete extra hard returns before centering a page.

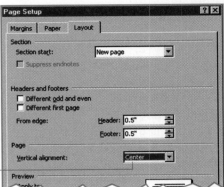

To center a page vertically:

1. Position the insertion point on the page to be centered.
2. From the File menu, select **Page Setup**. The Page Setup dialog box displays.
3. Click the **Layout** tab.
4. Click the **Vertical alignment** down arrow. Select **Center**; then click **OK**.

DRILL 1 **CENTER PAGE**

1. Open document **27b-d2**.
2. On the File menu, click **Page Setup**; then center the page vertically.

3. Click **Print Preview** to view the entire document, and check to ensure equal space exists at the top and bottom of the page.
4. Close Print Preview and save the document as **29a-drill1**. Close the document.

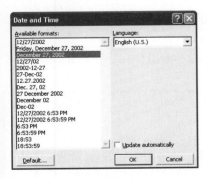

Date and Time

The current date and time can be inserted into documents using the **Date and Time** command from the Insert menu.

1. Choose **Date and Time** from the Insert menu.
2. Choose a format from the Available Formats box. Standard business format is the month-day-year format.

Note: The date is inserted as text and will not change. To update the date each time the document is opened, click the **Update Automatically** check box.

DRILL 2 **INSERT DATE**

1. Open a new document.
2. Key your name on the first line and align it at the right.
3. Insert the date using month-day-year format a DS below your name.

4. Return to left alignment and key the following sentence: **The date shown above is in standard business format.**
5. Save the document as **29a-drill2** and close it.

LESSON 42

Two-Page Report with Long Quotations

SKILLBUILDING

42a
Warmup
Key each line twice SS.

alphabetic 1 Two exit signs jut quietly above the beams of a razed skyscraper.
figures 2 Send 345 of the 789 sets now; send the others on August 1 and 26.
direct reach 3 I obtain many junk pieces dumped by Marvyn at my service centers.
easy 4 Enrique may fish for cod by the dock; he also may risk a penalty.
| 1 | 2 | 3 | 4 | 5 | 6 | 7 | 8 | 9 | 10 | 11 | 12 | 13 |

42b
Timed Writings
Key a 1' timing on each paragraph, and a 3' timing on all paragraphs.

 all letters

gwam 1' | 3'

Does a relationship exist between confidence and success? If you think it does, you will find that many people agree with you. However, it is very hard to judge just how strong the bond is.

When people are confident they can do a job, they are very likely to continue working on that task until they complete it correctly. If they are not confident, they give up much quicker.

People who are confident they can do something tend to enjoy doing it more than those who lack confidence. They realize that they do better work when they are happy with what they do.

	1'	3'
	12	4 42
	26	9 46
	38	13 50
	12	17 54
	24	21 58
	38	25 63
	12	29 67
	25	34 71
	37	37 75

1' | 1 | 2 | 3 | 4 | 5 | 6 | 7 | 8 | 9 | 10 | 11 | 12 | 13 |
3' | 1 | 2 | 3 | 4 |

FUNCTION REVIEW

42c

Review Indent

1. Open **indents** from the data files.
2. On page 1, increase the indent of paragraph 2.
3. On page 2, format the references with a hanging indent.
4. Save as **42c-drill1**.

DOCUMENT DESIGN

42d

Report Documentation

Reports must include the sources of all information used in the report. Documentation gives credit for published material, whether electronic or printed, that is quoted or closely paraphrased by the writer. The writer may document sources by using footnotes, endnotes, or internal citations. In this module, you will use internal citations and footnotes.

At the end of the report, the writer provides the reader with a complete alphabetical listing of all references. With this complete information provided in the references, the interested reader may locate the original source. You will learn to format a reference list in Lesson 43.

DOCUMENT DESIGN

Tabs

Tabs are used to indent paragraphs and align text vertically. Pressing the TAB key aligns text at the **tab stop**. *Word* has five types of tabs, which are listed below. The left, right, and center tabs are similar to paragraph alignment types. In this lesson, you will work with left and right tabs.

L	**Left tab**	Aligns text at the left.
⌐	**Right tab**	Aligns text at the right.
⊥	**Center tab**	Aligns text evenly on either side of the tab stop.
⊥.	**Decimal tab**	Aligns numbers at the decimal point.
I	**Bar tab**	Aligns text to the right of a vertical bar.

Tabs can be set and cleared on the Horizontal Ruler. The numbers on the ruler indicate the distance in inches from the left margin. The small gray lines below each half-inch position are the default tab stops. The Tab Alignment button at the left edge of the ruler indicates the type of tab. To change the tab type, click the Tab Alignment button.

Tab alignment   **Left tab**   **Right tab**

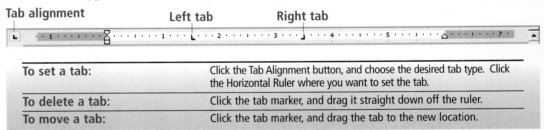

To set a tab:	Click the Tab Alignment button, and choose the desired tab type. Click the Horizontal Ruler where you want to set the tab.
To delete a tab:	Click the tab marker, and drag it straight down off the ruler.
To move a tab:	Click the tab marker, and drag the tab to the new location.

Tabs can also be set in the Tab dialog box (**Format** menu, **Tabs**). The Tab dialog box provides more options and allows you to set precise settings.

DRILL 3   **SET AND MOVE TABS**

1. Display the Horizontal Ruler if necessary (**View** menu, **Ruler**).

2. Set a left tab at 1.5" and a right tab at 3.5".

3. Key the first three lines of the drill. Press TAB at the beginning of each line.

4. Move the left tab to 1" and the right tab to 3". Key the last three lines. Save as **29a-drill3**. Print and close.

	Left tab 1.5"	Right tab 3.5"
Tab ⟶	Schneider	5,000
	Langfield	17,200
	Almich	9,500
	Left tab 1"	Right tab 3"
	McCoy	12,000
	Buswinka	198,250
	Oritz	500

DRILL 6 — MARGINS

1. Set 1" side margins. Key the paragraph below. Save as **41d-drill6**; then preview the document.

2. Position the insertion point at the beginning of sentence 4. Press ENTER twice.

3. With the insertion point in paragraph 2, change the top and side margins to 2". Preview the document.

4. At the end of sentence 4, press ENTER twice. Key and complete this sentence with the better response, (a) or (b).

The margin command affects the appearance of the (a) entire document (b) paragraph containing the insertion point.

5. Save the document again.

6. Change the left, right, and top margins to 1.5". Apply margin settings to the whole document.

7. Save the document as **41d-drill6b**.

Attractive document layout begins with margins set an equal distance from the left and right edges of the paper. When margins are equal, the document appears balanced. One exception to the equal-margin rule is in the formatting of reports bound at the left. To ensure the appearance of equal left and right margins in a leftbound report, you must add extra space to the left margin to allow for the binding.

DRILL 7 — COMBINED PRACTICE

1. Set 1.5" side margins.

2. Key the text below following the directions in the text.

3. Insert a manual page break as shown.

4. Insert page number at the top right. Do not print number on the first page.

5. Save as **41d-drill7**.

Indent

Type the following paragraph indented 0.5" from the left margin.

Long quotations of four lines or more are indented 0.5" from the left margin and single-spaced. A double-space or one blank line comes before and after the long quotation. The first line is indented an additional 0.5" if the quotation is the beginning of a paragraph.

·· Insert page break.

Hanging Indent

Key the following article as a reference in hanging indent style.

Falcon, Leah. "Reflections of an Echo Boomer." *Net Generation Magazine*, Vol. 2, No. 1, February 2003, 12–15.

APPLICATIONS

29b-d1
Tabs, Date, and Center Page

1. Open a new document. Change spacing to DS. Center the title on the first line. Apply bold and change font to 16-point Times New Roman.
2. On the second line, insert the current date using day-month-date-year format. Apply same format as the first line.
3. Set a left tab at 1.5" and a right tab at 4.5".
4. Key the document shown below. Center the page.
5. Preview and print. Save as **29b-d1**.

Starting Lineup

Saturday, December 28, 200-

Power Forward	Shanze J. Penn
Small Forward	Christina U. Perovic
Center	Teresa C. Gortman
Shooting Guard	Tonisha J. Burgess
Point Guard	Kelly O. Reese

29b-d2
Tabs, Date, and Center Page

1. Open a new document. Change spacing to DS. Center the title in all caps on the first line. Apply bold and change font to 14-point Times New Roman.
2. On the second line, insert the current date using standard business format. Apply same format as the first line.
3. Set a left tab at 1" and a right tab at 5".
4. Key the document shown below. Center the page.
5. Preview and print. Save as **29b-d2**.

Internet Groups on Campus

December 28, 200-

Name	Description
webdes	Web page design topics
biz	Business administration—all majors
bioeng	Biomedical engineers
sprtmg	Sports management
marband	Marching band

SKILLBUILDING

29c

Use the remaining class time to build your skills using the Skill Builder module within *Keyboarding Pro*. Continue with the next lesson.

Manual Page Break

When a page is filled with copy, the software automatically inserts a soft page break, which is indicated with a dotted line across the page when you are in Normal view.

You may need to begin a new page, however, before the page is filled. To insert a manual page break, press CTRL + ENTER. The software inserts a dotted line across the screen with the words "Page Break." The insertion point moves to the next page; the status line at the bottom of the screen indicates this change. A manual page break will not move as text is inserted or deleted.

To remove a manual page break, position the insertion point on the Page Break line and press DELETE.

DRILL 5   **MANUAL PAGE BREAK**

1. Key the text below.

2. Place the insertion point after the first set of goals. Insert a manual page break.

3. Continue keying page 2.

4. Use the Page Number command to insert number at the top of page. Do not print number on the first page.

5. Save as **41d-drill5**.

GOAL 1: MEMBERSHIP DEVELOPMENT

Objective: To increase membership.

Indent ⟶ **Plan**

    A. Review and evaluate membership benefits.

    B. Study avenues for additional membership benefits.

    C. Develop new membership markets.

Insert page break.

GOAL 2: STAFF DEVELOPMENT

Objective: To enhance performance and motivation of staff.

Indent ⟶ **Plan**

    A. Review and evaluate previous staff development programs.

    B. Survey staff to determine needs.

    C. Implement relevant staff development programs.

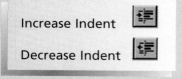

Increase Indent

Decrease Indent

Margins

Margins are the distance between the edge of the paper and the print. The default settings are 1.25" side margins and 1" top and bottom margins. Default margins stay in effect until you change them.

Help keywords:
Change page margins

To change the margins:

1. Click **File;** then **Page Setup**.

2. From the Margins tab, click the up or down arrows to increase or decrease the default settings.

3. Apply margins to the Whole document unless directed otherwise. Click **OK**.

LESSON 30

Skillbuilding and Editing Review

30a
Warmup
Key each line twice SS.

alphabetic 1	Gay expected to solve the jigsaw puzzle more quickly than before.
figures 2	Jane opened Rooms 16, 20, and 39 and locked Rooms 48, 53, and 57.
shift 3	Ted and I spent April in San Juan and May in St. Paul, Minnesota.
easy 4	The island is the shape of a big sleigh. Jake got clams for us.

| 1 | 2 | 3 | 4 | 5 | 6 | 7 | 8 | 9 | 10 | 11 | 12 | 13 |

30b
Technique Builders
Key each line twice SS.

Direct Reach words, phrases, and sentences

5 hung deck jump cent slope decide hunt serve polo brave cedar pump

6 no way | in tune | many times | jump in | funny times | gold plated | in sync

7 June and Cecil browsed in craft shops and found many funny gifts.

Adjacent Reach words, phrases, and sentences

8 Were pop safe sad quick column tree drew opinion excite guy point

9 We are | boil over | are we | few rewards | short trek | where are we going

10 Bert said he tries to shop where we can buy gas, oil, and treats.

30c
Speed Builders
Key each line twice; work for fluency.

11 Ken may go to the big lake to fish for sockeye and dig for clams.

12 Jan may go with us to visit the ancient chapel on the big island.

13 Their goal is to fix the bicycle or dismantle it to fit in a box.

14 A cow roams the cornfield, and fox, quail, and duck also roam it.

15 A neighbor bid by proxy for eighty bushels of corn and rye blend.

30d
Speed Check
Take two 3' timed writings.

I have a story or two or three that will transport you to	4
faraway places, to meet people you have never known, to see	8
things you have never seen, to feast on foods available only to a	12
few. I can help you to learn new skills you want and need; I can	17
inspire you, excite you, instruct you, and entertain you. I	21
answer your questions. I work with you to realize a talent, to	25
express a thought, and to determine just who and what you really	29
are and want to be. I help you to know words, to write, and to	33
read. I help you to understand the mysteries of the past and the	38
secrets of the future. I am your library. I hope I shall see	42
you often. You might find me online.	45

3' | 1 | 2 | 3 | 4 |

Hanging Indent

Hanging indent places the first line of a paragraph at the left margin and indents all other lines to the first tab. It is commonly used to format bibliography entries, glossaries, and lists. Hanging indent can be applied before text is keyed or after.

Help keywords
Hanging indent; paragraph; about text alignment and spacing

To create a hanging indent:

1. Display the Horizontal Ruler (click **View**; then **Ruler**).

2. From the Horizontal Ruler, drag the hanging indent marker to the position where the indent is to begin. ⟵ **Hanging Indent**

3. Key the paragraph. The second and subsequent lines are indented beginning at the marker. (*Shortcut:* CTRL + T, then key the paragraph; or select the paragraphs to be formatted as hanging indents, and press CTRL + T.)

DRILL 2   HANGING INDENT

1. Drag the Hanging Indent marker 0.5" to the right; then key the references that follow.

2. Turn Hanging Indent off by dragging the Hanging Indent marker back to the left margin.

3. Save the document as **41d-drill2**.

> Fowler, H. Ramsey and Aaron, Jane E. *The Little, Brown Handbook.* 6th ed. Boston: HarperCollins College Publishers, 1995.
>
> Osaji, Allison. "Know the Credibility of Electronic Citations." *Graduate Education Journal*, April 2000, 45–51.
>
> VandenBos, Gary R. "Software Helps Writers Conform to APA Style." *APA Monitor Online*, (1999) http://www.apa.org/monitor/jan99/soft.html (10 November 2000).
>
> Walters, Daniel S. dswalters2@umt.edu. "Final Report Available on Intranet." E-mail to Stephen P. Cobb, spcobb@umt.edu (14 September 2000).

DRILL 3   FORMAT TEXT WITH HANGING INDENT

1. Open **references** from the data files, and save it as **41d-drill3**.

2. Select the references, and format them with a hanging indent. (*Hint:* Try the shortcut.) Save the file again.

DRILL 4   FORMAT TEXT WITH HANGING INDENT

1. Open **glossary** from the data files, and save it as **41d-drill4**.

2. Select all the glossary entries, and format them with a hanging indent. Save the file again.

30e

Editing Review

DRILL 1   COMPOSE, PROOFREAD, AND EDIT

1. Key the ¶s filling in the information indicated.

2. Print the document; proofread it and mark any corrections needed using proofreaders' marks.

3. Correct the document and save it as **30e-drill1**.

4. Print a copy.

Review proofreaders' marks in 23f, page 55.

My name is (*student's name*). I am a (*class level*) at (*school*) located on (*street*) in (*city, state*). In addition to (*name of this course*), I am also enrolled in (*names of other courses; modify sentence if you are not enrolled in any other courses*). My instructor in this course is (*title and name*).

The reason I enrolled in this course is (*complete sentence*). What I like most about this course is (*complete sentence*). What I like least about this course is (*complete sentence*).

DRILL 2   EDIT SENTENCES AND PARAGRAPH

1. Key the text making the edits indicated by the proofreaders' marks.

2. Proofread and correct any errors.

3. Print the document and save it as **30e-drill2**.

16 Do you assess you~r~ writing skills as average, great, or mediocre?

17 You should also ask your instructor about *to assess* your writing skills.

18 Your instructor ~will know~ *may teach you* how to ~greatly~ improve your writing skills.

19 Do you ~always~ *take the time to* edit and proofread carefully things that you write?

20 few people who do not bother to edit there work are good writers.

21 Learning to edit effective *ly* may be just as important as writing well.

22 Another question to ask *answer* is: how important are writing skills?

23 Good writing skills are needed to be successful in most *any* careers.

24 You can improve your writing skills by making it a priority *to do so*.

25 Judge your writing ~only if~ *after* you have proofread and edited your work.

Take the time to carefully evaluate your completed work. Is the copy forma *t* ted attractively? Does it read ~good~ *well*? have your corrected all grammar and spelling errors? If your work does not impress you, it will not impress any one else.

Indent

When a writer paraphrases or quotes material longer than three lines from another source, the writer must set off the long quote from the rest of the report. Quoted material is set off by indenting it 0.5" from the left margin.

The Indent feature moves all lines of a paragraph to the next tab. In contrast, TAB moves only the first line of a paragraph to the next tab. Indent is a paragraph command. The Indent feature enables you to indent text from either the left or right margin or from both margins.

To indent text from the left margin:

1. Click the **Increase Indent** button on the toolbar. (*Shortcut:* CTRL + M)

2. Key the paragraph and press ENTER. The left indent will continue until you click the **Decrease Indent** button. (*Shortcut:* CTRL + SHIFT + M)

Indent can also be applied to text that has already been keyed.

Help keywords
*Increase the left indent
of an entire paragraph*

 Increase
Indent

 Decrease
Indent

DRILL 1   **INDENT**

1. Key the copy that follows. DS paragraph 1; strike TAB to indent the paragraph.
2. To format paragraph 2, at the left margin, click **Increase Indent**. Change to SS. Strike TAB, and then key paragraph 2.

3. For paragraph 3, click **Decrease Indent**; change to DS.
4. Save as **41d-drill1**.

However, the thrust to use e-mail almost exclusively is causing a tremendous challenge for both e-mail recipients and companies. DS

TAB   With the convenience of electronic mail resulting in its widespread use, many users are forsaking other forms of communication—face-to-face, telephone (including voice mail), and printed documents. Now companies are challenged to create clear e-mail policies and to implement employee training on effective use of e-mail (Ashford, 2000, 2). DS

Communication experts have identified problems that may occur as a result of misusing e-mail. Two important problems include information overload (too many messages) and inappropriate form of communication.

Indent ▶

APPLICATIONS

30f-d1
Rough Draft

1. Open a new document and change spacing to DS.
2. On the first line, center the title: **You Are What You Eat.** Apply bold and 14-point Arial type.
3. Use default font and point size (Times New Roman 12 point) and left-align for the remainder of the document.
4. Key the document making all edits indicated by the proofreaders' marks.
5. Set a right-align tab at 5 3/4" and key your name a DS below the last line of the document.
6. Insert the date using standard business format directly below your name.
7. Proofread and correct all errors.
8. Center the page.
9. Save as **30f-d1**, preview, and print.

A speaker said, "you are what you eat". the speaker didnot mean to imply that fast food make fast people, or that an hearty meal makes a person heart, or even that good food makes a person good? On the other hand, though, a healthfull diet does indeed make person healthier; and good health effects many things including performance, energy level, and attitude. Learning what to include in a healthful diet is the 1st step. The 2nd step is developing the discipline to apply that knowledge. The results are well worth the effort. IN fact, good health may be one of the most often over looked treasures within human existance.

30f-d2
Rough Draft

1. Key the following document DS making all corrections indicated by the proofreaders' marks.
2. Add the following title on the first line: **Sportsmanship and Athletics—An Oxymoron?** Format it in bold and Times New Roman 14 point.
3. Proofread, correct errors, preview, print, and save as **30f-d2**.

An oxymoron is a figure of speech that involve words of opposite meaning, such as an honest thief. Today many people are asking if sportsmanship in athletics is becoming an oxymoron. It fosters an attitude of honesty, ethical conduct, fair play, treating others with respect, and exhibition character worthy of emulation. Does this real describe the current state of intercollegiate athletics?

SKILLBUILDING

41a
Warmup
Key each line twice SS.

alphabetic	1	Jacki might analyze the data by answering five complex questions.
figures	2	Memo 67 asks if the report on Bill 35-48 is due on the 19th or the 20th.
shift	3	Plum trees on a hilly acre, in my opinion, create no vast estate.
easy	4	Did the foal buck? And did it cut the right elbow of the cowhand?

41b
Technique Builder
Key each line SS; DS between groups.

y/t	5	you yes yelp year yeild yellow yule yours symbol pray grassy money
	6	to at tent triek treat trestle tribute thirty match matter clutter
	7	Timothy printed a symbol, yacht, and yellowjacket for Mr. Forsyst.
g/h	8	got get giggle gargle gargoyle gangway engage eagle magic peg piggy
	9	he she her head harp hay heavy hearth homograph hyena high height
	10	Gail Hughes, a researcher, charted the height and weight of Hugh.

| 1 | 2 | 3 | 4 | 5 | 6 | 7 | 8 | 9 | 10 | 11 | 12 | 13 |

41c

Build Staying Power
Take two 3' writings on all ¶s.

    all letters

	gwam	1'	3'
In a recent show, a young skater gave a great performance.		12	4	69
Her leaps were beautiful, her spins were impossible to believe,		25	8	74
and she was a study in grace itself. But she had slipped during		38	13	78
a jump and had gone down briefly on the ice. Because of the high		51	17	82
quality of her act, however, she was given a third-place medal.		64	21	87
Her coach, talking later to a reporter, stated his pleasure		12	25	91
with her part of the show. When asked about the fall, he said		25	30	95
that emphasis should be placed on the good qualities of the per-		37	34	99
formance and not on one single blemish. He ended by saying that		50	38	104
as long as his students did the best they could, he would be		63	42	108
satisfied.		65	43	108
What is "best"? When asked, the young skater explained she		12	47	112
was pleased to have won the bronze medal. In fact, this perfor-		25	51	117
mance was a personal best for her; she was confident the gold		37	55	121
would come later if she worked hard enough. It appears she knew		50	60	125
the way to a better medal lay in beating not other people, but her		64	64	130
own personal best.		67	65	131

1'	1	2	3	4	5	6	7	8	9	10	11	12	13
3'		1			2			3			4		

Fans, coaches, media, student athletes, parents, and administrators often have a win-at-all-cost attitude. Disruptive and destructive fans shout obscenities and harrass officials as well as fans of opponents; they also destroy property. Trash-talking has become commonplace *a way of life* for student athletes. Parents are willing to lie and cheat to get there children in athletic programs. Coaches and administrators cheat, *or tolerate cheating* to recruit players and keep them academically eligible. Are these fair statements, or are they simply media ploys *designed* trying to sell newspapers and magazines and attract radio and television audiences?

Clearly, not all fans, student athletes, coaches, parents, and administrators exhibit unsportsmanlike conduct. However, *stet* numerous surveys indicate that most (70-80%) Americans believe that sportsmanship has significantly declined in recent years. Even if the figures are an exaggeration *ed*, intercollegiate athletics is *still* in trouble because of the public perception of poor sportsmanship.

Colleges offer expensive athletics program *s* because of the educational value and the equal opportunity they provide all students. Other wise, they could not justify expending vast amounts of money on athletics. Despite the myth to the contrary, less *fewer* than 40 intercollegiate athletics programs break *sp* even or make money.

- Format references using the hanging indent feature.
- Use typographic or special symbols to enhance the report.

Writers also take advantage of the online thesaurus for choosing the most appropriate word and the spelling and grammar features to ensure spelling and grammar correctness. Additionally, electronic desk references and style manuals are just a click away.

Finally, all the report needs is the title page. Effective writers know that it pays dividends to create a custom title page that truly reflects the quality of the report that it covers. Use page borders and shading as well as graphics to create an attractive title page.

Two simple steps followed in a systematic order will assist you in your goal to learn to win at writing. Knowing the approach is the first step; the second step is to practice, practice, and practice.

40e-d2
Title Page

1. Prepare a title page for the unbound report prepared in **40e-d1**. Set the left margin at 1.5".
2. Prepare the title page for **XYZ Employees by Jennifer Schoenholtz, Office Manager**. Center the page.
3. Save the title page as **40e-d2**.

SKILLBUILDING
40f

Use the remaining class time to build your Skills using the Skill Builder module within *Keyboarding Pro*.

Module 3: Checkpoint

Evaluate your understanding of this project by answering the questions below.

1. The_____ feature automatically moves text to the next line when one line is full.

2. The _____ feature enables you to see how a document will look when it is printed.

3. The _____ keyboard shortcut can be used to move to the beginning of a document.

4. Before character formats can be applied to existing text, the text must be_____.

5. The alignment used to begin and end all lines at the same position on the left and right margins is_____.

6. Use the _____ function to format a one-page document with the same amount of space in the top and bottom margin.

7. Standard business format for the date is the _____-_____-_____ format.

8. A green wavy line under text indicates a potential _____ error.

9. A potential spelling error is indicated by a(n) _____wavy line.

10. The _____ function reverses changes made in formatting or keying text.

Performance Assessment

Document 1

Rough-draft

1. Key the text shown at the right; make all corrections noted by proofreaders' marks.

2. Add the title **The Hassles of Air Travel**; format it in bold, 14-point type and center it.

3. Right-align your name a DS below the last line of the document. Insert the date on the line directly below your name.

4. Center the page.

5. Print and save the document as **checkpoint3-d1.**

The disaster at the world trade center in NEW York resulted in a significant increase in the hassle factor in air travel. Passengers today must arrive at the airport early to allow addition time to go through enhanced security procedures. Those procedures range from walking through metal detectors to complete searches of individuals and luggage.

Some passengers are frustrated by these changes in security procedures that are both time-consuming and annoying. Most passengers however recognize that they are essential for our safety.

DISCOVER

Insert file—Position insertion point where file is to be inserted. On the **Insert** menu, click **File**; select the desired file; click **Insert**.

1. Key the unbound report that follows. Position main heading at approximately 2". Set proper line spacing.

2. From the data disk, insert the file **writing** below the second paragraph. (*Note:* Be sure to position the insertion point where you want the text to appear before inserting the file.)

3. Format the first side heading *Researching* correctly.

4. Format the bulleted list SS with a DS between items.

5. Revise the side headings to make them parallel (grammatically consistent).

6. Insert page numbers; do not print the page number on page 1.

7. Apply Keep with next to protect side headings from being left alone at the bottom of a page.

8. Switch to Print Layout view to verify page numbers.

9. Save the report as **40e-d1**. Check the spelling, and print the document.

LEARN TO WIN AT WRITING

Being able to communicate effectively continues to be one of the most demanded work skills. Today's high demand for clear, concise, and logical communication makes it impossible for an employee to excuse himself or herself from writing by saying, "I'm just not a writer," or "I can't write."

Realizing you need to improve your writing skills is the first step to enhancing them. Then you must apply a systemized approach to writing as detailed in this report.

Insert the data file writing here.

The effective writer understands the importance of using technology to create an attractive document that adheres to correct style rules. Review the list below to determine your use of technology in the report writing process.

- Number preliminary pages of the report with small Roman numerals at the bottom center of the page.
- Number the report with Arabic numbers in the upper-right corner.
- Create attractive headers or footers that contain helpful information for the reader.
- Suppress headers, footers, and page numbering on the title page and on the first page of the report.
- Invoke the widow/orphan protection feature to ensure that no lines display alone at the bottom or top of a page.
- Use the block protection command to keep side headings from appearing alone at the bottom of the page.

continued

MODULE 4

Business Correspondence

- Learn standard memorandum format.
- Format letters in block letter style.
- Format letters in modified block style.
- Modify tabs.
- Create envelopes.
- Improve keying speed and accuracy.

LESSON 31   Interoffice Memo

SKILLBUILDING

31a
Warmup
Key each line twice SS.

alphabet 1 I quickly explained to two managers the grave hazards of the job.
figures 2 All channels—16, 25, 30, and 74—reported the score was 19 to 8.
shift 3 Maxi and Kay Pascal expect to be in breezy South Mexico in April.
easy 4 Did the man fight a duel, or did he go to a chapel to sign a vow?
| 1 | 2 | 3 | 4 | 5 | 6 | 7 | 8 | 9 | 10 | 11 | 12 | 13 |

gwam 3'

31b
Timed Writing
Take two 3' timings.

all letters

Hard work is required for job success. Set high goals and   4 43
devote time to the exact things that will help you succeed. Work   8 47
hard each day and realize you must be willing to make sacrifices.   13 51

Avoid being like the loser who says, "It may be possible, but   17 55
it's too difficult." Take on the attitude of the winner who says,   21 59
"It may be difficult, but it's possible." Count on working hard.   26 64

Also, seek mentors to pilot you in your long road to success.   30 69
They will encourage you and will challenge you to reach for higher   34 73
dreams even when you are very happy with where you are.   39 77

1' | 1 | 2 | 3 | 4 | 5 | 6 | 7 | 8 | 9 | 10 | 11 | 12 | 13 |
3' | 1 | 2 | 3 | 4 |

Report Format Guidelines

Reports are widely used in various environments. Study the information that follows:

Side margins: Default side margins for an unbound report. Set the left margin at 1.5" for a leftbound report.

Top margin: 2" for first page of report, preliminary pages, and Reference page; 1" on other pages.

Page numbers: Include page numbers for the second and succeeding pages of a report. Position at the top of the page (header), right alignment.

Single lines: Avoid single lines at the top or bottom of a report (called *widow/orphan lines*). Do not separate a side heading from the paragraph that follows between pages.

To format a report:

1. At the top of the document, change the line spacing to double. Strike ENTER three times to position the insertion point to leave an approximate 2" top margin.

2. Check that the font size is 12 point.

3. Insert page numbers. Suppress the page number on the first page.

4. Key the main heading in ALL CAPS. Strike ENTER twice, then select the heading and apply 14 point and bold. Center-align the heading.

5. Move the insertion point to below the heading, and begin to key the report.

6. Position the references on a new page. If necessary, insert a manual page break. Format the title REFERENCES in 14 point, bold, at approximately 2".

7. Protect side headings that may get separated from the related paragraph with the Keep with next feature.

8. View the report using Print Layout view.

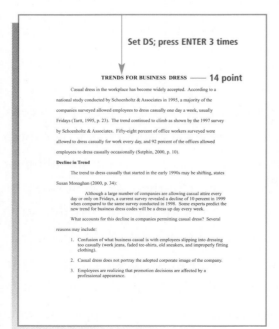

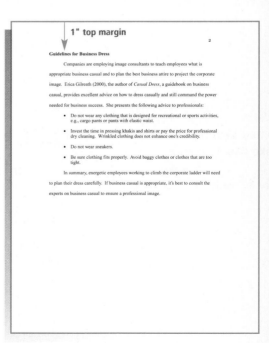

COMMUNICATION

31c

Proofread and Finalize a Document

Before documents are complete, they must be proofread carefully for accuracy. Error-free documents send the message that you are detail oriented and capable. Apply these procedures when processing all documents:

1. Use Spelling and Grammar to check spelling when you have completed the document.
2. Proofread the document on screen to be sure that it makes sense.
3. Preview the document, and check the overall appearance.
4. Save the document, and then print it.
5. Compare the document to the source copy (textbook), and check that text has not been omitted or added. Revise, save, and print if necessary.

DOCUMENT DESIGN

31d

Interoffice Memorandums

Messages sent to persons within an organization are called **memorandums** (memos for short). A popular memo form is an e-mail, which is mailed electronically. Memos are printed on plain paper and sent in plain or interoffice envelopes. Memos consist of the heading, a body, and one or more notations.

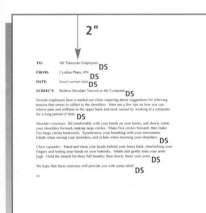

To format a memo:

1. Strike ENTER six times to position the first line of the heading at about 2".
2. Format the memo headings in bold and all caps. Turn off bold and all caps, and strike TAB once or twice after each heading to align the information. Generally, courtesy titles (Mr., Ms., etc.) are not used; however, if the memo is formal, the receiver's name may include a title.
3. Single-space the body of the memo. DS between paragraphs.
4. Add reference initials a DS below the body if the memo is keyed by someone other than the sender. Do not include initials when keying your own memo.
5. Items clipped or stapled to the memo are noted as attachments; items included in an envelope are enclosures. Key these notations a DS below the reference initials.

To format a distribution list:

When memos are sent to more than one person, list their names after TO:. Generally the names are listed in alphabetical order; some organizations, however, list the names in order of rank. For readability, key the names on separate lines. When sending the memo to many people, refer to a distribution list at the end of the memo. Example: TO: Task Force Members--Distribution Below. Indent the names on the distribution list to the first tab.

If you have any questions about these policies, please call me at any time.

xx

Distribution:
    Allen Bejahan
    Janet James
    Terry Johnson
    Ray Lightfoot

Two-Page Reports

SKILLBUILDING

40a
Warmup
Key each line twice SS.

alphabetic 1 Jayne Cox puzzled over workbooks that were required for geometry.
figures 2 Edit pages 308 and 415 in Book A; pages 17, 29, and 60 in Book B.
shift 3 THE LAKES TODAY, published in Akron, Ohio, comes in June or July.
easy 4 The town may blame Keith for the auditory problems in the chapel.
  | 1 | 2 | 3 | 4 | 5 | 6 | 7 | 8 | 9 | 10 | 11 | 12 | 13 |

40b
Technique Builder
Key at a controlled rate.

n/u 5 nun nut unbolt null unable nudge under nurture thunder numb shunt
    6 Uncle Hunter runs with me to hide under the bed when it thunders.
c/e 7 ecru cell echo ceil check cedar pecan celery secret receive price
    8 Once Cecilia checked prices for acceptable and special offerings.
b/r 9 brag barb brown carbon brain marble break herb brace gerbil brick
   10 Bradley will try to break the unbroken brown brood mare bareback.
n/y 11 many bunny irony grainy granny sunny phony rainy runny zany funny
   12 Aunt Nanny says rainy days are for funny movies and many candies.

COMMUNICATION

40c
Report Format Review

In Lesson 39 you learned the unbound report format. Check your understanding of the unbound report format by completing Drills 1 and 2 below. Refer to pp. 127–128 if you have questions.

DRILL 1   FORMAT REVIEW

Key each line below choosing the correct choice shown in parentheses. Use the numbering feature to number each statement. Save as **40c-drill1**.

1. The main heading that appears on the first page of a report is keyed approximately (1", 2") from the top of the page.
2. The main heading is keyed at the (center, left margin); the font size of the main heading is (14 point, 12 point).
3. The main heading is (bold, not bold); side headings are (bold, not bold).
4. Side headings are keyed at the (center, left margin); the font size of side headings is (14 point, 12 point).
5. Side margins of an unbound report are (default or 1", 1.5").

DRILL 2   PROOFREAD FOR CONSISTENCY

1. Open **Report3Key** from the data files and print; close this file.
2. Open **Report 3** and print. Proofread this report and mark any formats that are not consistent with the solution printed in step 1. Use the proofreaders' marks shown on page 55 to mark all corrections.
3. Correct the errors you marked.
4. Save as **40c-drill2** and print. Submit the edited copy and the final copy to your instructor.

31e-d1
Memo

1. Strike ENTER to position the insertion point at about 2" on the status line; key the memo and save as **31e–d1**.

2. Follow "Proofread and Finalize a Document" on page 99.

Interoffice Memo

2" **TO:** TAB TAB Loretta Howerton, Office Manager

FROM: TAB Lawrence Schmidt, OA/CIS Consultant

DATE: TAB Current date

SUBJECT: TAB Memorandums for Internal Correspondence

A memorandum is an internal communication that is sent within the organization. It is often the means by which managers correspond with employees and vice versa. Memos provide written records of announcements, requests for action, and policies and procedures.

Templates, or preformatted forms, are often used for keying memos. Templates provide a uniform look for company correspondence and save the employee the time of having to design and format each memo. Word processing software also has memo templates that can be customized. An example of a template is attached.

xx

Attachment

31e-d2
Memo

> **TIP**
> Use the Date command (**Insert** menu, **Date and Time**) to insert the current date.

> **TIP**
> If the first letter of your reference initials is automatically capitalized, point to the initial until the AutoCorrect options button appears. Click the button; then choose **Undo Automatic Capitalization**.

1. Key the memo and save as **31e-d2**.

words

TO:	Lonny Ashmyer DS	4
FROM:	Breton S. Vreede DS	9
DATE:	Current date	13
SUBJECT:	Wheelchair Access	19

Recently, I explained to you my efforts on a variety of projects to facilitate wheelchair entry into public buildings. I may have found a solution to one problem, Lonny; that is, how does someone open a large public door from a wheelchair? — 35 / 50 / 64 / 67

The answer may lie in the installation of an electrical signal similar to a garage door opener that can be activated from the chair. All signals would be identical, of course, permitting universal application. — 83 / 98 / 110

Please provide me with a rough estimate of the costs for conducting the necessary preliminary search, equipping a wheelchair, and tooling our factory to manufacture this item. — 125 / 139 / 146

xx — 146

39e-d2
Continued

Choosing a typeface

Typeface refers to the style of printing on the page.　　167

Matching the style or "feeling" of the type with the purpose　178

of the finished product is very important. For example,　190

a layout　　_include_　　_of_
you would not ~~want to~~ use a gothic or "old style" typeface　202

to promote a modern, high tech product. Consider the bold-　215

ness or lightness of the style, _and_ the readability factor, _and_　227

the decorativeness or simplicity. ¶ Mixing more than three　233

different typefaces on a page should also be avoided. Vary　251

the type sizes to give the effect of different type styles.　271

ital.
Bold and _italics_ can also be added for emphasis and vari-　275

ety, especially when only one type style is being used.　286

297

39e-d3
Title Page

TIP
Center Page:
Choose File menu,
Page Setup, Layout tab,
Vertical alignment: Center

✳ DISCOVER

Click and Type—Switch to
Print Layout View. Point to
the center of the page to
display centered text icon;
double-click and key.

1. Prepare a title page for the unbound report completed in 39e-d1. See the illustration on page 134.
2. Use bold and 14 point for all lines.
   ✳ 3. Center-align each line using the Click and Type feature.
4. Center the page vertically. Save the document as **39e-d3**.

ELECTRONIC MAIL GUIDELINES

↓8

Prepared for
McIngvale Communications, Inc.

↓8

Prepared by
Craig A. Oliver
Information Technology Manager

↓8

Current date

31e-d3
**Memo with
Distribution List**

1. Key both the memos below; both contain a distribution list.
2. Save as **31e-d3** and **31e-d4**.

TO: TAB   TAB Manufacturing Team--Distribution Below
DS

FROM: TAB Mei-Ling Yee, Administrative Assistant
DS

DATE: TAB Current date

SUBJECT: TAB Enrichment Seminar

As was stated by Robert Beloz in the January newsletter, *Focus for the New Year*, Foscari & Associates will be offering a series of enrichment seminars for its employees in the year ahead. If you have suggestions for seminars that would be beneficial to your team, please let me know.

We are proud to announce our first seminar offering, *First Aid and CPR*. Participants will be awarded CPR Certificates from the American Heart Association upon successful completion of this eight-hour course. If you are interested in taking this seminar, please call me at ext. 702 or send me an e-mail message by April 25.

Mark your calendar for this important seminar.

First Aid and CPR Enrichment Seminar
May 16 and 17
1:00-5:00 p.m.
Staff Lounge

xx

Distribution:
    Eddie Barnett
    Steve Lewis
    Dinah Rice
    Amy Sturdivant

31e-d4
**Memo with
Distribution List**

TO: Safety Officers--Distribution Below | FROM: Louis Cross | DATE: Current | SUBJECT: Safety Seminar

Mark your calendar for the *Safety Practices and Accident Prevention Seminar* that will be held on June 17, 200-, from 9:00 a.m. to 4:30 p.m. The seminar will be held at the Kellogg Center.

New OSHA regulations will be presented at this seminar, so it is extremely important for you as a safety officer to be in attendance. The seminar will be conducted by OSHA employees and professors from the University of New Mexico.

xx

Distribution:
    Lori Baker, Production
    George Markell, Maintenance
    Henry Otter, Human Resources

APPLICATIONS

39e-d1
Unbound Report

1. Key the model report on the previous page. Change the line spacing to double. Strike ENTER three times to position the main heading at about 2". Use default side margins.

2. Key the main heading in ALL CAPS. Strike ENTER once. Select the heading; then change the font size to 14-point bold and center-align the heading. (*Tip:* Striking ENTER before formatting the main heading prevents the format of the heading from being applied to the body of the report.)

3. After keying and formatting the report, save it as **35e-d1**.

39e-d2
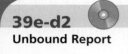
Unbound Report

1. Open **report2** from the data files.

2. Position the main heading at approximately 2.0"

3. Select the report and change the line spacing to double.

4. Correct the capitalization of the side headings and apply bold.

5. Make other edits shown in the report.

6. Save as **39e-d2**.

words

WHO CAN DESIGN A BETTER BROCHURE?
17

Producing a brochure with a professional appearance
29

requires careful creativity and planning. Not every one is
41

an accomplished paste-up artist who is capable of creating
50

a complex piece of printed art, but most skilled computer
62

users can create an attractive layout for a basic brochure.
66

Working with blocks
76

Work with copy and illustration in blocks. Type body
87

of text copy, leaving plenty of space for illustrations and
99

headlines. The blocks should then be arranged in a orderly
101

and eye appealing manner.
112

Using a small a small size type (or font) is not recommended.
122

In most cases, use a font that is 12 point or larger to
133

make the document easy to read. Copy that is arranged in
143

more than one column is also more attractive. Try not to key
147

copy across the full width of a page. Preferably break the
160

page into smaller columns of copy and intersperse with photos or
163

illustrations.
167

LESSON 32 — Review Memo and E-Mail

SKILLBUILDING

32a
Warmup
Key each line twice SS.

alphabet	1	Extra awards given by my employer amazed Jo, the file clerk.
figures	2	I will be on vacation June 4-7, October 3, 5, 8, and December 6-9.
shift	3	Sue, May, Al, Tom, and Jo will meet us at the Pick and Save store.
easy	4	Ask the girl to copy the letter for all the workers in the office.

| 1 | 2 | 3 | 4 | 5 | 6 | 7 | 8 | 9 | 10 | 11 | 12 | 13 |

DOCUMENT DESIGN

32b

Electronic Mail

Electronic mail (or **e-mail**) is an informal message that is sent by one computer user to another computer user. To be able to send or receive e-mail, you must have an e-mail address, an e-mail program, and access to the Internet.

Heading: Accurately key the e-mail address of the receiver and supply a specific subject line. The date and your e-mail address will display automatically.

Attachments: Documents can be sent electronically by attaching the file to the recipient's e-mail message. The attached file can then be opened and edited by the recipient.

Body: SS the body of an e-mail; DS between paragraphs. Do not indent the paragraphs.

Formatting: Do not add bold or italic or vary the fonts. Do not use uppercase letters for emphasis. Use emoticons or e-mail abbreviations with caution (e.g., ;- for wink or BTW for by the way).

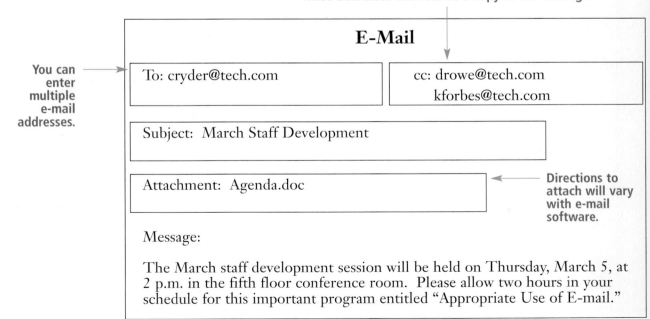

These addresses will receive a copy of the message.

E-Mail

You can enter multiple e-mail addresses.

To: cryder@tech.com

cc: drowe@tech.com
kforbes@tech.com

Subject: March Staff Development

Attachment: Agenda.doc

Directions to attach will vary with e-mail software.

Message:

The March staff development session will be held on Thursday, March 5, at 2 p.m. in the fifth floor conference room. Please allow two hours in your schedule for this important program entitled "Appropriate Use of E-mail."

DOCUMENT DESIGN DOCUMENT DESIGN DOCU-

Set DS; Press ENTER 3 times

about 2"

ELECTRONIC MAIL GUIDELINES ← 14pt

Electronic mail, a widely used communication channel, clearly has three major advantages—time effectiveness, distance effectiveness, and cost-effectiveness. To reap full benefit from this popular and convenient communication medium, follow the basic guidelines regarding the creation and use of e-mail.

Side heading

E-mail Composition

Although perceived as informal documents, e-mail messages are business records. Therefore, follow effective communication guidelines: write clear, concise sentences;

Default or 1" ... break the message into logical paragraphs; and double-space between paragraphs. Spell ... Default or 1"

check e-mail messages carefully, and verify punctuation and content accuracy. Do limit e-mail messages to one idea per message, and preferably limit to one screen. Include a subject line that clearly defines the e-mail message.

Side heading

E-mail Practices

Although many people are using e-mail, some individuals do not use it as their preferred method of communication and may check it infrequently. To accomplish tasks more effectively, be aware of individuals' preferred channels of communication and use those channels. Consider an e-mail message the property of the sender, and forward only with permission. Some senders include a note in the signature line that reminds recipients not to forward e-mail without seeking permission.

APPLICATIONS

Follow these directions for completing all documents in Lesson 32:

Without Internet access: Complete all documents as memos.

With an e-mail address: Complete the documents in your e-mail software and send them.

With Internet access but no e-mail address: Your instructor will assist you in setting up a free e-mail account and address.

32c-d1
E-mail Message

1. Key the following e-mail message to your instructor.
2. Key **Assignment 1 from (Your Name)** as the subject line.
3. Send the message.

Consider the following when choosing an appropriate e-mail password.

1. Do not choose a password that is named after a family member or a pet.

2. Do not use birth dates as a password.

3. Choose a combination of letters and numbers; preferably, use uppercase and lowercase letters, e.g., TLQ6tEpR.

4. Do not share your password with anyone.

5. Do not write your password on a piece of paper and leave it by your computer or in your desk drawer.

32c-d2
E-mail Message with Copy Notation

1. Key the following e-mail message to your instructor.
2. Copy the message to one student in your class.
3. Key **Assignment 2 from (Your Name)** as the subject line.
4. Send the message.

Follow these guidelines when composing e-mail.

1. Do not use bold or italic or vary fonts.

2. Do not use uppercase for emphasis.

3. Use emoticons or e-mail abbreviations with caution (e.g., :) for smile or BTW for by the way).

4. Write clear, concise messages that are free of spelling and grammatical errors.

5. Do not send an e-mail message in haste or anger. Think about the message carefully before clicking the Send button.

39d
Report Format Guides

Main heading

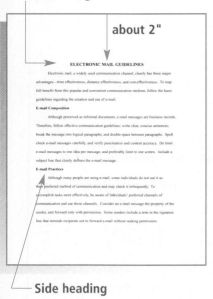

about 2"

Side heading

Unbound Report Format

Reports prepared without binders are called **unbound reports**. Unbound reports may be attached with a staple or paper clip in the upper-left corner.

Margins, Spacing, and Page Numbers

Margins: Margins are the distance between the edge of the paper and the print. Use the preset default top, side, and bottom margins on unbound reports. (Note: You will position the main heading by pressing ENTER.)

Font size and spacing: Use 12-point size for readability. Generally, educational reports are double spaced (DS) and business reports are single spaced (SS). Indent paragraphs 0.5" when the body of the report is DS. Begin the paragraphs at the left margin when the report is SS, and DS between paragraphs.

Enumerated items: Align bulleted or numbered items with the beginning of a paragraph. SS each item and DS between items.

Page numbers: The first page of a report is not numbered. The second and succeeding pages are numbered in the upper-right corner in the header position (0.5").

Headings

Headings have a hierarchy. Spacing and font size indicate the level of heading. The main heading informs readers of the report title. Side headings within the report break a lengthy report into smaller, easier-to-understand parts.

Main heading: Strike ENTER to position the main heading at about 2". The status bar will show at 2.1". Center and key the title in ALL CAPS. Use 14 point and bold.

At 2.1"	Ln 7	Col 1

Side headings: Key at left margin in bold. Capitalize the first letters of main words; DS above and below side headings if the report is SS.

Title Page

The cover or title page should have a concise title that identifies the report to the reader. A title page includes the title of the report, the name and title of the individual or the organization for which the report was prepared, the name and title of the writer, and the date the report was completed.

Center-align each line and center the page vertically. Allow near equal space between parts of the page (strike ENTER about eight times).

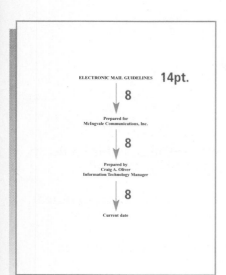

32c-d3
Interoffice Memo with Distribution List

1. Key the memo below. Add your reference initials.

2. Indent the names on the Distribution List to the first tab.

   Distribution:
   Allen Bejahan
   Janet James
   Terry Johnson
   Ray Lightfoot

3. Save as **32c-d3**.

		words
TO:	Team Leaders -- Distribution Below	8
FROM:	J. Mac Chandler, Office Manager	15
DATE:	Current date	19
SUBJECT:	New Multimedia Lab Available June 12	29

We are pleased to announce the opening of our new Multimedia Lab effec- 43
tive June 12. The lab is in the front office just beyond the Advertising 58
Department. The lab has four new computers with full multimedia capa- 72
bility, two laser disc players, a VCR, two presentation projection devices, 87
two scanners, and various color and laser printers. 97

Use this lab if your computer is too small for your job, too slow, or too 112
limited to handle a specific job. Just complete the sign-up sheet located 127
adjacent to the equipment. Projection equipment and two laptop com- 141
puters may be checked out for presentations. Please reserve this equipment 156
twenty-four hours in advance. 162
176

32c-d4
Memo with Proofreaders' Marks

1. Key the memo; make changes as shown.

2. Use your reference initials.

3. Save as **32c-d4**.

		words
TO: J. Ezra Bayh		4
FROM: Greta Sangtree		8
DATE: Current date		13
SUBJECT: Letter-Mailing Standards		20

chk sp

Recently the post office delivered late a letter that ⟩ *, because of the delay,* 35
caused us some (embarassment). To avoid recurrence, please 47
ensure that all administrative assistants and mail person- 58
nel follow postal service guidelines. 67

U.S.

Perhaps a refresher seminar on correspondence guidelines is 79
in in order. Thanks for you help. *(for your* 86

LESSON 39

Unbound Report with Title Page

SKILLBUILDING

39a
Warmup
Key each line twice SS.

alphabetic	1	The explorer questioned Jack's amazing story about the lava flow.
fig/sym	2	I cashed Cartek & Bunter's $2,679 check (Check #3480) on June 15.
1st/2d finger	3	Hugh tried to go with Katrina, but he did not have time to do so.
easy	4	The eighty firms may pay for a formal audit of their field works.

| 1 | 2 | 3 | 4 | 5 | 6 | 7 | 8 | 9 | 10 | 11 | 12 | 13 |

39b
Troublesome Pairs
Key each line once; repeat if time permits.

TECHNIQUE TIP
Keep hands and arms still as you reach up to the third row and down to the first row.

t	5	it cat pat to top thin at tilt jolt tuft mitt flat test tent felt
r	6	fur bur try roar soar ram trap rare ripe true rear tort corral
t/r	7	The track star was triumphant in both the third and fourth heats.
m	8	me mine memo mimic named clam month maximum mummy summer remember
n	9	no snow ton none nine ninety noun mini mind minnow kennel evening
m/n	10	Men and women in management roles maximize time during commuting.
o	11	of one odd coil book oink cool polo crop soap yoyo option noodle
i	12	in it if did idea bike fix site with fill ilium indigo initiative
o/i	13	To know if you rock while giving a speech, stand on a foil sheet.
a	14	an as am is ask arm pass task team haze value salsa manage animal
s	15	so as sip spy must shape class shawl sister system second synergy
a/s	16	Assistants must find names and addresses for a class action suit.
e	17	he we me she they seal feel green there energy desire screensaver
i	18	is it in icon kite site tired unit limit feline service invisible
e/i	19	Initial triage services are limited to solely emergency patients.

39c

Timed Writings
1. Take two 1' timings; key as rapidly as you can.
2. Take one 2' timing. Try to maintain your 1' rate.

  all letters

gwam 1' 2'

	1'	2'
The value of an education has been a topic discussed many	12	6	48
times with a great deal of zest. The value is often measured in	25	12	54
terms of costs and benefits to the taxpayer. It is also judged	37	19	61
in terms of changes in the individuals taking part in the	49	24	67
educational process. Gains in the level of knowledge, the	61	30	72
development and refinement of attitudes, and the acquiring of	73	36	79
skills are believed to be crucial parts of an education.	84	42	84

1' | 1 | 2 | 3 | 4 | 5 | 6 | 7 | 8 | 9 | 10 | 11 | 12 | 13 |
2' | 1 | 2 | 3 | 4 | 5 | 6 |

Block Letter Format

SKILLBUILDING

33a
Warmup

Keep fingers curved, hands quiet as you key each line twice SS.

1st finger
1 My 456 heavy brown jugs have nothing in them; fill them by May 7.
2 The 57 bins are numbered 1 to 57; Bins 5, 6, 45, and 57 are full.

2d finger
3 Ed decided to crate 38 pieces of cedar decking from the old dock.
4 Mike, who was 38 in December, likes a piece of ice in cold cider.

3d finger
5 Polly made 29 points on the quiz; Wex 10 points. Did they pass?
6 Sall saw Ezra pass 200 pizza pans to Sean, who fixed 20 of them.

| 1 | 2 | 3 | 4 | 5 | 6 | 7 | 8 | 9 | 10 | 11 | 12 | 13 |

33b
Timed Writing

Take two 3' timings.

  all letters

gwam 3'

So now you are operating a keyboard and don't you find it   4 | 38
amazing that your fingers, working with very little visual help,   8 | 43
move easily and quickly from one key to the next, helping you to   13 | 47
change words into ideas and sentences. You just decide what you   17 | 51
want to say and the format in which you want to say it, and your   21 | 56
keyboard will carry out your order exactly as you enter it. One   26 | 60
operator said lately that she sometimes wonders just who is most   30 | 64
responsible for the completed product—the person or the machine.   34 | 69

3' | 1 | 2 | 3 | 4 | 5 |

FUNCTION REVIEW

33c

Date and Time

The current date can be inserted into a document by using the Insert Date and Time feature.

To insert the date:

1. Place the cursor at the position the date is to be inserted.
2. Select **Date and Time** from the Insert menu.
3. Select the desired format from the Date and Time dialog box; click **OK**.

Center Page

Copy can be centered vertically on the page by using the Center Page command. To center the copy on the page, choose **Page Setup** from the File menu. Click the **Layout** tab, click the **Vertical Alignment** drop list arrow, and choose **Center**.

DRILL 1

INSERT DATE AND CENTER PAGE

1. Key your first and last name on the page; strike ENTER twice.
2. Insert the current date; select the format *March 5, 2003*.
3. Center the page and print. Do not save.

TECHNIQUE TIP
You can also insert a page break by pressing CTRL + Enter or choosing **Page Break** from the Insert menu.

Line and Page Breaks

Pagination or breaking pages at the appropriate location can easily be controlled using two features: Widow/Orphan control and Keep with next.

Widow/Orphan control prevents a single line of a paragraph from printing at the bottom or top of a page. A check mark displays in this option box indicating that Widow/Orphan control is "on" (the default).

Keep with next prevents a page break from occurring between two paragraphs. Use this feature to keep a side heading from being left alone at the bottom of a page. To use Keep with next:

1. Select the side heading and the paragraph that follows.

2. Click **Format**; then **Paragraph**.

3. From the Line and Page Breaks tab, select **Keep with next**. Click **OK**. The side heading moves to the next page.

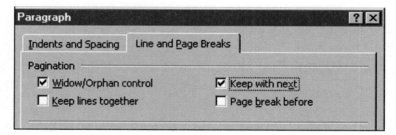

DRILL 4   **LINE AND PAGE BREAKS**

1. Open **keep with next** from the data files. Save as **38c-drill4**.

2. Select the heading **Friday, October 24** (include all lines of heading) and the paragraph that follows. Apply the **Keep with next** command.

3. Use the Insert command to insert number at the top of page. Suppress the page number on the first page.

4. Save and print.

APPLICATIONS

38d-d1
Report with Page Numbers, Bullets and Page Breaks

1. Open **report1** from the data files. Save it as **38d-d1**.

2. Key the following bulleted items just above the section *And the Final Report*.
    *   Italicize titles of complete publications.
    *   Use quotation marks with parts of publications.
    *   Months and certain locational words may be abbreviated.

3. Insert the number at the top of page. Suppress the page number on the first page.

4. Select the heading *In Conclusion* and the paragraph that follows. Apply the Keep with next command.

5. Change to Print Layout view to verify the page numbers and page breaks.

6. Save and print.

33d

Block Letter

Business Letters

Business letters are used to communicate with persons outside of the business. Business letters carry two messages: one is the tone and content; a second is the appearance of the document. Appearance is important because it creates the critical first impression. Stationery, use of standard letter parts, and placement should convey that the writer is intelligent, informed, and detail minded.

Stationery

Letters should be printed on high-quality (about 24-pound) letterhead stationery. Standard size for letterhead is $8^{1}/_{2}$" x 11". Envelopes should match the letterhead in quality and color.

Letter parts

Businesspeople expect to see standard letter parts arranged in the proper sequence. The standard parts are listed below. Other letter parts may be included as needed.

Letterhead: Preprinted stationery that includes the company name, logo, address, and other optional information such as a telephone number and fax number.

Dateline: Date the letter is prepared.

Letter address: Complete address of the person who will receive the letter. Generally, the address includes the receiver's name, company name, street address, city, state (followed by one space only), and ZIP code. Include a personal title (*Mr.*, *Ms.*, *Dr.*) with the person's name. Key the address four lines below the dateline, and capitalize the first letter of each word.

Salutation: Key the salutation, or greeting, a double space (DS) below the letter address. If the letter is addressed to an individual, include a courtesy title with the person's last name. If the letter is addressed to a company, use *Ladies and Gentlemen*.

Body: Begin the body, or message, a DS below the salutation. Single-space (SS) paragraphs and DS between paragraphs.

Complimentary closing: Begin the complimentary closing a DS below the body. Capitalize only the first letter of the closing.

Writer's name and title: Key the writer's name and job title four lines below the complimentary closing to allow space for the writer's signature. Key the name and title on either one or two lines, whichever gives better balance to the signature block. Separate the writer's name and title with a comma if they are on one line.

Reference initials: Key the initials of the typist in lowercase letters a DS below the typed name and title. If the writer's initials are also included, key them first in ALL CAPS followed by a colon (BB:xx).

Block Format

In block format, all letter parts are keyed at the left margin. For most letters, use open punctuation, which requires no punctuation after the salutation or the closing. For efficiency, use the default settings and features of your software when formatting letters.

Side margins: Default (1.25") or 1".

Dateline: Position the date at about 2" (strike ENTER six times) or at least 0.5" below the letterhead. If the letter is short, center the page vertically. To avoid interfering with the letterhead, do not center long letters or letters containing many extra parts.

Spacing: SS paragraphs; DS between them. Follow the directions for spacing between other letter parts provided above.

DRILL 2 — DATA FILES AND BULLETS

The CD-ROM in the back of your textbook contains extra files you will use in this course. This text refers to these files as **data files**. They are organized by module. A CD icon appears with the drill or application heading when a data file is used.

1. Ask your instructor how to access the files, or install the files on the hard drive following the instructions on the CD-ROM. When the files are installed, locate the data path or folder where these files are stored.

2. Double-click the **Module 5** folder to open it. Open the file **bullets**.

3. Select the bulleted items, and convert them to numbers.

4. Add a blank line between each numbered item without adding an additional number by pressing SHIFT + ENTER at the end of each item.

5. Save as **38c-drill2**.

Page Numbers

Help keywords:

Page numbers, Add page number, Add basic page numbers to headers or footers

The Page Number command automatically inserts the correct page number on each page. Page numbers may be positioned automatically in the header position (0.5" at top of page) or in the footer position (bottom of page). To enable the number not to print on the first page, you will remove the ✓ before Show number on first page box.

Print Layout view is designed to view page numbers and other features as they will print. Select Print Layout from the View menu to view page numbers.

To insert page numbers:

1. From the **Insert** menu, choose **Page Numbers**; the Page Numbers dialog box displays.

2. Select **Top of page (Header)** in the Position box.

3. Select **Right** in the Alignment box (default).

4. Remove the check (✓) in the **Show number on first page** box. Click OK.

5. Choose **Print Layout** from the **View** menu to view the page numbers.

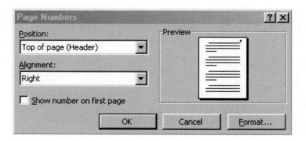

DRILL 3 — PAGE NUMBERS

1. Open **page numbers** from the data files.

2. Use Page Numbers command to insert number at top of page. Remove the ✓ in Show number on first page box.

3. Use Print Layout view to verify page numbers (**View, Print Layout**).

4. Save as **38c-drill3**.

2.1"

E-Market, Group
10 East Rivercenter Boulevard
Covington, KY 41016-8765

Dateline Current date ↓4

Letter address Mr. Ishmal Dabdoub
Professional Office Consultants
1782 Laurel Canyon Road
Sunnyvale, CA 93785-9087 **DS**

Salutation

Dear Mr. Dabdoub **DS**

Body Have you heard your friends and colleagues talk about obtaining real-time stock quotes? real-time account balances and positions? Nasdaq Level II quotes? extended-hours trading? If so, then they are among the three million serious investors that have opened an account with E-Market. **DS**

We believe that the best decisions are informed decisions made in a timely manner. E-Market has an online help desk that provides information for all levels of investors, from beginners to the experienced serious trader. You can learn basic tactics for investing in the stock market, how to avoid common mistakes, and pick up some advanced strategies. **DS**

Stay on top of the market and your investments! Visit our Web site at http://www.emarket.com to learn more about our banking and brokerage services. E-Market Group is the premier site for online investing. **DS**

Sincerely ↓4   **Complimentary Closing**

Margaritta Gibson

Writer's name
Title Ms. Margaritta Gibson
Marketing Manager **DS**

Reference initials xx

38c

Bullets   Numbering

Numbered and bulleted lists are commonly used to emphasize information in reports, newspapers, magazine articles, and overhead presentations. Use numbered items if the list requires a sequence of steps or points. Use bullets or symbols if the list contains an unordered listing. *Word* automatically inserts the next number in a sequence if you manually key a number.

Single-space bulleted or numbered items if each item consists of one line. If more than one line is required for any item, single-space the list and double-space between each item. Study the illustrations shown below.

Help keywords:
Bullets, Numbering

- Word processing
- Spreadsheet
- Database
- Presentation
- Desktop publishing

1. Preheat oven to 350°.
2. Cream butter and sugar; add eggs.
3. Add flour.

To create bullets or numbers:

1. Key the list without bullets or numbers. Select the list and click the **Bullets** or **Numbering** button on the Formatting toolbar. If a double space is required between items, press SHIFT + ENTER at the end of each line.

2. To add or remove bullets or numbers, click the **Bullets** or **Numbering** button.

3. To convert bullets to numbers or vice versa, select the items to change and click either the **Bullets** or **Numbering** button.

DRILL 1   BULLETS

1. Key the text below as a single list; do not key the bullets.

2. Apply bullets to the list by selecting the text to be bulleted and clicking the **Bullets** button.

3. Convert the bullets to numbers. Select the bulleted items and click the **Numbering** button.

4. Add **Roll Call** as the second item.

5. Delete the number before *Next Meeting*.

6. Save the document as **38c-drill1** and print it.

- Call to Order
- Reading and Approval of the Minutes
- Announcements
- Treasurer's Report

- Membership Committee Report
- Unfinished Business
- New Business
- Adjournment
- Next Meeting: November 3, 200-

33e-d1
Block Letter

| At 2.1" | Ln 7 | Col 1 |

1. Key the model letter on page 107 in block format with open punctuation. Begin with the date.
2. Strike ENTER to position the dateline about 2.1" on the status bar. The position will vary depending upon the font size.
3. Insert the current date using the Date and Time feature.
4. Include your reference initials. If the first letter of your initials is automatically capitalized, point to the initial until the AutoCorrect Option button appears, click the button, and then choose Undo Automatic Capitalization.
5. Follow the proofreading procedures outlined in Lesson 31. Use Print Preview to check the placement.
6. Use Show/Hide to compare paragraph markers with the model at the left. Print the letter when you are satisfied. Create the folder **Module 4 Keys** and save the letter as **33e-d1** in this folder. Save all drills and documents for Module 4 in the **Module 4 Keys** folder.

33e-d2
Block Letter

1. Key the letter below in block format with open punctuation. Use Date and Time to insert the current date. Add your reference initials in lowercase letters.
2. Save the letter as **33e-d2**. Proofread and print the letter. Keep the document displayed for the next exercise.

↓2.1"
Current date ↓4

Ms. Alice Ottoman
Premiere Properties, Inc.
52 Ocean Drive
Newport Beach, CA 92747-6293 ↓2

Dear Ms. Ottoman ↓2

Internet Solutions has developed a new technique for you to market your properties on the World Wide Web. We can now create 360-degree panoramic pictures for your Web site. You can give your clients a virtual spin of the living room, kitchen, and every room in the house. ↓2

Call today for a demonstration of this remarkable technology. Give your clients a better visual understanding of the property layout—something your competition doesn't have. ↓2

Sincerely ↓4

Lee Rodgers
Marketing Manager ↓2

xx

33e-d3
Block Letter and
Center Page

1. Document **33e-d2** should be displayed on your screen. Save it as **33e-d3**.
2. Replace the letter address with the one below in proper format.
   Ms. Andrea Virzi, J P Personnel Services, 2351 West Ravina Drive, Atlanta, GA 30346-9105
3. Supply the correct salutation. Turn on **Show/Hide (¶)**. Delete the six hard returns above the dateline. Align the page at vertical center (**File, Page Setup**). Proofread and save. Use Print Preview to view placement. Note that a short letter looks more attractive centered on the page rather than positioned at 2.1".

Simple Reports

- Format two-page reports with references and title pages.
- Indent long quotations and bibliography entries appropriately.
- Insert page numbers.
- Apply bullets and numbers.
- Insert and edit footnotes.

LESSON 38 — Skillbuilding and Report Basics

SKILLBUILDING

38a
Warmup
Key each line twice SS.

alphabetic	1	Dave Cagney alphabetized items for next week's quarterly journal.
figures	2	Close Rooms 4, 18, and 20 from 3 until 9 on July 7; open Room 56.
up reaches	3	Toy & Wurt's note for $635 (see our page 78) was paid October 29.
easy	4	The auditor is due by eight, and he may lend a hand to the panel.

| 1 | 2 | 3 | 4 | 5 | 6 | 7 | 8 | 9 | 10 | 11 | 12 | 13 |

gwam 1' | 3'

38b
Timed Writings
Take two 3' timings.

 all letters

	1'	3'
Have simple things such as saying please, may I help you, and	12	4
thank you gone out of style? We begin to wonder when we observe	25	8
front-line workers interact with customers today. Often their bad	39	13
attitudes shout that the customer is a bother and unimportant. But	52	17
we know there would be no business without the customer. So what	66	22
can be done to prove to customers that they really are the king?	79	26
First, require that all your staff train in good customer	12	30
service. Here they must come to realize that their jobs exist for	25	35
the customer. Also, be sure workers feel that they can talk to	38	39
their bosses about any problem. You do not want workers to talk	51	43
about lack of breaks or schedules in front of customers. Clients	64	48
must always feel that they are kings and should never be ignored.	77	52

1' | 1 | 2 | 3 | 4 | 5 | 6 | 7 | 8 | 9 | 10 | 11 | 12 | 13 |
3' | 1 | | 2 | | 3 | | 4 |

Block Letters with Envelopes

SKILLBUILDING

34a
Warmup
Key each line twice SS.

alphabetic 1 Buddy Jackson is saving the door prize money for wax and lacquer.
figures 2 I have fed 47 hens, 25 geese, 10 ducks, 39 lambs, and 68 kittens.
one hand 3 You imply Jon Case exaggerated my opinion on a decrease in rates.
easy 4 I shall make hand signals to the widow with the auditory problem.

| 1 | 2 | 3 | 4 | 5 | 6 | 7 | 8 | 9 | 10 | 11 | 12 | 13 |

34b
Rhythm Builder
Key lines 5–8 twice.
Take two 30" timings
on lines 9 and 10.

Balanced-hand words, phrases, and sentences.

5 am an by do go he if is it me or ox or so for and big the six spa
6 but cod dot dug eye end wit vie yam make also city work gage them

7 is it| is it| is it he| is it he| for it| for it| paid for it| it is she
8 of it| pay due| pay for| paid me| paid them| also make| such as| may end

9 Sue and Bob may go to the zoo, and he or she may pay for the gas.
10 Jim was sad; Ted saw him as we sat on my bed; we saw him get gas.

| 1 | 2 | 3 | 4 | 5 | 6 | 7 | 8 | 9 | 10 | 11 | 12 | 13 |

COMMUNICATION

34c

Letter Addresses and Salutations

The salutation, or greeting, consists of the person's personal title (*Mr.*, *Ms.*, or *Mrs.*) or professional title (*Dr.*, *Professor*, *Senator*, *Honorable*), and the person's last name. Do not use a first name unless you have a personal relationship. The salutation should agree in number with the addressee. If the letter is addressed to more than one person, the salutation is plural.

	Receiver	Salutation
To individuals	Dr. Alexander Gray	Dear Dr. Gray
	Dr. and Mrs. Thompson	Dear Dr. and Mrs. Thompson
To organizations	TMP Electronics, Inc.	Ladies and Gentlemen
Name unknown	Advertising Manager	Dear Advertising Manager

DRILL 1
PRACTICE LETTER PARTS

1. Review the model document on page 107 for correct placement of letter parts.
2. Key the letter parts for each activity, spacing correctly between parts. In the first exercise, strike ENTER six times to begin the dateline at 2.1"; use the Date and Time feature.
3. Press ENTER five times between drills. Do not save the drills.
4. Take a 2' timing on each drill. Repeat if you finish before time is up.

A Current date

Ms. Joyce Bohn, Treasurer
Citizens for the Environment
1888 Hutchins Ave.
Seattle, WA 98111-2353

Dear Ms. Bohn

B Please confirm our lunch date.

Sincerely yours

James D. Bohlin
District Attorney

xx

Skill Builder Lesson E

1. Open *Keyboarding Pro*, Skill Builder module. Complete Lesson E with the Speed Emphasis.

2. Print your Lesson Report if requested by your instructor.

3. Complete the Skill Builder lessons on your own or as directed by your instructor.

DRILL 8

WORD BEGINNINGS

In the Open Screen, key each row once; strive for accuracy. Repeat.

br
1 bright brown bramble bread breath breezes brought brother broiler
2 In February my brother brought brown bread and beans from Boston.

exe
3 exercises exert executives exemplify exemption executed exemplary
4 They exert extreme effort executing exercises in exemplary style.

bt
5 doubt subtle obtains obtrusion subtracts indebtedness undoubtedly
6 Extreme debt will cause more than subtle doubt among my creditors.

ny
7 tiny funny company nymph penny nylon many anyone phony any brainy
8 Anyone as brainy and funny as Penny is an asset to their company.

| 1 | 2 | 3 | 4 | 5 | 6 | 7 | 8 | 9 | 10 | 11 | 12 | 13 |

DRILL 9

TIMED WRITINGS

1. Take a 1' writing on each ¶.
2. Take a 3' writing on both ¶s.

Option: Key the timing as a Diagnostic Writing in *Keyboarding Pro 4* or from *MicroPace Pro*:

Filename **SB3-T9**

gwam 1' | 3'

Many people believe that an ounce of prevention is worth a | 12 | 4
pound of cure. Care of your heart can help you prevent serious | 25 | 8
physical problems. The human heart is the most important pump ever | 38 | 13
developed. It constantly pushes blood through the body tissues. | 51 | 17
But the layers of muscle that make up the heart must be kept in | 64 | 23
proper working order. Exercise can help this muscle to remain in | 77 | 26
good condition. | 84 | 27

Another important way of keeping a healthy heart is just to | 12 | 31
avoid habits which are considered detrimental to the body. Food | 25 | 35
that is high in cholesterol is not a good choice. Also, use of | 38 | 39
tobacco has quite a bad effect on the function of the heart. You | 51 | 44
can minimize your chances of heart trouble by avoiding these bad | 64 | 48
health habits. | 67 | 49

1' | 1 | 2 | 3 | 4 | 5 | 6 | 7 | 8 | 9 | 10 | 11 | 12 | 13 |
3' | 1 | 2 | 3 | 4 |

NEW FUNCTIONS

34d

Envelopes

The envelope feature can insert the delivery address automatically if a letter is displayed; postage can even be added if special software is installed. The default is a size 10 envelope (4⅛" by 9½"); other sizes are available by clicking the Options button on the Envelope tab. An alternative style for envelope addresses is uppercase (ALL CAPS) with no punctuation.

> Ms. Alice Ottoman
> Premiere Properties, Inc.
> 52 Ocean Drive
> Newport Beach, CA 92747-6293

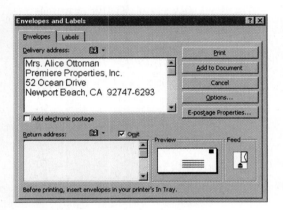

To generate an envelope:

1. With the letter you have created displayed, click **Tools** on the menu, and then **Letters and Mailings**. Click **Envelopes and Labels,** and if necessary, click the **Envelopes** tab. The mailing address is automatically displayed in the Delivery address box. (To create an envelope without a letter, follow the same steps, but key the address in the Delivery address box.)

2. If you are using business envelopes with a preprinted return address (assume you are), click the Return address Omit box. To include a return address, do not check the Omit box, click in the Return address box, and enter the return address.

   Note: To format a letter address on the envelope in all caps, click **Add to Document** to attach the envelope to the letter, and then edit the address.

Change Case

Change Case enables you to change the capitalization of text that has already been keyed.

Sentence case capitalizes the first letter of the first word of a sentence.

Lowercase changes all capital letters to lowercase letters.

Uppercase changes all letters to uppercase.

Title case capitalizes the first letter of each word.

Toggle case changes all uppercase letters to lowercase and vice versa.

To change case, select the text to be changed, choose **Change Case** from the Format menu, and then choose the appropriate option.

DRILLS 2–3

CREATE ENVELOPE

1. Create an envelope for the addressee in Drill 1 on page 109.

2. Attach the envelope to a blank document.

3. Save the document as **34d-drill2.**

4. Open **33e-d2**. Create and attach an envelope to the letter.

5. Select the entire address and convert it to uppercase. Delete the punctuation.

6. Save the document as **34d-drill3** and print it. Your instructor may have you print envelopes on plain paper.

Skill Builder Lesson D

1. Open *Keyboarding Pro*, Skill Builder module. Complete Lesson D with the Speed Emphasis.
2. Print your Lesson Report if requested by your instructor.

DRILL 6

ADJACENT KEY REVIEW
Key each row once; strive for accuracy. Repeat.

1 nm many enmity solemn kl inkling weekly pickle oi oil invoice join
2 iu stadium medium genius lk milk talk walks uy buy buyer soliloquy
3 mn alumni hymn number column sd Thursday wisdom df mindful handful
4 me mention comment same fo found perform info le letter flew files

5 The buyer sent his weekly invoices for oil to the group on Thursday.
6 Mindful of the alumni, the choirs sang a hymn prior to my soliloquy.
7 An inmate, a fogger, and a genius joined the weekly talks on Monday.
8 They were to join in the talk shows to assess regions of the Yukon.

| 1 | 2 | 3 | 4 | 5 | 6 | 7 | 8 | 9 | 10 | 11 | 12 | 13 |

DRILL 7

TIMED WRITINGS
1. Take a 1' writing on each ¶.
2. Take a 3' writing on both ¶s.

Option: Key the timing as a Diagnostic Writing in *Keyboarding Pro 4* or from *MicroPace Pro:*

Filename SB3-T7

	gwam	1'	3'

All people, in spite of their eating habits, have two major — 12 — 4
needs that must be met by their food. They need food that — 24 — 8
provides a source of energy, and they need food that will fill — 37 — 12
the skeletal and operating needs of their bodies. Carbohydrates, — 50 — 17
fats, and protein form a major portion of the diet. Vitamins and — 63 — 21
minerals are also necessary for excellent health. — 72 — 24

Carbohydrates make up a major source of our energy needs. — 12 — 28
Fats also serve as a source of energy and act as defense against — 25 — 32
cold and trauma. Proteins are changed to amino acids, which are — 38 — 37
the building units of the body. These, in turn, are utilized to — 51 — 41
make most body tissue. Minerals are required to control many — 64 — 46
body functions, and vitamins are used for normal growth and aid — 78 — 50
against disease. — 79 — 51

1' | 1 | 2 | 3 | 4 | 5 | 6 | 7 | 8 | 9 | 10 | 11 | 12 | 13 |
3' | 1 | 2 | 3 | 4 |

APPLICATIONS

34e-d1
Edit Letter

1. Open letter **33e-d1**, save it as **34e-d1**, and then make the changes shown below.
2. Center the letter vertically. Use **Show/Hide** to remove any extra paragraph markers (¶).
3. Change the date to the current date, preview the letter, and print one copy.

~~Mr. Ishmal Dabdoub~~ Dr. Arthur Goralsky
~~Professional Office Consultants~~ Global Enterprises, Inc.
~~1782 Laurel Canyon Road~~ 2000 Corporate Way
~~Sunnyvale, Ca 93785~~ Lake Oswego, OR 97035

Dear ~~Mr. Dabdoub~~ Dr. Goralsky

Have you heard your friends and colleagues talk about obtaining real-time stock quotes? real-time account balances and positions? Nasdaq Level II quotes? extended-hours trading? If so, then they are among the ~~three~~ *four* million serious investors that have opened ~~an~~ accounts with ~~E-Market~~. *E-Trade*

E-Trade We believe that the best decisions are informed decisions made in a timely manner. ~~E-Market~~ has an online help desk that provides information for *strategies* all levels of investors, from beginners to the experienced serious trader. You can learn basic ~~tactics~~ for investing in the stock market, how to ~~avoiding~~ common mistakes, and ~~picking~~ up some advanced strategies.

etrade Stay on top of the market and your investments! Visit our Web site at http://www. ~~emarket~~.com to learn more about our banking and brokerage services ~~E-Market Group~~ is the premier site for online investing. *E-Trade*

Sincerely

~~Ms. Margaritta Gibson~~ Keisha Knight
Marketing Manager

xx

Skill Builder Lesson C

1. Open *Keyboarding Pro*, Skill Builder module. Complete Lesson C with the Speed Emphasis. If you have already completed Lesson C, go on to the next uncompleted lesson.
2. Print your Lesson Report if requested by your instructor.

DRILL 4

BALANCED-HAND COMBINATIONS

Practice the reaches for fluency.

1	an anyone brand spans th their father eighth he head sheets niche
2	en enters depends been nd end handle fund or original sport color
3	ur urban turns assure to took factory photo ti titles satin still
4	ic ice bicycle chic it item position profit ng angle danger doing
5	I want the info in the file on the profits from the chic bicycle.
6	The original of the color photo she took of the factory is there.
7	Assure them that anyone can turn onto the road to the urban area.
8	The color of the title sheet depends on the photos and the funds.

| 1 | 2 | 3 | 4 | 5 | 6 | 7 | 8 | 9 | 10 | 11 | 12 | 13 |

DRILL 5

TIMED WRITING

1. Take a 1' writing on each ¶.
2. Take a 3' writing on both ¶s.

Option: Key the timing as a Diagnostic Writing in *Keyboarding Pro 4* or from *MicroPace Pro:*

Filename **SB3-T5**

	gwam	1'	3'
Practicing basic health rules will result in good body condi-	12	4
tion. Proper diet is a way to achieve good health. Eat a variety	26	9
of foods each day, including some fruit, vegetables, cereal pro-	38	13
ducts, and foods rich in protein, to be sure that you keep a bal-	51	17
ance. Another part of a good health plan is physical activity,	64	21
such as running.	67	22
Running has become popular in this country. A long run is a	12	27
big challenge to many males and females to determine just how far	26	31
they can go in a given time, or the time they require to cover a	38	35
measured distance. Long runs of fifty or one hundred miles are on	52	40
measured courses with refreshments available every few miles.	64	44
Daily training is necessary in order to maximize endurance.	76	48

| 1' | 1 | 2 | 3 | 4 | 5 | 6 | 7 | 8 | 9 | 10 | 11 | 12 | 13 |
| 3' | | 1 | | 2 | | 3 | | 4 | |

34e-d2
Block Letter

1. Use the Date feature to insert the current date.

2. Center the page vertically. Proofread and check the spelling. Preview the letter and check the placement. Save the letter as **34e-d2** and print one copy.

Current date | Mr. Trace L. Brecken | 4487 Ingram Street | Corpus Christi, TX 78409-8907 | Dear Mr. Brecken

We have received the package you sent us in which you returned goods from a recent order you gave us. Your refund check, plus return postage, will be mailed to you in a few days.

We are sorry, of course, that you did not find this merchandise personally satisfactory. It is our goal to please all of our customers, and we are always disappointed if we fail.

Please give us an opportunity to try again. We stand behind our merchandise, and that is our guarantee of good service.

Cordially yours | Mrs. Margret Bredewig | Customer Service Department | xx

34e-d3
Block Letter

1. Follow the directions for **34e-d2**. Save the letter as **34e-d3** and print one copy.

Current date | Mrs. Rose Shikamuru | 55 Lawrence Street |Topeka, KS 66607-6657 | Dear Mrs. Shikamuru

Thank you for your recent letter asking about employment opportunities with our company. We are happy to inform you that Mr. Edward Ybarra, our recruiting representative, will be on your campus on April 23, 24, 25, and 26 to interview students who are interested in our company.

We suggest that you talk soon with your student placement office, as all appointments with Mr. Ybarra will be made through that office. Please bring with you the application questionnaire the office provides.

Within a few days, we will send you a company brochure and more information about our offices; plant; salary, bonus, and retirement plans; and the beautiful community in which we are located. We believe a close study of this information will convince you, as it has many others, that our company builds futures as well as small motors.

If there is any other way we can help you, please write to me again.

Yours very truly | Miss Myrle K. Bragg | Human Services Director | xx

34e-d4
Envelopes

1. Open each of the following documents and create an envelope: **34e-d1**, **34e-d2**, **34e-d3**. Print each envelope; do not save.

Skill Builder Lesson B

1. Open *Keyboarding Pro*, Skill Builder module. Complete Lesson B with Speed Emphasis. If you have already completed Lesson B, go on to the next uncompleted lesson.

2. Print your Lesson Report if requested by your instructor.

DRILL 2

BALANCED-HAND COMBINATIONS

Practice the reaches for fluency.

1 to today stocks into ti times sitting until ur urges further tour
2 en entire trend dozen or order support editor nd and mandate land
3 he healthy check ache th these brother both an annual change plan
4 nt into continue want of office softer roof is issue poison basis

5 My brother urged the editor to have an annual health check today.
6 The manager will support the change to order our stock annually.
7 The time for the land tour will not change until further notice.
8 Did the letter mention her position or performance in the office?

| 1 | 2 | 3 | 4 | 5 | 6 | 7 | 8 | 9 | 10 | 11 | 12 | 13 |

DRILL 3

SKILL TRANSFER PARAGRAPHS

Follow the directions for Drill 2 on p. 124.

To save timings, use a filename that identifies the timing such as **xx-sb3-drill3-t1** (your initials, Skill Builder 3 Drill3-Timing1).

gwam   1' | 3'

Most of us, at some time, have had a valid reason to complain—   12 | 6

about a defective product, poor service, or perhaps being tired of   26 | 13

talking to voice mail. Many of us feel that complaining, however,   39 | 20

to a firm is an exercise in futility and don't bother to express   52 | 26

our dissatisfaction. We just write it off to experience and   64 | 32

continue to be ripped off.   70 | 35

Today more than at anytime in the past consumers are taking some   12 | 6

steps to let their feelings be known—and with a great amount of   25 | 13

success. As a result, many firms are becoming more responsive to   38 | 19

the needs of the consumer. complaints from customers alert firms   51 | 26

to produce or service defect and there by cause action to be taken   65 | 33

for their benefit. of all   70 | 35

1' | 1 | 2 | 3 | 4 | 5 | 6 | 7 | 8 | 9 | 10 | 11 | 12 | 13 |
3' | 1 | 2 | 3 | 4 |

SKILLBUILDING

35a
Warmup
Key each line twice SS.

alphabet	1	Jacky Few's strange, quiet behavior amazed and perplexed even us.
figures	2	Dial Extension 1480 or 2760 for a copy of the 3-page 95-cent book.
double letters	3	Ann will see that Edd accepts an assignment in the school office.
easy	4	If I burn the signs, the odor of enamel may make a toxic problem.

| 1 | 2 | 3 | 4 | 5 | 6 | 7 | 8 | 9 | 10 | 11 | 12 | 13 |

DOCUMENT DESIGN

35b

Modified Block Format

In modified block letter format, the dateline and the closing lines begin at the center point of the page. Paragraphs may be blocked or indented to the first tab stop; however, it is more efficient not to indent paragraphs. Set a tab at the center of the page to key the date and the closing lines. To determine the position of the tab, subtract the side margins from the center of the paper.

4.25"	Center of the paper
−1.25"	Margins
3"	Tab setting

Letter Parts

In Lesson 33 you learned the standard letter parts. Listed below are optional parts.

Enclosure notation: If an item is included with a letter, key an enclosure notation a DS below the reference initials. Press TAB to align the enclosures. Variations include:

Enclosures: Check #831
             Order form

Enclosures: 2

Copy notation: A copy notation c indicates that a copy of the document has been sent to the person listed. Key the copy notation a DS below the reference initials or enclosure notation. Press TAB to align the names.

   ┌**Tab**
c ▼ Hillary Stevens
   David Schmidt
   Doug Overland

DOCUMENT DESIGN   DOCUMENT DESIGN   DOCUMENT DESIGN   DOCMENT

Skill Builders 3

Skill Builder Lesson A

1. Open *Keyboarding Pro*, Skill Builder module. The Skill Builder section includes 20 lessons of increasing difficulty that will help you build keying speed and improve control.

2. You can choose to emphasize speed or accuracy as you complete a lesson. Choose **Speed**. Click on the Emphasis displayed at the bottom of the Lesson menu to toggle between Speed and Accuracy. (Not available if preferences are locked.) Or use the Preferences option before you choose a lesson to change the emphasis (choose **Edit** from the menu bar).

3. Complete Lesson A, or the first lesson that you have not completed. A red check mark will display to the left of any lesson completed.

4. Print your Lesson Report if requested by your instructor.

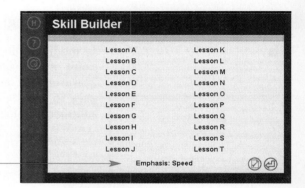

Click Emphasis to change to Accuracy

DRILL 1
SKILL TRANSFER PARAGRAPHS

1. Key a 1' writing on each paragraph. Compare your *gwam*. Type additional 1' writings on the slower timing.

2. Repeat these steps for 2'.

   To save timings in the Open Screen, use a filename that identifies the timing such as **xx-sb3-drill1-t1** (your initials, Skill Builder 3 Drill1-Timing1).

	gwam	1'	3'

There are many qualities which cause good employees to stand | 12 | 6

out in a group. In the first place, they keep their minds on the | 25 | 13

task at hand. Also, they often think about the work they do and | 38 | 19

how it relates to the total efforts of the project. They keep | 52 | 26

their eyes, ears, and minds open to new ideas. | 60 | 30

Second, good workers may be classed as those who work at a | 13 | 6

steady pace. Far too many people, work by fits and pieces. They | 25 | 13

begin one thing, but then they allow themselves to be easily taken | 39 | 19

away from the work at hand. At lot of people are good starters, | 52 | 26

but many less of them are also good finishers. | 60 | 30

1'	1	2	3	4	5	6	7	8	9	10	11	12	13
3'		1			2			3			4		

NATIONAL
ASSOCIATION OF
INFORMATION
PROCESSING
PROFESSIONALS

Left tab 3"
Current date   ↓
                 4

Mr. Richard Harrison
Jobs-OnLine, Inc.
7490 Oregon Avenue
Arvada, CO 80002-8765 **DS**

Dear Mr. Harrison
                 DS

Please consider this personal invitation to join the National Association of Information
Processing Professionals (NAIPP). Membership is offered to the top 25 percent of the
graduating class. NAIPP is a nonprofit organization comprised of technical
professionals who are striving to stay current in their field. Member benefits include:
                                                                                DS

Career Development Opportunities—Resume preparation services, job search
program, 120-day internship in many cities, and access to our online job bulletin board.
                                                                                DS

Educational Benefits—Industry Standard Skill Testing and Credentialing, discounts on
continuing education courses at "Curriculum Approved" colleges and universities, and
online recertification programs. **DS**

Professional Benefits—Discounts on technical publications and computer hardware,
competitive rates for medical and hospitalization insurance, retirement and financial
planning programs, and free international travel services.
                                                                DS

Sign on to our Web site at http://www.naipp.org to learn more about our organization.
Enclosed is a parking pass for the Multimedia Symposium on February 27.
                                                                            DS

Sincerely ↓
         4

Lorraine Beasly, President
NAIPP Board of Directors
                        DS

LB:xx
     DS
Enclosure
        DS
c Adam Learner

DRILL 1

CAPITALIZATION

Review the rules and examples on the previous page. Then key the sentences, correcting all capitalization errors. Number each item and DS between items. Save as **capitalize-drill 1.**

1. according to one study, the largest ethnic minority group online is hispanics.
2. the american author mark twain said, "always do right; this will gratify some people and astonish the rest."
3. the grand canyon was formed by the colorado river cutting into the high-plateau region of northwestern arizona.
4. the president of russia is elected by popular vote.
5. the hubble space telescope is a cooperative project of the european space agency and the national aeronautics and space administration.
6. the train left north station at 6:45 this morning.
7. the trademark cyberprivacy prevention act would make it illegal for individuals to purchase domains solely for resale and profit.
8. consumers spent $7 billion online between november 1 and december 31, 2003, compared to $3.1 billion for the same period in 2002.
9. new students should attend an orientation session on wednesday, august 15, at 8 a.m. in room 252 of the perry building.
10. the summer book list includes *where the red fern grows* and *the mystery of the missing baseball.*

DRILL 2

CAPITALIZATION

1. Open the file **capitalize2** from the data files and save it as **capitalize-drill2**.
2. Follow the specific directions provided in the data file. Remember to use the correct proofreaders' marks:

≡	Capitalize	sincerely
lc	Lowercase	My Dear Sir

3. Resave and print. Submit the rough draft and final copy to your instructor.

DRILL 3

CAPITALIZATION OF LETTER PARTS

Key the letter parts using correct capitalization. Number each item and DS between each. Save as **capitalize-drill3**.

1. dear mr. petroilli
2. ladies and gentlemen
3. dear senator kuknais
4. very sincerely yours
5. dear reverend Schmidt
6. very truly yours
7. cordially yours
8. dear mr fong and miss landow
9. respectfully yours
10. sincerely
11. dear mr. and mrs. Green
12. dear service manager

DRILL 4

CAPITALIZATION

1. Open the file **capitalize4** from the data files. Save it as **capitalize-drill4**.
2. This file includes a field for selecting the correct answer. You will simply select the correct answer. Follow the specific directions provided in the data file.
3. Resave and print.

APPLICATIONS

35c-d1
Modified Block Letter

1. Open a new document; set a left tab at 3". Insert the date at the top of the page at the tab. Key the letter on the previous page in modified block format. After keying the enclosure notation, strike ENTER twice and set a left tab at .5"; then key the copy notation.
2. Center vertically. Save as **35c-d1**, preview, and print.

35c-d2
Modified Block Letter

1. Add your reference initials and a copy notation to your instructor.
2. Proofread carefully, save the letter as **35c-d2**, and print.

Current date ↓4

Ms. Ana Gonzalez
One-Stop Printing Co.
501 Madison Road
Cincinnati, OH 45227-6398

Dear Ms. Gonzalez

Do you know that more and more people are opting to go on a shopping spree on the Internet rather than the mall? Businesses, ranging from small mom and pop stores to global multinational corporations, are setting up shop on the Web if they haven't already. They are selling goods, services, and themselves!

Consumers expect businesses to have a Web site. Those that don't will give their business to their competitor.

E-Business, Inc. has helped hundreds of businesses nationwide establish their business on the Internet. May we help you integrate your online and offline sales strategies? Call us today at 800-555-0100 and arrange for one of our consultants to analyze your e-commerce strategies to increase your volume. ↓2

Sincerely yours ↓4

Ellen Soey
Marketing Manager ↓2

35c-d3
Modified Block Letter

Key the letter in modified block format; center vertically. Save, preview before printing, and print.

words

Current date | Dr. Burtram M. Decker | 800 Barbour Ave. | 10
Birmingham, AL 35208-5333 | Dear Dr. Decker   19

The Community Growth Committee offers you its sincere   30
thanks for taking an active part in the sixth annual Youth   41
Fair. We especially appreciate your help in judging the   53
Youth of Birmingham Speaks portion of the fair and for   64
contributing to the prize bank.   70

Participation of community leaders such as you makes this   81
event the annual success it has become. We sincerely hope   93
we can seek your help again next year.   101

Cordially | Grace Beebe Hunt | Secretary | HNJ:xx   110

Communication Skills 1

Capitalize:

1. **First word of a sentence and of a direct quotation.**

   We were tolerating instead of managing diversity.

   The speaker said, "We must value diversity, not merely recognize it."

2. **Proper nouns**—specific persons, places, or things.

   Common nouns: continent, river, car, street

   Proper nouns: Asia, Mississippi, Buick, State St.

   Exception: Capitalize a title of high distinction even when it does not refer to a specific person (e.g., President of the United States).

3. **Derivatives** of proper nouns and capitalize **geographical** names.

   Derivatives: American history, German food, English accent, Ohio Valley

   Proper nouns: Tampa, Florida, Mount Rushmore

4. **A personal or professional title** when it precedes the name; capitalize a title of high distinction without a name.

   Title: Lieutenant Kahn, Mayor Walsh, Doctor Welby

   High distinction: the President of the United States,

5. **Days of the week, months of the year, holidays, periods of history, and historic events.**

   Monday, June 8, Labor Day, Renaissance

6. **Specific parts of the country** but not compass points that show direction.

   Midwest   the South   northwest of town   the Middle East

7. **Family relationships** when used with a person's name.

   Aunt Carol   my mother   Uncle Mark

8. **A noun preceding a figure** except for common nouns such as line, page, and sentence.

   Unit 1   Section 2   page 2   verse 7   line 2

9. **First and main words of side headings, titles of books, and works of art.**
   Do not capitalize words of four or fewer letters that are conjunctions, prepositions, or articles.

   Computers in the News   *Raiders of the Lost Ark*

10. **Names of organizations and specific departments** within the writer's organization.

    Girl Scouts   our Sales Department

11. **The salutation of a letter and the first word of the complimentary closing.**

    Dear Mr. Bush   Ladies and Gentlemen: Sincerely yours,
    Very cordially yours,

Correspondence Review

36a
Warmup
Key each line twice SS.

alphabetic 1 Perhaps Max realized jet flights can quickly whisk us to Bolivia.
fig/sym 2 Send 24 Solex Cubes, Catalog #95-0, price $6.78, before April 31.
1st finger 3 The boy of just 6 or 7 years of age ran through the mango groves.
easy 4 The auditor did sign the form and name me to chair a small panel.

| 1 | 2 | 3 | 4 | 5 | 6 | 7 | 8 | 9 | 10 | 11 | 12 | 13 |

36b
Review Letter Parts
Arrange the letter parts correctly for a modified block letter. Ignore top margin requirements. Press ENTER five times between activities.

1 Sincerely yours | Manuel Garcia | Council President | MG:xx | c Ron N. Besbit

2 Yours truly | Ms. Loren Lakes | Secretary General | xx | Enclosure | c Libby Uhl

3 Ms. Mara Pena | 8764 Gold Plaza | Lansing, MI 48933-8312 | Dear Ms. Pena

36c

Modifying Tabs

Tabs can be added or moved in existing documents. When adding tabs to an existing document, you must first select all portions of the document where the new tab(s) will be applied; then set the additional tab(s). When moving a tab, first select all the text that will be affected. If you fail to select all the text, then only the tab that your cursor is on will be moved.

DRILL 1   ADDING TAB TO EXISTING DOCUMENT

1. Open **33e-d1**.
2. Select the entire letter by clicking the **Edit** menu and choosing **Select All**.
3. Set a left tab at 3.0".
4. Tab the appropriate lines to format this letter in modified block letter format.
5. Save as **36c-drill1**. Leave the document on the screen.

DRILL 2   MOVING A TAB

1. **36c-drill1** should still be displayed on the screen.
2. Select the entire letter (**Edit, Select All**).
3. Drag the tab on the ruler from 3.0" to 3.25".
4. Save as **36c-drill2**.

Module 4: Checkpoint

1. A(n) _____ is a form of written communication that is used primarily for internal communication.

2. _____ is a method of transmitting documents and messages via the computer system.

3. If several people are to receive a copy of a memo, key a(n) _____ list at the end of the memo.

4. When a business letter is addressed to a company, the correct salutation is _____.

5. Use 1.25" or _____ side margins for a business letter.

6. Letters are positioned vertically on the page by using the _____ command.

7. When keying a modified block letter, set a tab at the center point of the page, which is _____.

8. When an item is included with a letter, a(n) _____ notation is keyed a DS below the reference initials.

9. Use the _____ menu to create envelopes.

10. The _____ notation is used to indicate that a copy of the letter is being sent to another person.

Performance Assessment

Document 1
Modified Block Letter

1. Use the text at the right to create a modified block letter. Include letter parts as necessary.

2. The letter is to:
   Ms. Sharon Jens
   Western Regional
   Manager
   Acune, Inc.
   5450 Signal Hill Rd.
   Springfield, OH 45504-5440
   The letter is from **Troy Compton**.

Document 2
Memo

1. Key the same message as a memo to **Laura Riedel** from **Troy Compton**. Use the current date and **May Seminar** as the subject line.

2. Add a copy notation to **Jessica Smith**.

The keynote speaker for our annual sales conference this year will be Dr. Helen McBride, from the University of Southern California. She will be giving her opening speech at 2:00 p.m. on Tuesday, May 25, 200–.

Dr. McBride, a well-known psychologist who has spent a lot of time researching and writing on employee productivity, will address "Stress Management." I am sure you will find her speech to be both informative and entertaining.

A copy of Dr. McBride's resume is enclosed for use in preparing news releases and announcements for the sales conference.

36d-d1 and 36d-d2
Modified-Block Letter and Envelopes

1. Format the letter in modified block format. Insert the current date at 2.1".
2. Supply the correct salutation, a complimentary closing, and your reference initials. Add an enclosure line and a copy notation to **Laura Aimes, Sales Representative**.
3. Proofread carefully. Preview for good placement. Save as **36d-d1**. Print.
4. Attach an envelope to the letter, and save it again as **36d-d2**.

Ms. Mukta Bhakta
9845 Buckingham Road
Annapolis, MD 21403-0314

Thank you for your recent inquiry on our electronic bulletin service. The ABC BBS is an interactive online service developed by All Business Communication to assist the online community in receiving documents via the Internet.

All Business Communication also provides a *Customer Support Service* and a *Technical Support Team* to assist bulletin board users. The Systems Administrators will perform various procedures needed to help you take full advantage of this new software.

For additional information call:

Customer and Technical Support
Telephone: 900-555-0112
9:00 a.m.-5:00 p.m., Monday-Friday, Eastern Time

Please look over the enclosed ABC BBS brochure. I will call you within the next two weeks to discuss any additional questions you may have.

Alex Zampich, Marketing Manager

36d-d3
Memo with Tab

1. Key the following memo in correct format (see Lesson 31).
2. After keying the second paragraph, strike ENTER twice. Set a tab at 2.5", and key the last several lines. Save the document as **36d-d3**.

TO:	All Sunwood Employees
FROM:	Julie Patel, Human Relations
DATE:	Current date
SUBJECT:	Eric Kershaw Hospitalized

We were notified by Eric Kershaw's family that he was admitted into the hospital this past weekend. They expect that he will be hospitalized for another ten days. Visitations and phone calls are limited, but cards and notes are welcome.

A plant is being sent to Eric from the Sunwood staff. Stop by our office before Wednesday if you wish to sign the card. If you would like to send your own "Get Well Wishes" to Eric, send them to:

Left tab 2.5" ——— Eric Kershaw
County General Hospital
Room 401
Atlanta, GA 38209-4751

37c-d1
Enrichment
Block-Format Letter
Supply the salutation.

words

Current date | AMASTA Company, Inc. | 902 Greenridge Drive | Reno, NV · 13
69505-5552 · 19

We sell your videocassettes and have since you introduced them. Several · 33
of our customers now tell us they are unable to follow the directions on the · 49
coupon. They explain that there is no company logo on the box to return to · 64
you as you requested. · 68

What steps should we take? A copy of the coupon is enclosed, as is a · 82
Super D Container. Please read the coupon, examine the box, and then let · 97
me know your plans for extricating us from this problem. · 109

Sincerely yours | John J. Long | Sales Manager | Enclosures: 2 · 122

37c-d2
Modified-Block Letter
Supply the salutation.

words

Current date | Mr. John J. Long, Sales Manager | The Record Store | 9822 · 11
Trevor Avenue | Anaheim, CA 92805-5885 · 22

With your letter came our turn to be perplexed, and we apologize. When · 36
we had our refund coupons printed, we had just completed a total redesign · 51
program for our product boxes. We had detachable logos put on the · 65
outside of the boxes, which could be peeled off and placed on a coupon. · 79

We had not anticipated that our distributors would use back inventories · 94
with our promotion. The cassettes you sold were not packaged in our new · 108
boxes; therefore, there were no logos on them. · 118

I'm sorry you or your customers were inconvenienced. In the future, · 131
simply ask your customers to send us their sales slips, and we will honor · 146
them with refunds until your supply of older containers is depleted. · 160

Sincerely yours | Bruna Wertz | Sales and Promotions Dept. | xx · 173

37c-d3
Memo with Distribution List

1. Key the memo to **Continuing Education Committee—Distribution List Below**. It is from **Alberto Valenzuela**; **May Seminar** is the subject line.

2. The distribution list is as follows: **John Patterson, Facilities Manager; Shawna Thompson, Regional Manager; Ed Vandenberg, Advertising Manager**

gwam

I have invited Lynda A. Brewer, Ph.D., Earlham · 33
College, Richmond, Indiana, to be our seminar · 42
leader on Friday afternoon, May 10. · 50
 Dr. Brewer, a well-known psychologist who has · 59
spent a lot of time researching and writing in the · 69
field of ergonomics, will address "Stress Management." · 80
 Please make arrangements for rooms, speaker accom- · 90
modations, staff notification, and refreshments. · 100
I will send you Dr. Brewer's vita for use in pre- · 110
paring news releases. · 114

closing lines · 139

36d-d4
**Rough-Draft Letter
Block Format**

1. Key the following letter in block format. Apply what you have learned about correct letter placement and letter parts.
2. Save the document as **36d-d4**, and print one copy.

Mr. John Crane
5760 Sky Way
Seattle, WA *05671-0321* — a   sp

Would you like to invest in a company that will provide you with 180% ^ *a*   *sp*

return on your investment? Consider investing in a ~~company~~ *firm* that specializes in

importing and exporting with China. China's domestic product (GDP) is

expected to be over a trillion dollars. ^ *gross*

(bold & italic)
Ameri-Chinois has made a significant number of business arrangements

with key organizations in China to source goods and to participate in global two-

way trade. Trade between China and other ~~countries~~ is expected to grow over
the rest of the world
sp
20% this year. China's exports are expected to rise to $244 billion in the year

2004. Imports ~~will~~ grow to $207 billion. *are expected to*

Contact Lawrence Chen at Century Investments to learn how you can be

an investor in the growing company of Ameri-Chinois. The current price is

$0.52; the targeted price is $9.00. Call today! *per share*

800-555-0134 ⌐ Sincerely

⌐ Lawrence Chen

36d-d5
Edit Modified Block Letter

1. Open **36d-d4**; and save it as **36d-d5**. Select the letter address, and then delete it.
2. Address the letter to: **Mr. Tom K. Onehawk, 139 Via Cordoniz, Evansville, IL 44710-3277.** Supply an appropriate salutation.
3. Add **Please study the enclosed portfolio and then** at the beginning of paragraph 3. Be sure to change the *c* in contact to lowercase.
4. Add an enclosure notation.

36d-d6
Move Tab

1. Open **36d-d3**.
2. Select the last four lines of the memo.
3. Move the tab from position 2.5" to 3.0". This moves the last four lines to 3.0".
4. Save as **36d-d6**.

Assessment

SKILLBUILDING

37a
Warmup
Key each line twice SS.

alphabetic 1 Johnny Willcox printed five dozen banquet tickets for my meeting.
fig/sym 2 Our check #389 for $21,460—dated 1/15/01—was sent to O'Neil & Co.
1st finger 3 It is true Greg acted bravely during the severe storm that night.
easy 4 In the land of enchantment, the fox and the lamb lie by the bush.

| 1 | 2 | 3 | 4 | 5 | 6 | 7 | 8 | 9 | 10 | 11 | 12 | 13 |

37b
Timed Writings
Take two 3' timings.

 all letters

gwam 3'

Many young people are quite surprised to learn that either lunch or dinner is included as part of a job interview. Most of them think of this part of the interview as a friendly gesture from the organization.

The meal is not provided just to be nice to the person. The organization expects to use that function to observe the social skills of the person and to determine if he or she might be effective doing business in that type of setting.

What does this mean to you if you are preparing for a job interview? The time spent reading about and learning to use good social skills pays off not only during the interview but also after you accept the job.

	4	48
	8	52
	13	56
	15	58
	18	62
	22	66
	27	71
	30	73
	33	77
	38	81
	42	86
	44	87

1' | 1 | 2 | 3 | 4 | 5 | 6 | 7 | 8 | 9 | 10 | 11 | 12 | 13 |
3' | 1 | | 2 | | 3 | | 4 |

APPLICATIONS

37c
Assessment

Continue button

Check button

General Instructions: Format the letters in the style indicated; add additional letter parts if necessary. Use the Date and Time feature for the current date. Add a proper salutation and your reference initials for all letters. Position each letter at 2.1". Check spelling, preview for proper placement, and carefully proofread each letter before proceeding to the next document.

With CheckPro: *CheckPro* will keep track of the time it takes you to complete the entire production test, compute your speed and accuracy rate on each document, and summarize the results. When you complete a document, proofread it, check the spelling, and preview for placement. When you are completely satisfied with the document, click the Continue button to move to the next document. You will not be able to return and edit a document once you continue to the next document.   Click the **Check** button when you are ready to error-check the test. Review and/or print the document analysis results.

Without CheckPro: On the signal to begin, key the documents in sequence. When saving documents, name them in the usual manner (for example, **37c-d1**). When time has been called, proofread all documents again, identify errors, and determine *g-pwam*.

$$g\text{-}pwam = \frac{\text{total words keyed}}{25'}$$

Reference Guide

Capitalize

1. First word of a sentence and of a direct quotation.

   We were tolerating instead of managing diversity.
   The speaker said, "We must value diversity, not merely recognize it."

2. Names of proper nouns—specific persons, places, or things.

   Common nouns: continent, river, car, street
   Proper nouns: Asia, Mississippi, Buick, State St.

3. Derivatives of proper nouns and geographical names.

   American history   English accent
   German food   Ohio Valley
   Tampa, Florida   Mount Rushmore

4. A personal or professional title when it precedes the name or a title of high distinction without a name.

   Lieutenant Kahn   Mayor Walsh
   Doctor Welby   Mr. Ty Brooks
   Dr. Frank Collins   Miss Tate
   the President of the United States

5. Days of the week, months of the year, holidays, periods of history, and historic events.

   Monday, June 8   Labor Day   Renaissance

6. Specific parts of the country but not compass points that show direction.

   Midwest   the South   northwest of town

7. Family relationships when used with a person's name.

   Aunt Helen   my dad   Uncle John

8. Noun preceding a figure except for common nouns such as *line, page,* and *sentence.*

   Unit 1   Section 2   page 2   verse 7   line 2

9. First and main words of side headings, titles of books, and works of art. Do not capitalize words of four or fewer letters that are conjunctions, prepositions, or articles.

   Computers in the News   *Raiders of the Lost Ark*

10. Names of organizations and specific departments within the writer's organization.

    Girl Scouts   our Sales Department

Number Expression

General guidelines

1. Use **words** for numbers *one* through *ten* unless the numbers are in a category with related larger numbers that are expressed as figures.

   He bought three acres of land. She took two acres.
   She wrote 12 stories and 2 plays in the last 13 years.

2. Use **words** for approximate numbers or large round numbers that can be expressed as one or two words. Use **numbers** for round numbers in millions or higher with their word modifier.

   We sent out about three hundred invitations.
   She contributed $3 million dollars.

3. Use **words** for numbers that begin a sentence.

   Six players were cut from the ten-member team.

4. Use **figures** for the larger of two adjacent numbers.

   We shipped six 24-ton engines.

Times and dates

5. Use **words** for numbers that precede o'clock (stated or implied).

   We shall meet from two until five o'clock.

6. Use **figures** for times with *a.m.* or *p.m.* and days when they follow the month.

   Her appointment is for 2:15 p.m. on July 26, 2000.

7. Use **ordinals** for the day when it precedes the month.

   The 10th of October is my anniversary.

Money, percentages, and fractions

8. Use **figures** for money amounts and percentages. Spell out *cents* and *percent* except in statistical copy.

   The 16% discount saved me $145; Bill, 95 cents.

9. Use **words** for fractions unless the fractions appear in combination with whole numbers.

   one-half of her lesson   5 1/2   18 3/4

Addresses

10. Use **words** for street names First through Tenth. Use **figures** for ordinals for streets above Tenth. Use **figures** for house numbers other than number **one.** (If street name is a number, separate it from house number with a dash.)

    One Lytle Place   Second Ave.   142—534 St.

Puncuation

Use an apostrophe

1. To make most singular nouns and indefinite pronouns possessive (add **apostrophe** and **s**).

   computer + 's = computer's   Jess + 's = Jess's
   anyone's   one's   somebody's

2. To make a plural noun that does not end in s possessive (add **apostrophe** and **s**).

   women + 's = women's   men + 's = men's
   deer + 's = deer's   children + 's = children's

3. To make a plural noun that ends in s possessive. Add only the **apostrophe**.

   boys + ' = boys'   managers + ' = managers'

4. To make a compound noun possessive or to show joint possession. Add **apostrophe** and **s** to the last part of the hyphenated noun.

   son-in-law's   Rob and Gen's game

5. To form the plural of numbers and letters, add **apostrophe** and **s**. To show omission of letters or figures, add an **apostrophe** in place of the missing items.

   7's   A's   It's   add'l

Use a colon

1. To introduce a listing.

   The candidate's strengths were obvious: experience, community involvement, and forthrightness.

2. To introduce an explanatory statement.

   Then I knew we were in trouble: The item had not been scheduled.

Use a comma

1. After an introductory phrase or dependent clause.

   After much deliberation, the jury reached its decision.
   If you have good skills, you will find a job.

2. After words or phrases in a series.

   Mike is taking Greek, Latin III, and Chemistry II.

3. To set off nonessential or interrupting elements.

   Troy, the new man in MIS, will install the hard drive.
   He cannot get to the job, however, until next Friday.

4. To set off the date from the year and the city from the state.

   John, will you please reserve the center in Billings, Montana, for January 10, 2000.

5. To separate two or more parallel adjectives (adjectives could be separated by and instead of a comma).

   The loud, whining guitar could be heard above the rest.

6. Before the conjunction in a compound sentence. The comma may be omitted in a very short sentence.

   You must leave immediately, or you will miss your flight.
   We tested the software and they loved it.

7. Set off appositives and words of direct address.

   Karen, our team leader, represented us at the conference.
   Paul, have you ordered the CD-ROM drive?

Use a hyphen

1. To show end-of-line word division.

2. In many compound words—check a dictionary if unsure.
   - Two-word adjectives before a noun:

     two-car family
   - Compound numbers between twenty-one and ninety-nine.
   - Fractions and some proper nouns with prefixes/suffixes.

     two-thirds   ex-Governor   all-American

Use italic or underline

1. With titles of complete literary works.

   College Keyboarding   *Hunt for Red October*

2. To emphasize special words or phrases.

   What does *professional* mean?

Use a semicolon

1. To separate independent clauses in a compound sentence when the conjunction is omitted.

   Please review the information; give me a report by Tuesday.

2. To separate independent clauses when they are joined by conjunctive adverbs (*however*, *nevertheless*, *consequently*, etc.).

   The traffic was heavy; consequently, I was late.

3. To separate a series of elements that contain commas.

   The new officers are: Fran Pena, president; Harry Wong, treasurer; and Muriel Williams, secretary.

Use a dash

1. To show an abrupt change of thought.

   Invoice 76A—which is 10 days overdue—is for $670.

2. After a series to indicate a summarizing statement.

   Noisy fuel pump, worn rods, and failing brakes—for all these reasons I'm trading the car.

Use an exclamation point

After emphatic interjections or exclamatory sentences.

Terrific!   Hold it!   You bet!   What a great surprise!

Proofreading procedures

Proofread documents so that they are free of errors. Error-free documents send the message that you are detail-oriented and a person capable of doing business. Apply these procedures after you key a document.

1. Use Spelling.
2. Proofread the document on screen to be sure that it makes sense. Check for these types of errors:
   - Words, headings, and/or amounts omitted.
   - Extra words or lines not deleted during the editing stage.
   - Incorrect sequence of numbers in a list.
3. Preview the document on screen using the Print Preview feature. Check the vertical placement, presence of headers or footers, page numbers, and overall appearance.
4. Save the document again and print.
5. Check the printed document by comparing it to the source copy (textbook). Check all figures, names, and addresses against the source copy. Check that the document style has been applied consistently throughout.
6. If errors exist on the printed copy, revise the document, save, and print.
7. Verify the corrections and placement of the second printed copy.

Word division

With the use of proportional fonts found in current word processing packages, word division is less of an issue. Occasionally, however, you will need to make decisions on dividing words, such as when using the Columns function. The following list contains generally accepted guidelines for dividing words.

1. Divide words between syllables only; therefore, do not divide one-syllable words.

2. **Short words:** Avoid dividing short words (five letters or fewer).

   area   since   bonus   ideal

3. **Double consonants:** Divide words with double consonants between the double letters unless the root word ends with the double letters. In this case, divide after the second consonant.

   mis-sion   trim-ming   dress-ing   call-ing

4. **One-letter syllables:** Do not divide after a one-letter syllable at the beginning of a word or before a one- or two-letter syllable at the end of a word; divide after a one-letter syllable within a word.

   enough   abroad   starter   friendly
   ani-mal   sepa-rate   regu-late

5. **Two single-letter syllables:** Divide between two single-letter syllables within a word.

   gradu-ation   evalu-ation

6. **Hyphenated words:** Compound words with a hyphen may be divided only after the hyphen.

   top-secret   soft-spoken   self-respect

7. **Figures:** Avoid dividing figures presented as a unit.

   #870331   190,886   1/22/02

8. **Proper nouns:** Avoid dividing proper nouns. If necessary, include as much of the proper noun as possible before dividing it.

   Thomas R./Lewiston *not* Thomas/R. Lewiston
   November 15,/2002 *not* November/15, 2002

Proofreaders' marks

Mark	Meaning	Mark	Meaning
#	Add horizontal space	/ or *lc*	Lowercase
||	Align		Move left
(wavy underline)	Bold		Move right
Cap or ≡	Capitalize		Move up
	Close up		Move down
	Delete	#	Paragraph
^	Insert	*sp*	Spell out
˅ ˄	Insert quotation marks	*tr*	Transpose
___	Underline or italic		
stet or ···	Let it stand; ignore correction		

Addressing procedures

The envelope feature inserts the delivery address automatically if a letter is displayed. Title case, used in the letter address, is acceptable in the envelope address. An alternative style for envelopes is uppercase with no punctuation.

Business letters are usually mailed in envelopes that have the return address preprinted; return addresses are printed only for personal letters or when letterhead is not available. The default size of *Word* is a size 10 envelope (4 1/8" by 9 1/2"); other sizes are available using the Options feature.

When preparing an envelope using an electronic typewriter, follow the spacing guidelines below:

Small envelope. On a No. 6 3/4 envelope, place the address near the center—about 2 inches from the top and left edges. Place a return address in the upper left corner.

Large envelope. On a No. 10 envelope, place the address near the center—about line 14 and .5" left of center. A return address, if not preprinted, should be keyed in the upper left corner (see small envelope).

An address must contain at least three lines; addresses of more than six lines should be avoided. The last line of an address must contain three items of information: (1) the city, (2) the state, and (3) the ZIP Code, preferably a 9-digit code.

Place mailing notations that affect postage (e.g., REGISTERED, CERTIFIED) below the stamp position (line 8); place other special notations (e.g., CONFIDENTIAL, PERSONAL) a DS below the return address.

Folding and inserting procedures

Large envelopes (No. 10, 9, 7 3/4)

Step 1	Step 2	Step 3
	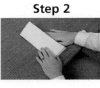	

Step 1: With document face up, fold slightly less than 1/3 of sheet up toward top.

Step 2: Fold down top of sheet to within 1/2" of bottom fold.

Step 3: Insert document into envelope with last crease toward bottom of envelope.

Small envelopes (No. 6 3/4, 6 1/4)

Step 1	Step 2	Step 3

Step 1: With document face up, fold bottom up to 1/2" from top.

Step 2: Fold right third to left.

Step 3: Fold left third to 1/2" from last crease and insert last creased edge first.

Window envelopes (full sheet)

Step 1	Step 2	Step 3

Step 1: With sheet face down, top toward you, fold upper third down.

Step 2: Fold lower third up so address is showing.

Step 3: Insert document into envelope with last crease toward bottom of envelope.

Two-letter state abbreviations

Alabama, AL	Florida, FL	Kentucky, KY	Montana, MT	Ohio, OH	Texas, TX
Alaska, AK	Georgia, GA	Louisiana, LA	Nebraska, NE	Oklahoma, OK	Utah, UT
Arizona, AZ	Guam, GU	Maine, ME	Nevada, NV	Oregon, OR	Vermont, VT
Arkansas, AR	Hawaii, HI	Maryland, MD	New Hampshire, NH	Pennsylvania, PA	Virgin Islands, VI
California, CA	Idaho, ID	Massachusetts, MA	New Jersey, NJ	Puerto Rico, PR	Virginia, VA
Colorado, CO	Illinois, IL	Michigan, MI	New Mexico, NM	Rhode Island, RI	Washington, WA
Connecticut, CT	Indiana, IN	Minnesota, MN	New York, NY	South Carolina, SC	West Virginia, WV
Delaware, DE	Iowa, IA	Mississippi, MS	North Carolina, NC	South Dakota, SD	Wisconsin, WI
District of Columbia, DC	Kansas, KS	Missouri, MO	North Dakota, ND	Tennessee, TN	Wyoming, WY

Letter parts

Letterhead. Company name and address. May include other data.

Date. Date letter is mailed. Usually in month, day, year order. Military style is an option (day/month/year: 17/1/02).

Letter address. Address of the person who will receive the letter. Include personal title (*Mr.; Ms.; Dr.*); name; professional title, company, and address.

Salutation. Greeting. Corresponds to the first line of the letter address. Usually includes name and courtesy title; use *Ladies and Gentlemen* if letter is addressed to a company name.

Body. Message. SS; DS between paragraphs.

Complimentary close. Farewell, such as *Sincerely.*

Writer. Name and professional title. Women may include a personal title.

Initials. Identifies person who keyed the document (for example, *tr*). May include identification of writer (*ARB:trr*).

Enclosure. Copy is enclosed with the document. May specify contents.

Copy notation. Indicates that a copy of the letter is being sent to person named.

Envelope

IMAGE MAKERS
5131 Moss Springs Rd.
Columbia, SC 29209-4768

Ms. Mary Bernard, President
Bernard Image Consultants
4927 Stuart Avenue
Baton Rouge, LA 70808-3519

Block letter (open punctuation)

Professional Office Consultants, Inc.
584 Castro St.
San Francisco, CA 94114-2201
415-555-8725
415-555-8775 (FAX)

Dateline — January 17, 200-
DS

Letter address — Ms. Amanda Castillo, Office Manager
Teletel Corporation
24 Technology Dr.
Irvine, CA 92865-9845
DS

Salutation — Dear Ms. Castillo
DS

Body — Thank you for selecting Professional Office Consultants, Inc. to assist with the setup of your new corporate office. You asked us for a recommendation for formatting business letters. We highly recommend the block letter style because it is easy to read.

This letter is keyed in block format. As you can see, all lines begin at the left margin. Most letters can be keyed using default side margins and then centered vertically on the page for attractive placement. The block letter format is easy to key because tabs are not required.

We think that you will be happy using the block letter format. Over 80 percent of businesses today are using this same style.

Complimentary close — Sincerely
DS

Writer's Title — Anderson Cline
OA & CIS Consultant
DS

Reference initials — tr

Letter placement table

Length	Dateline position	Margins
Short: 1-2 ¶ls	Center page	Default
Average: 3-4 ¶ls	Center page or 2.1"	Default
Long: 4+ ¶ls	2.1" (default + 6 hard returns)	Default

Default margins or a minimum of 1".

Modified block letter (mixed punctuation)

IMAGE MAKERS
5131 Moss Springs Road
Columbia, SC 29209-4768
(803) 555-0127

October 27, 200-

Ms. Mary Bernard, President
Bernard Image Consultants
4927 Stuart Ave.
Baton Rouge, LA 70808-3519

Dear Ms. Bernard:

The format of this letter is called modified block. Modified block format differs from block format in that the date, complimentary close, and the signature lines are positioned at the center point.

Paragraphs may be blocked, as this letter illustrates, or they may be indented from the left margin. We suggest you block paragraphs when you use modified block style so that an additional tab setting is not needed. However, some people who use modified block format prefer indented paragraphs.

Although modified block format is very popular, we recommend that you use it only for those customers who request this letter style. Otherwise, we urge you to use block format, which is more efficient, as your standard style.

Both formats are illustrated in the enclosed *Image Makers Format Guide.* Please note that the block format is labeled "computer compatible."

Sincerely,

Patrick R. Ray
Communication Consultant

tr

Enclosure

Copy notation — c Scot Card, Account Manager

Personal business letter

Janna M. Howard
587 Birch Cir.
Clinton, MS 39056-0587
(601) 555-4977

Current date

> The return address may be keyed immediately above the date, or you may create a personal letterhead as shown here.

Mrs. Linda Chandler
Financial News
32 North Critz St.
Hot Springs, AR 71913-0032

Dear Mrs. Chandler

My college degree in office systems technology and my graphics design job experience in the United States and Taiwan qualify me to function well as a junior graphic designer for your newspaper.

As a result of my comprehensive four-year program, I am skilled in the most up-to-date office suite packages as well as the latest version of desktop publishing and graphics programs. In addition, I am very skilled at locating needed resources on the information highway. In fact, this skill played a very important role in the design award that I received last month.

My technical and communication skills were applied as I worked as the assistant editor and producer of the *Cother Alumni News*. I understand well the importance of meeting deadlines and also in producing a quality product that will increase newspaper sales.

After you have reviewed the enclosed resume, I would look forward to discussing my qualifications and career opportunities with you at *Financial News*.

Sincerely

Janna M. Howard

Enclosure

Resume

JANNA M. HOWARD

Temporary Address (May 30, 2000)   **Permanent Address**
587 Birch Cir.   328 Fondren St.
Clinton, MS 39056-0587   Orlando, FL 32801-0328
(601) 555-4977   (407) 555-3834

CAREER OBJECTIVE	To obtain a graphic design position with an opportunity to advance to a management position.
EDUCATION	*B.S. Office Systems Technology*, Cother University, Mobile, Alabama. May 1998. Grade-point average: 3.8/4.0. Serve as president of Graphic Designers' Society.

SPECIAL SKILLS

Environments:	*Microsoft Windows®* and *Macintosh®*
Application software:	*Microsoft Office Professional®/ Windows 95®, PageMaker®, CorelDraw®, Harvard Graphics®*
Internet:	*Netscape®, Mosaic®*
Keyboarding skill:	70 words per minute
Foreign language:	Chinese
Travel:	Taiwan (two summers working as graphic design intern)

EXPERIENCE

Cother University Alumni Office, Mobile, Alabama. Assistant editor and producer of the *Cother Alumni News*, 1997 to present.
• Work 25 hours per week.
• Design layout and production of six editions.
• Meet every publishing deadline.
• Received the "Cother Design Award."

Cother Library, Mobile, Alabama. Student Assistant in Audiovisual Library, 1996-1997.
• Worked 20 hours per week.
• Created *Audiovisual Catalog* on computerized database.
• Processed orders via computer.
• Prepared monthly and yearly reports using database.
• Edited and proofed various publications.

REFERENCES   Request portfolio from Cother University Placement Office.

Standard memo

1.5"

Tab (1" from left margin)

TO: Executive Committee
                                            DS
FROM: Colleen Marshall

DATE: November 8, 200-

SUBJECT: Site Selection
                                            DS
Please be prepared to make a final decision on the site for next year's Leadership Training Conference. Our staff reviewed the students' suggestions and have added a few of their own. The following information may be helpful as you make your decision:
                                            DS
1.   New York and San Francisco have been eliminated from consideration because of cost factors.
                                            DS
2.   New Orleans is still open for consideration even though we met there three years ago. New Orleans has tremendous appeal to students.

3.   Charleston, San Antonio, and Tampa were suggested by students as very desirable locations for the conference.

Site selection will be the first item of business at our meeting next Wednesday. I'm attaching various hotel brochures for each site.
                                            DS
xx
       DS
Attachments

Standard memo with distribution list

1.5"

Tab (1" from left margin)

TO: Team Leaders
                                            DS
FROM: Form Paragraph Task Force

DATE: Current

SUBJECT: Initial Meetings with Task Force
                                            DS
The task force assigned the responsibility for developing form paragraphs to use in key departments of our company plans to work in your department beginning two weeks from today. Please assign two representatives from your department to coordinate the work with us. DS

The procedure that the Executive Committee asked us to follow is to collect samples of typical correspondence, meet with departmental representatives to collect additional information, and then to prepare a draft of the form paragraphs for review. After we receive your feedback on the draft copy, we will schedule a meeting to finalize the paragraphs.

Matthew Redfern has been assigned as the task force coordinator for your department. Please direct all communications about the project to him.
       DS
xx
       DS
Distribution List:
       Nestor Garcia, Claims
       Roberta Layman, Underwriting
       Rosa Romero, Agency Services
       Diana Wang, Business Services

Standard unbound report

Margins: *Top 2"* for first page and reference pages; 1" for succeeding pages; *Side 1"* or default, *bottom 1"*.

Spacing: *Educational reports*: DS, paragraphs indented .5". *Business reports*: SS, paragraphs blocked with a DS between.

Page numbers: Second and subsequent pages are numbered at top right of the page. DS follows the page number.

Main headings: Centered; ALL CAPS, 14 pts.

Side headings: Bold; main words capitalized; DS above and below.

Paragraph headings: Bold; capitalize first word, followed by a period.

NOTE: Styles may also be used for headings.

Report documentation

Internal citations: Provides source of information within report. Includes the author's surname, publication date, and page number (Bruce, 2002, 129).

Footnotes: References cited in a report are often indicated within the text by a superscript number (...story[1]) and a corresponding footnote with full information at the bottom of the same page where the reference was cited.

Bibliography or references: Lists all references, whether quoted or not, in alphabetical order by authors' names. References may be formatted on the last page of the report if they all fit on the page; if not, list on a separate, numbered page.

First page of unbound report

Set DS; press enter 3 times

TRENDS FOR BUSINESS DRESS —— 14 point

Casual dress in the workplace has become widely accepted. According to a national study conducted by Schoenholtz & Associates in 1995, a majority of the companies surveyed allowed employees to dress casually one day a week, usually Fridays (Tarr, 1995, p. 23). The trend continued to climb as shown by the 1997 survey by Schoenholtz & Associates. Fifty-eight percent of office workers surveyed were allowed to dress casually for work every day, and 92 percent of the offices allowed employees to dress casually occasionally (Surphin, 2000, p. 10).

Decline in Trend

The trend to dress casually that started in the early 1990s may be shifting, states Susan Monaghan (2000, p. 34):

Although a large number of companies are allowing casual attire every day or only on Fridays, a current survey revealed a decline of 10 percent in 1999 when compared to the same survey conducted in 1998. Some experts predict the new trend for business dress codes will be a dress up day every week.

What accounts for this decline in companies permitting casual dress? Several reasons may include:

1. Confusion of what business casual is with employees slipping into dressing too casually (work jeans, faded tee-shirts, old sneakers, and improperly fitting clothing).

2. Casual dress does not portray the adopted corporate image of the company.

3. Employees are realizing that promotion decisions are affected by a professional appearance.

Second page of unbound report

0.5"

2

Guidelines for Business Dress

Companies are employing image consultants to teach employees what is appropriate business casual and to plan the best business attire to project the corporate image. Erica Gilreath (2000), the author of *Casual Dress*, a guidebook on business casual, provides excellent advice on how to dress casually and still command the power needed for business success. She presents the following advice to professionals:

- Do not wear any clothing that is designed for recreational or sports activities, e.g., cargo pants or pants with elastic waist.
- Invest the time in pressing khakis and shirts or pay the price for professional dry cleaning. Wrinkled clothing does not enhance one's credibility.
- Do not wear sneakers.
- Be sure clothing fits properly. Avoid baggy clothes or clothes that are too tight.

In summary, energetic employees working to climb the corporate ladder will need to plan their dress carefully. If business casual is appropriate, it's best to consult the experts on business casual to ensure a professional image.

Reference page

0.5"

3

2.1"

REFERENCES —— 14 pt.

Gilreath, Erica. "Dressing Casually with Power." < http://www.dresscasual.com> (23 March 2001).

Monaghan, Susan. "Business Dress Codes May Be Shifting." *Business Executive*, April 2000, pp 34-35.

Surphin, Rachel. "Your Business Wardrobe Decisions are Important Decisions." *Business Management Journal*, January 2000, pp. 10-12.

Tarr, Kelsey. "Companies Support Business Casual Dress." *Management Success*, June 1995, pp. 23-25.

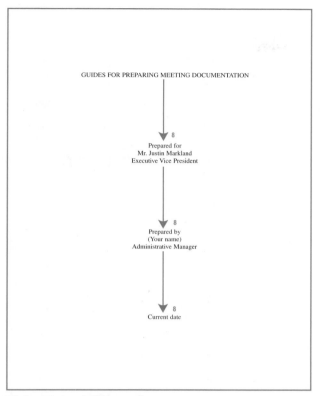

Title page—leftbound

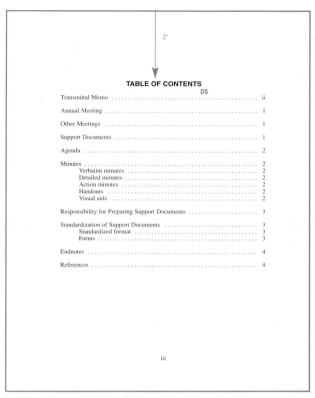

Table of contents—leftbound

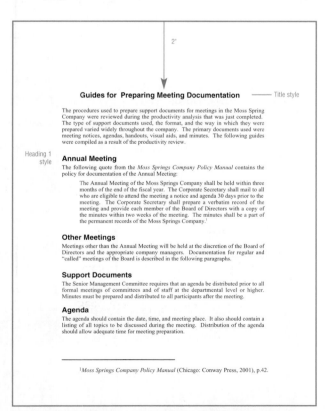

First page of leftbound report (with styles)

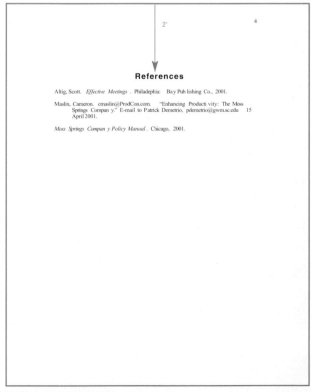

Reference Page

FUNCTION SUMMARY

Function	Menu Command	Keyboard Shortcut	Toolbar Button
Alignment: Left, Center, Right, Justify	Format, Paragraph, Indents and Spacing tab		▤ ▤ ▤ ▤
AutoCorrect	Tools, AutoCorrect Options		
Bold	Format, Font, Font tab	CTRL + B	**B**
Borders: Page	Format, Borders and Shading, Page Border tab		
Borders: Paragraph	Format, Borders and Shading, Borders tab		
Bullets	Format, Bullets and Numbering		▤
Center Page	File, Page Setup, Layout tab		
Change Case	Format, Change Case		
Clip Art and Images	Insert, Picture, Clip Art		🖼
Close Document	File, Close		✕
Columns—New	Insert, Break, Column break		
Columns—Create	Format, Columns		▥
Columns—Balance	Insert, Break, Continuous section break		
Copy	Edit, Copy	SHIFT + F2	
Cut	Edit, Cut	CTRL + X	📋
Date and Time	Insert, Date and Time, select format		✂
Exit	File, Exit		
Find	Edit, Find	CTRL + F	✕
Font	Format, Font		
Font: Color	Format, Font, select color		Times New Roman ▾
Font: Size	Format, Font, select size		A ▾
Font: Style	Format, Font, select style		12 ▾
Footnote	Insert, Reference, Footnote		
Graphic: Move	Select graphic; click Text Wrapping button; choose a wrapping option; point to graphic; and drag to desired position.		
Graphic: Size	Select graphic; drag resize handle. Double-click graphic; Format Picture dialog box, choose Size tab; enter dimensions.		
Graphic: Wrap Text	Select graphic, Format, Format Picture; select wrapping style.		
Hanging Indent	Format, Paragraph, Indents and Spacing tab	CTRL + T	
Help	Help, Microsoft Word Help	F1	❓
Indent	Format, Paragraph, Indents and Spacing tab		▤ Increase Indent / ▤ Decrease Indent

Function	Menu Command	Keyboard Shortcut	Toolbar Button
Italic	Format, Font		[I]
Keep with next	Format, Paragraph, Line and Page Breaks tab		
Line Spacing	Format, Paragraph, Indents and Spacing tab		[≡▾]
Margins	File, Page Setup, Margins tab		
New Document	File, New	CTRL + N	[▯]
Numbering	Format, Bullets and Numbering		[≣]
Open Document	File, Open	CTRL + O	[⌐]
Page Break	Insert, Break, Page Break	CTRL + ENTER	
Page Numbers	Insert, Page Numbers		
Paste	Edit, Paste	CTRL + V	[▤]
Print	File, Print	CTRL + P	[⎙]
Print Preview	File, Print Preview	CTRL + F2	[▦]
Redo	Edit, Redo	CTRL + Y	[↷▾]
Replace	Edit, Replace		
Save As/Save	File, Save As or File, Save	F12/CTRL + S	[▯]
Shading	Format, Borders and Shading, Shading tab		
Show/Hide			[¶]
Space after Paragraph	Format, Paragraph, Indents and Spacing tab		
Special Characters	Insert, Symbol, Special Characters tab		
Spelling and Grammar	Tools, Spelling and Grammar	F7	[▧]
Symbols	Insert, Symbol, Symbols tab		
Tables: Adjust Column Width	Table, Table Properties, Column tab		
Tables: AutoFormat	Table, Table AutoFormat		
Tables: Change Row Height	Table, Table Properties, Row		
Tables: Create	Insert, Table		[▢]
Tables: Delete Rows or Columns	Click in the row or column to be deleted, Table, Delete, Rows or Columns		
Tables: Insert Rows or Columns	Position insertion point, Table, Insert, Rows Above or Row Below or Columns to the Left or Columns to the Right		
Tables: Merge Cells	Select cells, click Table, Merge Cells.		[▣]
Tabs: Set	Horizontal Ruler; set Tab Alignment, click Ruler; Format, Tabs		
Thesaurus	Tools, Language, Thesaurus	SHIFT + F7	
Underline	Format, Font		[U]
Undo	Edit, Undo Typing	CTRL + Z	[↶▾]
Widow/Orphan	Format, Paragraph, Line and Page Breaks tab		